Chicano Politics

Maurilio Vigil

University Press
of America™

"The Chicano's relationship to the United States
Government is like that of a foster child to a
mother. Naturally, the deepest love and affection
of the mother goes to her natural child. This
means that the foster child goes unnoticed or
unattended, until its cries force the mother's
attention."

Reies Lopez Tijerina
(personal interview, 1972)

PREFACE

To Americans witnessing the 1976 Democratic National Convention in New York City in July, 1976 one of the most noteworthy differences or innovations was the unprecedented important role played by ethnic minorities in the nominating process of the Presidential nominee of one of the major political parties.

It all began with Texas' black Representative Barbara Jordan's stirring and dramatic keynote address which opened the convention, and continued with the selection of Los Angeles' black Mayor Thomas Bradley as one of the four permanent co-chairpersons of the Convention. The climax came in Presidential nominee Jimmy Carter's acceptance speech when he referred to the "vitality" which had been contributed to the "pluralistic" American society by the "diversity" of America's ethnic minorities.

Even more unique was the important role of Chicanos, one of the more recently active minorities, in the process. New Mexico's Governor Jerry Apodaca, who had endorsed Georgia's Governor Carter and campaigned for him in the California primary was made one of Carter's regional flour managers for the convention.

More importantly, Apodaca served along with Bradley as permanent co-chairperson, presiding over the ccnvention during the crucial nominating and seconding speeches. So impressive was Apodaca's performance that members of the "Latino coalition caucus" circulated a petition which secured seventy delegate signatures (more than the fifty required) calling for the nomination of Apodaca for the Vice Presidency. Only Apodaca's refusal to sign the approval form (because of his commitment to support Carter's choice) prevented his name from being placed in nomination and the setting of a precedent for Chicanos in national politics.

Chicanos were also visible in several other respects in the convention. Grace Olivarez, the Chicana and feminist leader and Director of the New Mexico State Planning Office presented the Democratic Party's welfare reform plank to the convention.

Cesar Chavez, leader of the United Farm Workers Organizing Committee delivered the nominating speech for California Governor Edmund "Jerry" Brown.

Following the acceptance speech by nominee Jimmy Carter both Governor's Apodaca and Raul Castro of Arizona were among the national Democratic Party leaders who were called to the speaker's platform to pose with Carter before the national television audience.

All of these instances represented the new threshold achieved in American politics by the ethnic group once regarded as politically docile and apathetic and commonly regarded as the nation's "forgotten Americans" or "forgotten people."

The factors, forces, events, leaders and organizations that have been instrumental in the political transformation of the Chicano since the 1960's in American society certainly merit serious analyses and study.

Maurilio E. Vigil

September, 1976

TABLE OF CONTENTS

INTRODUCTION

This work has evolved from a long and painstaking maturation process that I have personally experienced in my study of American politics and the place which it holds for the powerless. In essence, I feel it is a testimonial to that system, since I am convinced that the American system is - with all its procedural imperfections - the best functioning democracy.

It is my belief that the most that can reasonably be expected of a democracy in practical terms is that individuals operating individually or through groups, be allowed the maximum opportunity for political influence. Notwithstanding the "idealized" American political arena, and how often the reality deviates from this idealized norm, I am convinced that the American political system does provide the avenue for even the most powerless to achieve a measure of political influence. I am also convinced that most Americans - perhaps to their own detriment - do not truly understand how our system really functions. Most Americans for example do not understand the political push and pull of special interest groups and their effect on the policy process.

Most Americans live - unfortunately - in an idealized

dream world about American politics where our best leaders are picked in a truly democratic process and that these leaders are altruistically motivated by humanitarian and egalitarian principles in pursuit of the public interest.

Thus Americans cannot cope with or understand the realities of the system - the excesses of political corruption manifested by Watergate, the political subordination and exclusion of minorities, the vast inequality in wealth.

Perhaps it is this lack of true understanding by Americans as a whole about the political system that has contributed to the evolution of the modern American corporate state. Perhaps the idealized view engendered a feeling of passivity, among Americans, that since the system was so good idealistically little activity was required on their part to achieve its true meaning. While most Americans harbored thoughts of an idealized democracy, operating under principles of liberty, equality and freedom, these powerful special interests who understood its operation were systematically and actively tipping the scales of public policy in their favor.

It is my view that the democracy in our system lies in the fact that the powerless - the American consumer, the economically disadvantaged, the subordinated minorities - can, by organized and cohesive action generate a countervailing political force that will adjust the previous imbalances of the system.

It is my view that American democracy requires an active not a passive temper. The system will respond - it will either respond to the personal selfish interest of powerful special interests, or it will respond to a broader range of publics.

It is my view that America's minorities are best served by educating them about the true nature of American politics and how they might more effectively function in it through conventional styles of political action, than by offering patronizing explanations of racial or cultural deficiencies that make it difficult for them to success- fully partake of the system.

The theme that pervades this work is that Chicanos have been systematically excluded from American politics as a result of a combination of historical circumstances (colonialization) and antecedent cultural characteristics (such as a hierarchical tradition), in other words, factors that can be analyzed and explained systematically. However, the group by undergoing a different political acculturation is capable of functioning viably in American politics.

The text is of course ideally suited for Chicano politics, but it will find, I think, application in courses on Ethnic studies, especially those dealing with ethnic politics. It will fit in with studies on Chicano history and sociology. The work, I feel, can also be useful as special topic supplementary reading in courses on American Government and Politics, U. S. History, and southwestern state histories on New Mexico, California, Texas, Arizona and Colorado.

When first confronted by the challenge of preparing material for and developing a course on Chicano politics I was overwhelmed by the great task of organizing, systematically, the many varied topics and concepts that I felt were essential in a relevant treatment of the topic. The greatest task it seemed lay in integrating the often conflicting topics into an interrelated whole.

Little comfort was gained by looking at traditional textbooks or courses in political science since rarely had these treated a single ethnic group, but instead treated different political variables, topics and approaches. There are in vogue today two ways of studying politics. One is to focus on the institutions of government - the constitution, the presidency, the courts, the congress, state and local government, political parties and so on. The emphasis quite often in this type of study or analysis is on formal, legal, philosophical perspectives. The second mode of political study is broadly described as the "behavioral" approaches which emphasize empirical or actually observed behavior of the most important political actor - man.

It seemed to me that any valid treatment of the political activity of a single group would have to take a third or alternate perspective, that would take into account elements of both the institutional and behavioral approaches that were appropriate in describing or explaining all of the politically relevant elements about the group.

The organization and structure ultimately adopted encompasses an attempt to address all the elements which I felt were relevant to a course on Chicano politics. How was this accomplished? It seems logical to me that if the target for analysis is a group, in this case, an ethnic group, then the main questions "politically" about the group would be the same kinds of questions that have been the focus - though in different levels of analysis - of political scientists in general. That is to say, political scientists have been interested in questions about patterns of leadership, voting behavior, political socialization, political culture, ideology, organizations and politics and so on.

What I have attempted in this work then is to bring together the most current information and data about the most important topics in Chicano politics. Obviously, in light of the paucity of information in some topics I have found it necessary to present my own insights and perspectives derived from my own exhaustive study of the subject, and from several years of revising topics and notes for what is probably one of the first courses on Chicano politics in the country initiated at Highlands University in 1972.

The work begins appropriately with a look at the theoretical questions of the study. Any political study is an empty exercise unless some attention is given to the broad implications made or inferred. In this chapter an effort is made to relate the topic of Chicano politics to the timely subject of ethnic politics or group politics, and their relationship to American society or evolving theories of American democracy. This will help illustrate why ethnic or group politics is a legitimate field of study in American politics, and will offer one paradigm about what form that study might follow. It will establish the theme for the remaining chapters.

The second chapter will provide a brief profile of the Chicanos with emphasis on the historical presence and evolution of the group in American society. The perspective will be the "making" of that minority group, or the socio-

economic and political factors that made the Chicano the
group that it is today.

The third chapter will touch on the main elements of
Chicano political ideology or political thought, with an
effort to explore Chicano political culture and the
unique socialization patterns that led to Chicano political
culture or ideology.

Chapter four will explore numerous categories and
examples of Chicano organizations, and will offer some
insights as to their political importance to the Chicano
community. Organization is perceived as the sine qua non
for the success of the ethnic group in politics, and the
importance of organization is integrated into an elaboration of the model presented in Chapter I.

Chapter five will explore the main "political" organizations that have been developed by Chicanos. The
emphasis will be on the independent Chicano political
parties. Examples of early ethnic Chicano parties will
be offered concluding of course with a review of the
development of La Raza Unida Party which will be appraised
with other possible alternative strategies as a force for
future political change.

Chapter six will be devoted to exploring the patterns
of leadership that have emerged from the Chicano community,

and how the various "styles" have served their respective purposes.

Chapter seven treats the patterns of political behavior of the Chicano with emphasis on voting behavior the most useful standard of general political behavior. This chapter will attempt to relate the political culture elements that shaped voting behavior and speculate as to factors and forces that may alter the situation.

The final chapter will attempt to bring all of the preceding themes together in a realistic assessment of the political prospects for the group in American society.

CHAPTER I

CHICANOS IN AMERICAN POLITICS: A PARADIGM

No piece of political behavior research is content
to describe the universe of politics, no matter how
realistic or reliable the description. The goal
is the explanation of why people behave politically
as they do and why as a result political processes
and systems function as they do. There are many
methods of explanation. Whatever they are they
require theorizing activity.* Heinz Eulau, 1963

Relationship of Research to Theory

Modern political analysis - perhaps because of the

demand for rigor and systematic political inquiry demanded

by the behaviorist revolution in American political analysis

- has come to appreciate more and more the importance of

theory and its relationship to political inquiry. It is

no longer enough to describe events, it is now necessary to

attempt to explain political phenomena in a way that will

relate to some level (low, middle range, or general) of

theory. Quite appropriately then, the first concern of

this work is to suggest some broad theoretical relation-

ship between the subject discussed - Chicano politics -

and American politics in general. Is Chicano politics a

natural manifestation of politics as practiced in the

American milieu? Or is Chicano politics an aberration,

*Heinz Eulau, The Behavioral Persuasion in Politics
(New York: Random House, 1963), 24.

a temporary thing, and as such not worthy of note? Finally, can the study of Chicano politics lend support to recent efforts to focus attention on the need for alternate theories of democracy that would account for the influence of pressure groups?.

Why Chicano Politics?

There are several areas of theoretical concern that are of interest in Chicano politics. Chapter 3, for example, will explore possible theories about Chicano political socialization patterns and political culture that may help "explain" patterns of Chicano political behavior.

Probably the most important theoretical question that needs exploring, however, is "Why Chicano politics?" or for that matter why Ethnic politics or Group politics? The traditional scholar will normally scoff at such frivolous distinctions and of their mention in application to American politics. American society is after all a democracy, and there is no need for distinctions of this sort. Traditionally, concern with or mention of such phrases as "black power," "red power," "woman power," "brown power" have not only been viewed as un-American, but as going against the very fabric of American democracy. Naturally, theories that attempted to integrate or consider these as "political phenomena" were themselves classed as radical ideologies.

Fortunately the myopia that has existed generally among the American public and traditionalists has not been shared by many social scientists. Especially behaviorist political scientists and sociologists, have been concerned about the poverty of traditional explanations of American democracy, and have begun to trod unfamiliar paths in seeking alternative explanations or theories of American democracy, especially theories that would account for the influence of pressure groups in the policy process.

Alternative Theories of Democracy

Robert Dahl and E. E. Schattschneider[1] are two of the giants in political science whose behaviorist studies have prompted them to speculate on the viability of traditional theories, and to offer alternative theories in their place. Dahl and Schattschneider have been especially concerned about the problem or threat which the gap between the formal and the real in democratic theory has had upon the American public, speculating that perhaps a very real challenge to American democracy might exist if people do not truly understand their form of government and how it works. Schattschneider especially has warned that tradi-

tional democratic theory has held expectations of citizens
that are not reasonable in expecting citizens to be
"rational arbiters of the details of public policy."[2]   In
describing the policy process in the United States, Dahl
has said that "the making of governmental decisions is not
a majestic march of great majorities united upon certain
matters of basic policy.   It is the steady appeasement of
relatively small groups."[3]

Traditional theories of American democracy grounded
as they have been on egalitarian presumptions, notions of
majority rule and the presumption of altruistic leaders
acting on the basis of the public good have simply not
been consistent with the reality of American politics.

Such theories may contribute to disenchantment of the
mass American public with their system of government when
events such as Watergate - which perhaps reflect the
natural excesses of the American policy process - occur.
Traditional theories create an idealized or utopian model
of the American decision-making structure whereby policies
are the direct result of the public will as manifested by
the majority principle.   Policy makers collectively make
decisions on altruistic motives or based on what is "good"
(as measured by the majority will) for the American public.
The idealized model of course does not account for the

central importance of money in the American electoral process; it does not account for the fact that roughly forty per cent of the populace rarely participate in politics (by voting) and that a larger percentage are basically ignorant of the candidates, the parties and the issues; it does not account for the fact that because of legal (Blacks, Native Americans, Chicanos) and cultural (women) factors large segments of the American population have systematically been politically subordinated, or deprived of an active and viable place in American politics; it finally does not account for intensity of activity, knowledge, resources and skills which well organized groups have employed successfully in forging public policies, even if those policies favored the private and narrow interests of small groups and were inconsistent with what was "good" for the mass public.

One of the arguments of this work is that part of the reason for the subordinate political position of Chicanos and other minorities is a lack of a clear understanding of the true workings of the American political system. It is argued that the idealized conception of American politics engenders a passive rather than an active citizenry. Americans feel, and quite rationally in light of past party history, that the workings of government will go on with or without their active input. The public in general believes that active participation has little measurable effect on the policies of government, and as such do not feel compelled to participate in politics other than their semi-annual expenditure of energy to cast a not always informed vote.[4] Perhaps all of this is as expected, in light of the highly undisciplined, decentralized, non-doctrinaire nature of American political parties.

The fact of the matter is that a clearer and more realistic picture of American politics will reveal that the political system is amenable and receptive to citizen influence, especially if it emanates as a systematic, well-organized, well planned, knowledgable pressure group effort. Perhaps, a most "democratic" aspect of American democracy is the "openness" and wide-leeway that the system affords a multiplicity of groups of all kinds to operate without restraints in pursuit of private (selfish?) motives in the public domain.

The point then is that perhaps Chicanos (and other minorities) have on the basis of the idealized system held the expectation that government would respond to their needs simply because of the high ideals and altruism purported by the system, and that little if any activity was expected on their part to accomplish that end.

While the possibility that some progress may result in this way is not dismissed, it is argued that measurable change will probably occur more rapidly if the group actively participates in pursuit of that change.

The reason for exploring the validity of alternate theories of American democracy in this context has now become clear. If one is to consider realistically the importance of ethnic or Chicano politics it is probably done best in the context of a model that illustrates the validity of group influence in the American policy process. One should bear in mind that in doing so one is not opting for an anti-democratic theory or criticizing as undemocratic the American system. On the contrary, the democratic nature of our political system is being reemphasized, and re-inforced, by looking at it realistically, since this per-spective may enable groups that have not attempted or been able to influence the system to begin to do so.

It could be argued that there have existed two dimensions to American politics, the formal or idealized and the real. Those that have depended on and placed their faith in the formal model have had less impact on and benefitted from government than those who have understood the real political process and employed practical political strategies to gain preferential treatment in that real system. Part of what has occurred in American politics in the last century that has transformed the American system into the modern corporate state has been a tipping of the scales toward the corporate interests. This occurred because groups pursuing those interests came to understand the system and were able to move it towards their own objectives by employing the needed resources, skills and incentives, to accomplish their ends. A countervailing force had until recently (as in the consumer movement) not appeared to balance the policy spectrum.

Chicanos in American Politics: A Conceptual Framework

There are at present a number of models among them those promulgated by Robert Dahl (polyarchy), E. E. Schattschneider (conflict), David Truman (group theory), David Easton (systems theory as applied to political systems), and Sociologist William Newman's theory (American pluralism)[5] that might conceivably be employed as a conceptual framework depicting the position and prospect of an ethnic group in American society. The model depicted in the foregoing pages can correctly be viewed as a hybrid of the various models, since it takes ideas and concepts from these and other sources.

Central to an effort to develop a conceptual framework

that can account for the status and prospects of a minority group is the task of arriving at some conception of the society and the relationship of the minority group to other groups in the system. William Newman in a recent synthesis of the central concepts of American race and cultural relations, has described American society as a highly pluralistic society characterized by a majority-minority group interactive process. The elements of group stratification in American society are not of the elite-mass configuration which one would find in less developed, closed societies, but nevertheless results in a stratified ranking between groups on the basis of social character-istics, political resources, and skills (class, status and power).[6]

Chicanos like other minority groups are a "minority" group not only in a numerical sense, but are a subordinate minority because of a lack of political power and because they exhibit racial and cultural characteristics at variance with the norms of the traditionally dominant WASP group.

The prospect that this condition of Chicanos and other minorities might change as a result of presumed assimilation-ist tendencies is not encouraging according to Newman. The popularity of the traditional "homogenizing" tendency of American society, and the presumption that distinctions

among Americans are slowly disappearing, prompted Newman
to explore various views on the subject. In Newman's view
the melting pot or as he describes it, "amalgamation",
illustrated by the formula $A + B + C = D$, has not exactly
occurred in American society. The blending of different
racial, cultural and ethnic groups has not resulted in an
altogether "better" hybrid as has traditionally been assumed.
Nor has assimilation $(A + B + C = A)$ been the case, since
many minority groups have resisted the pattern of WASP
conformity and instead retained elements of their own
antecedent cultures. Cultural pluralism $(A + B + C = A +
B + C)$ of more recent vogue correctly illustrates the
minority group's tendencies to retain their antecedent
culture, but ignores vestiges of change that occur among
groups as they come in contact with others in American
society.

Better footing is gained, says Newman, by looking at
Daniel Moynihan's and Nathan Glazer's conception in Beyond
the Melting Pot $(A + B + C = A_1 + B_1 + C_1)$ where the authors
compromise between retention of some antecedent cultural
characteristics while adopting some vestiges of change.
But Newman rejects Glazer and Moynihan's suggestion that
assimilation is a single process. Newman agrees with

Milton Gordon, <u>Assimilation</u> <u>in</u> <u>American</u> <u>Life</u>, that there are a number of elements in the assimilationist process which might preclude eventual assimilation or amalgumation. In other words, Newman concludes that the pluralistic character of American race and cultural relations may well continue in spite of popular notions to the contrary.

What all of this means, according to Newman, is that rather than social order lying in prospect as the consensus theorists have advocated, that perhaps a continuation of social dynamism or change may continue to be the case in American society as the conflict theorists have suggested.[7]

What essentially has occurred in American society and probably continue to occur says Newman is "social conflict." The notion of social conflict takes Newman to the same description of American society provided by Dahl, Schattschneider and others.

The central argument of the conflict theorists is that society is comprised of a wide array of power sources including groups of many kinds (racial, ethnic, religious, ideological, cultural, occupational, regional and so on) sizes and structures. The many groups can be conceived as publics or minorities, and operate under different social structures in pursuit of goals and objectives that may or may not intersect.

Newman argues:

> . . .societies that, for lack of a better
> label, have here been labeled pluralistic,
> evidence a never-ending 'web of affiliations,'
> and conflicts. Groups that at one point in
> time may be allies, may later be antagonists.
> Every public issue, every new occasion for con-
> flict, stimulates a rearrangement of group
> relationships. It is indeed rare that any one
> issue or conflict will completely bisect such a
> society. In this sense pluralistic societies
> evidence a special kind of social order in which
> the multiple allegiances and conflicts between
> groups produce a kind of creative tension, a
> tension that is at once ordered and yet conflict
> ridden.[8]

The groups may come in contact with each other in

conflict as a result of competition over attempts to

influence government.

The centripetal pull of government as a target of

political influence is understandable, since American govern-

ment has come to play such a vital influence over people's

lives.

> . . .Armed with legality and legitimacy,
> American governments can and do acquire vast
> resources. They can and do use these resources
> not only to punish but also to reward; they
> allocate job salaries, grants, contracts, pay-
> mènts, and other benefits in infinite variety. . .
> Because governments are extraordinarily in-
> fluential they are inevitably the objects of
> influence. To influence the conduct of govern-
> ment is to influence the way it uses its powers
> of compulsion, coercion, punishment; its capacity
> to render actions legal or illegal, legitimate
> or illegitimate, its ability to allocate rewards,
> benefits, privileges, handicaps, wealth, incomes,
> influence and power itself. It is easy to see

then, why few things are fought over with more
persistence, vigor and bloodshed than the
conduct of government.[9]

What factors influence the success of the various

groups in attempting to influence government? Robert Dahl

has outlined the most important factors. Dahl maintains

that the position of the adversaries and their allies, the

amount and quality of the resources (wealth, time, organ-

ization, access to decision makers, numbers), skills and

incentives which each side can bring to bear in the struggle

and the degree or type of change, all influence the degree

of success of a group in a political struggle in American

politics. Contributing to a group's chances of success are

the multiplicity of access points provided by the American

system with its federal structure (national, state and local

governments), and its separation of powers (the legislature,

the courts, the executive and the executive agencies).[10]

What about possible strategies which an ethnic group

might employ? The nature of the model herein described

would not constrain a group to conventional styles of politics

(that is political party activity, pressure group lobbying,

electoral activity), but would include unconventional

(radical) styles such as confrontation, disruption, protest,

demonstration, boycott, sit-ins and picketing.

Of the two strategies, the conventional forms would probably yield greater long-term benefit and the radical styles more immediate responses.

Having perceived the basic elements of our theoretical model, one can focus attention on its applicability to the situation of the specific ethnic group, in this case the Chicano.

First of all, it can be argued that the limited general success recorded by Chicanos in influencing American government[11] is probably attributed to its inability to marshall those resources (numbers, cohesion, organization, time) skills and incentives available to it, in sufficient quantities to yield some success. Attempts to explain why this has been the case among Chicanos will be reserved to later chapters of this work.

For the present, it is appropriate to speculate about those factors and forces that might contribute to creating a viable ethnic group capable of wielding political influence. Of the basic resources mentioned by Dahl, those that would seem essential to Chicanos would be numbers and cohesion, because of its obvious lack of capital. Since cohesion would be a product of high levels of individual identification with the group as the authors of The American Voter have maintained, the goal of the ethnic group is

enhancing intensity of subjective identification to the
extent where ethnicity prevails over other of the individual's
associations or identifications.

Chart A is designed to depict in a very simplified form
the complex process by which an individual Chicano's ethnic
association might be translated into intense identification
and collectively into group solidarity and influence.

The top of the Chart depicts the typical associations
or identification of most Chicanos (or American citizens
for that matter), and the potential support an individual
might render any group with which he is identified. The
center left portion of the chart depicts the aforementioned
factors that will influence degree of group success. The
center right (top) portion speculates on those factors that
will weigh heavily in determining the ethnic group's
viability. The center right (bottom) portion illustrates
how ethnic organizations (political or otherwise) occupy a
central position in enhancing or contributing to those
elements (center left) that will influence the degree of
success of a group. The bottom portion replicates David
Easton's conception of the political system and illustrates
how a multiplicity of groups through inputs (demands and
expectations) are involved in an effort to influence the

CHART A

ETHNIC GROUPS IN AMERICAN POLITICS:
A PARADIGM

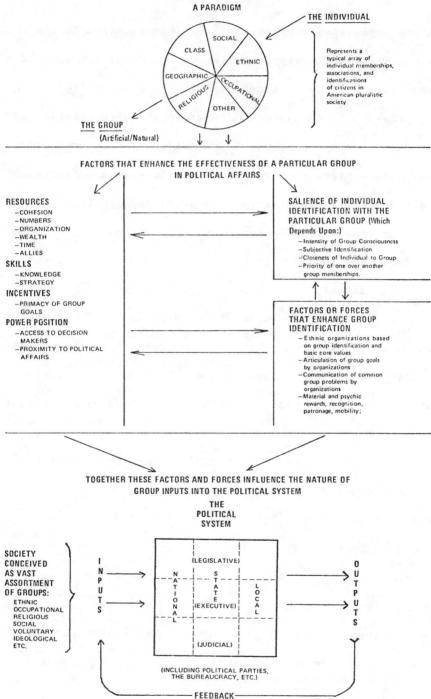

THE INDIVIDUAL

SOCIAL
CLASS
ETHNIC
GEOGRAPHIC
OCCUPATIONAL
RELIGIOUS
OTHER

Represents a
typical array of
individual memberships,
associations, and
identifications
of citizens in
American pluralistic
society

THE GROUP
(Artificial/Natural)

FACTORS THAT ENHANCE THE EFFECTIVENESS OF A PARTICULAR GROUP
IN POLITICAL AFFAIRS

RESOURCES
  −COHESION
  −NUMBERS
  −ORGANIZATION
  −WEALTH
  −TIME
  −ALLIES

SKILLS
  −KNOWLEDGE
  −STRATEGY

INCENTIVES
  −PRIMACY OF GROUP
   GOALS

POWER POSITION
  −ACCESS TO DECISION
   MAKERS
  −PROXIMITY TO POLITICAL
   AFFAIRS

**SALIENCE OF INDIVIDUAL
IDENTIFICATION WITH THE
PARTICULAR GROUP (Which
Depends Upon:)**
  −Intensity of Group Consciousness
  −Subjective Identification
  −Closeness of Individual to Group
  −Priority of one over another
   group memberships.

**FACTORS OR FORCES
THAT ENHANCE GROUP
IDENTIFICATION**
  −Ethnic organizations based
   on group identification and
   basic core values
  −Articulation of group goals
   by organizations
  −Communication of common
   group problems by
   organizations
  −Material and psychic
   rewards, recognition,
   patronage, mobility;

TOGETHER THESE FACTORS AND FORCES INFLUENCE THE NATURE OF
GROUP INPUTS INTO THE POLITICAL SYSTEM

THE
POLITICAL
SYSTEM

**SOCIETY
CONCEIVED
AS VAST
ASSORTMENT
OF GROUPS:**
  ETHNIC
  OCCUPATIONAL
  RELIGIOUS
  SOCIAL
  VOLUNTARY
  IDEOLOGICAL
  ETC.

INPUTS

(LEGISLATIVE)

NATIONAL   STATE   LOCAL

(EXECUTIVE)

(JUDICIAL)

OUTPUTS

(INCLUDING POLITICAL PARTIES,
THE BUREAUCRACY, ETC.)

FEEDBACK

policy process at different levels and boundaries of government in a way that will increase its share of values, rewards and benefits from the political system.

The prominent position of the ethnic organization is
evident in the chart. Not only does the ethnic organization
(whether explicitly political or not) serve as an instrument of interest aggregation (cohesion) but it also serves
to articulate the interest in the form of pressure group
activity.

Summary

This chapter has established the theoretical conceptual
framework for this work. Chicano politics is perceived
as a very appropriate and natural phenomenon of American
politics. American politics is characterized as an open
and pluralistic system composed of a vast array of private
interests or publics engaged in constant interaction (competition, conflict, conciliation) in an effort to influence
the policy process. Public policies are the direct result
of this conflict pattern. The degree of success of groups
in influencing policy is dependent upon practical considerations - resources, skills, incentives - which can be
brought to bear in the struggle. Chicanos have been unable to influence the system because of their inability to

marshall these resources, skills and incentives. A paradigm was presented which depicts how the situation might change.

While this first chapter has speculated on theoretical implications, its relationship to the practical considerations of Chicano politics will become evident in the remaining chapters which not only describe specific Chicano political activity, but analyze it in the context of the theoretical and long-range importance to the Chicano.

NOTES

[1]Robert A. Dahl, A Preface to Democratic Theory
(Chicago: University of Chicago Press, 1956); E. E.
Schattschneider, The Semisovereign People: A Realist's
View of Democracy (New York: Holt, Rinehart and Winston,
1960), and Karl Deutsch, The Nerves of Government.

[2]See Schattschneider, Chapter 8.

[3]Dahl, 147.

[4]See Robert A. Dahl, Modern Political Analysis
(Prentice Hall, 1970), 77-84.

[5]Robert Dahl, Democracy in the United States: Promise
and Performance (Chicago: Rand McNalley, 1972), Chapter 6;
Schattschneider, The Semisoverign People, op cit; David
Truman, The Governmental Process (New York: Alfred A.
Knopf, 1951); William Newman, American Pluralism; A Study
of Minority Groups and Social Theory (New York: Harper and
Row, 1973.

[6]Newman, op. cit. 9-31.

[7]Ibid., 41-87.

[8]Ibid., 182-183.

[9]Dahl, Democracy in the U.S., 387-388.

[10]Ibid., 387-398.

[11]This general statement is made with the exception
of New Mexico's Chicanos.

FURTHER SUGGESTED READING

Robert A. Dahl. A Preface to Democratic Theory. Chicago:
    University of Chicago Press, 1956.

_____. Democracy in the United States: Promise
    and Performance. Chicago: Rand McNally, 1972.

David Easton. The Political System: An Inquiry into the
    State of Political Science. New York: Alfred A.
    Knopf, 1953.

Milton Gordon. Assimilation in American Life. New York:
    Oxford University Press, 1964.

Edgar Litt. Ethnic Politics in America. Dallas: Scott,
    Foresman and Co., 1970.

S. J. Makielski. Beleaguered Minorities: Cultural Politics
    in America. San Francisco: W. H. Freeman and Co., 1973.

William Newman. American Pluralism. New York: Harper and
    Row, Publishers, 1973.

E. E. Schattschneider. The Semisoverign People: A Realists
    View of Democracy in America. New York: Holt Rinehart
    and Winston, 1960.

CHAPTER II

CHICANOS: A HISTORICAL PROFILE

> Unlike such groups as the Italians, the Irish, the Poles, the Spanish-Americans of the Southwest are not truly an immigrant group, for they are in their traditional home. As an Indian the Spanish-Mexican was here from time immemorial; and his Spanish forebearers were in this region long, long before John Smith and his fellows pioneered in Virginia. In other words, historically and culturally he belongs here.* George Sanchez, n.d.

Prior to embarking on a long dissertation on the Chicanos and their politics, it is appropriate to identify the group or at least establish the parameters of the Chicano group considered here, and to trace the important historical forces and events that moulded the Chicano political culture of today.

Unlike other minority groups whose physical and cultural distinctiveness provide an easily identifiable characteristic of ethnic identification, the Chicanos are not always as easily identified. Nor does the group always subscribe to a universal designation which would enhance ready identification.

---

*George I. Sanchez, The Chicago Jewish Forum, XX, No. 2, 3.

Ethnic Labels

Chicanos or Mexican Americans, as they are interchangeably called here, have been known historically under several
different designations (some of which persist today)
creating some confusion among outside observers and the
group itself about just who constitutes the group, and
perhaps raising doubts about the cohesiveness of the group.
"Spanish-Americans" is a term that has been preferred in
referring to the group in New Mexico, stemming from both an
effort to reject unfavorable association with the stereotyped image of Mexicanness, as well as the debatable
assumption that the "Spanish" colonizers and early Governors
in New Mexico were not "Mexicans." In Texas, the lower
middle class organizers of the League of United Latin
American Citizens preferred usage of the term "Latin
Americans," and that term has had limited acceptance as
well. The designation "la raza," perhaps stemming from
Jose Vasconcelos' writings has had wide acceptance,
especially as an in-group designation. The term has been
embraced as a designation by leaders of La Raza Unida Party
and Rodolfo "Corky" Gonzales. Reies Lopez Tijerina offered
his alternate designation of "Indo-Hispano" which has had
limited use among supporters of the Alianza. The term
"Mexican-Americans" has on the other hand been accepted in

California, Arizona and parts of Texas, probably because of the high proportion of Mexican immigrants in these states. The U.S. Bureau of the Census has reflected the ambivalence, referring to the group alternately as Hispanics, Spanish-surnamed, and Spanish-speaking.

Tom Pino and Daniel Valdez offered little help in their analysis of the problems of multiple designations, offering still another term "Hispano" as a more suitable universal designation for the group.[1] The problem of the several designations is that often, members of the group have been violently opposed to certain designations, thus if there is something to the notion that a common label or designation is important to internal cohesion, then the Chicanos are lacking in this respect.

The terms herein used interchangeably in referring to the group will be Chicanos and Mexican Americans. The term "Chicano" is used because it manifests the new political awareness and activism that has been manifested in the Chicano movement of the 1960's and 1970's. The term has not been accepted by older and perhaps more conservative Mexican Americans, and is more popular among the young activists. The term emerged as a result of contraction and pronunciation in Spanish of the name of the Aztec Indians also known as the Mexicas (Mexicas - Mexicano - Xicano - Chicano) that lived in pre-Columbian Mexico.[2]

The previous usage of the term in the United States, was primarily as an in-group designation especially among young "pachucos" as part of the pachuco language in referring to Mexican Americans. How it came to be applied to the current movement is a mystery, but the reason is not, in light of its activist connotation. The term Mexican American is technically the most correct term, first of all, other ethnic minorities are referred to by the hyphenated arrangement based on their previous nationality. "Mexican American" can correctly be applied to Mexican Americans emerging from "Spanish" origins (in New Mexico) since these people became Mexicans when Mexico gained independence from Spain in 1821 and thus were Mexicans when the American occupation of the Southwest took place in 1846. Moreover, the bulk of the Mexican American population in the U.S. owe their origins to immigration from Mexico or descendance therefrom.

Location and Numbers

The consideration of Chicanos encompassed in this work thus includes Mexican-Americans of which the primary concentration is in California, Texas, New Mexico, Arizona and Colorado, with smaller numbers interspersed throughout the country. It excludes consideration of Cubans and Puerto Ricans in other states, primarily because the needed elements of political community among all Spanish language and Spanish surnamed groups in the country have not yet developed.

Chicanos number, according to the 1970 U.S. Census, 4,667,975 persons in the five southwestern states where they are concentrated, and where they constitute 12.9% of the population, making it the largest ethnic minority in that region. The total Chicano population of the United States is probably between five and six million, a more accurate figure not easily arrived at due to the huge number of illegal aliens living in the U.S. and because of traditionally inaccurate U.S. Census figures. The greatest number of Chicanos, 2.2 million, live in California where they make up 11.1% of the state's population. Los Angeles alone has nearly 1 million Chicanos. Texas' Chicano population is 1.6 million and constitutes 14.9% of the total state population. The main concentration of Chicanos in Texas is in the southern counties of the state and cities such as San Antonio, El Paso and Corpus Christi. New Mexico's Chicanos number 324,248 but more significantly,

31.9% of the state population. In New Mexico the population is also concentrated in the north and north central
region comprising majorities in a number of counties.
Arizona has 246,390 Chicanos (13.9%) and Colorado 211,585
(9.6%).[3] In Arizona the main Chicano concentrations are
in south and west Phoenix, Tucson and Nogales. Colorado's
Chicanos are concentrated in southeast Denver and in
numerous smaller southern Colorado communities.

Were the numbers of Chicano population well distributed
throughout the country they would hardly present a potentially
viable political force. The fact that they are concentrated
in the Southwest, and especially in two of the more significant states (California and Texas) in population and
electoral votes adds measurably to the importance of the
Chicano group. Moreover, the concentration of this population in specific regions of these states enhances its
potential importance in local and state politics.

Although some Chicanos continue to live in rural areas
in some states such as New Mexico and Colorado, they are
not a rural population. Over 80% of the Chicano population
resides in urban areas.

Socio-Economic Status

In terms of socio-economic condition, aside from the

Native Americans no American ethnic minority is more economically depressed than Chicanos. The 1970 census showed
that 15% of all Mexican American families had incomes less
than $4,000 (the nationally established poverty level).
Unemployment among Chicanos is double that of the rest of
the population.[4] The income and unemployment figures are
deceptive however, as they cloud the more acute problems
the minority group faces in especially depressed areas. In
New Mexico's Mora County, for example, where 94.6% of the
population is Mexican American, unemployment was 25 percent
and per capita income $1,420; 52.4% of the population was
eligible for food stamps and 19.7% were receiving welfare
assistance.[5]

Statistics released by the U.S. Commission on Civil
Rights recently have continued to reflect the continued
concentration of Chicanos in the unskilled laboring trades
and with generally lower pay for similar kind of employment
(whether laborer or professional). Studies of illiteracy
have shown Chicanos with illiteracy rates seven times
higher than the general population and that Chicanos have
achieved median schooling of 7.1 years compared to 12.1
for the Anglo population.

Origins and Diversity

Two separate factors account for the emergence of the Mexican American population in the United States. First, a minority of Chicanos can claim descendance from Mexican colonists, the occupants of the southwestern states when the territory was annexed by the United States following the Mexican War. The great majority of Mexican Americans became Americans by immigration or from descendance from Mexican immigrants to this country after the Mexican War. The pattern of Mexican immigration has remained unchecked in spite of recent efforts to restrict it. Mexican immigration into the United States was not restricted until 1968 when the immigrant quota system was applied to western hemisphere countries. Prior to that time, and especially during the depression era the opportunity for economic advantage in the United States served as a constant magnet, drawing Mexican laborers who provided American business with a ready supply of cheap labor in all forms of industry and agriculture. The Bracero program,1951-1964, helped regulate the flow of immigrants, and its cessation in 1964 served more to encourage illegal entry than to eliminate migration.

The Making of the Chicano Minority

Although it is well known that the origins of the Mexican Americans in the United States go back further than

the earliest English settlement at Jamestown, it is appropriate to begin our historical profile of the Chicanos
with the passing of the New Mexico territory from Mexico
to the United States. Thus the focus of this profile is
the "making of the Mexican-American minority," and the
emphasis is on the patterns of contact (conflict) that
characterized relations between the Mexicans and the
American in the southwest. The first significant point is
that the Mexican American like the Native American became
a minority initially by conquest, which was followed by a
period of American colonialism during the territorial period.
Subsequent immigration, primarily of the poorest of the
poor from Mexico, only exacerbated the swelling ranks of
subordinated Mexican Americans in the Southwest. It is
significant to note, that the Southwest which the Army of
the West under General Stephen Watts Kearny encountered
was still very much a frontier region of Mexico. The
colonial enterprise which had been begun first by Juan de
Oñate (in 1598) had been interrupted by the Pueblo Revolt,
(1680) then rekindled under Don Diego de Vargas (1692) had
proceeded very slowly because of the marauding tribes of
Navajo, Apache and Ute which lived in New Mexico and
Arizona. Because of the vast expanse of its territories

the northern provinces of New Spain had been neglected first by Spain and later by Mexico, which provided only meager military support to the struggling villages or outposts along the Rio Grande.

The relatively sparse population (approx. 75,000) of the Southwest is reflective of this "frontier" character of the region. New Mexico, the most advanced had approximately 60,000 people, with approximately 5,000 in Texas, 7,500 in California and 1,000 in Arizona.[6] In New Mexico, the evolving nature of some military outposts such as Santa Fe into thriving commercial centers indicated that progress toward more advanced form of life was occurring in the 1850's. Also, some enterprising Mexican patrones had begun to accumulate vast holdings of land and livestock. The bulk of the population was however - by and large- comprised of small dirt farmers who banded together in community grants and extracted a subsistence out of their land in spite of the vicissitudes of nature and the threat of marauding Indians.

Thus was the situation when the Mexican War transferred the vast territories of the west from Mexico to the United States. The coming of the U.S. government did not drastically alter conditions in the Southwest initially, aside from

the fact that American territorial governors were now
primarily Anglos. The U.S. government in the Treaty of
Guadalupe Hidalgo very beneficently embraced the Mexicans
as American citizens, encouraging them to remain, and
offered the additional incentive of recognizing as legal,
Spanish and Mexican grants of land that had been made to
the people. The American government also provided a more
effective military force which increased protection of outposts, thus enhancing further colonial development and
progress.

The pattern of development following the American
occupation took a somewhat different pattern in the different states because of the size of population and because
of events that influenced each state's history as will be
shown, but in all cases the Mexican American population
fared very poorly, becoming a politically, socially and
economically subordinate group. Essentially, the pattern,
though varying in time lapse, was one in which the Mexican,
essentially a poor dirt farmer and sheep raiser operating
under a subsistence economy but possessed of his land,
began to lose his land primarily but not exclusively to
Anglo-American land speculators, large scale farmers and
ranchers, railroad and mining executives and the like,

through legal and illegal machinations. With the loss of
his land the Mexican became a "peon" a laborer, essentially
unskilled in all but those trades which he had traditionally
performed for himself - farming, sheep raising, and work
as a cowhand. The Mexican thus entered the labor market
under the worst kind of conditions and his economic status
reflected it. As economics dictates social position, the
cycle of subordinate status was soon complete. The Mexican's
economic position of course dictated the kind of housing,
educational opportunity, standard of living which he could
afford, and this generally categorized him among the poorest
of the poor. The Mexican became victim of a stereotyped
image, he became a dirty Mexican, a greaser, he was characterized as lazy, lethargic, unambitious, fatalistic and
so on. The Mexican became victim of prejudice and discrimination because of his ethnicity, his language, his
dark skin, and patterns of behavior, all factors that
deviated from norms of the dominant group. Thus the normal
avenues of opportunity, education, a skilled trade, a better
job, politics, eluded the Chicano and cast him into a cycle
of poverty and subordination, which generally characterizes
the group even today. The plight of the domestic Mexican
was only complicated by the immigrant Mexicans, who generally were in a similar or worse position, and whose entry

into the U.S. flooded the ranks of unskilled laborer, while swelling the numbers of the impoverished minority in the states.

In Texas, the conflict between the Anglo American and the Mexican often was clouded by conflicts over land, range wars, sheep versus cattle grazing, and so on. The cattle industry already begun by the Mexicans was taken over by cattle barons who turned the industry into a large scale marketing venture by fencing large tracts of range land and initiating the long drive. Sheep ranching endeavors, often the main enterprise of Mexicans (because of the utility of sheep for wool and meat), were sharply curtailed as a result of range wars. At the same time in other parts of Texas, large scale farmers introduced the cash crop, cotton, requiring large plantations. In both situations much of the land was acquired by systematically depriving the Mexican landowner. Between 1840 and 1854, as Paul Taylor has observed, Anglos had taken over all but one Mexican land grant in Texas.[7] In both cases mentioned above, the former Mexican landowner provided the needed supply of cheap labor. Thus the economic and racial subordination foreshadowed the political subordination of the Mexican in Texas.

The conflict in California took on a little different flavor because of the California gold strike of 1849. The

migration of hundreds of thousands of new settlers transformed that state almost overnight. When the new sources
of gold had been exhausted and were no longer available,
prospectors and others turned their attention to farming
and livestock raising and other pursuits. The Californios,
as the California Mexicans were called, soon saw their land
holdings depleted and in the hands of Anglo land speculators
and barons. The Chicano was thus excluded politically from
an active participation almost from the time California
became a state in 1850.

In Arizona, an altogether different pattern occurred.
Most of the early development in that state came at the
impetus of Anglos, especially those representing mining
interests, as the names of the cities - Phoenix, Flagstaff,
Prescott, Winslow, Tucson, - indicate. The Mexican in this
situation entered primarily as an immigrant laborer, thus
his subordinate status was foregone. From the start the
Mexican laborer lived in a designated part of the company
town, attended segregated churches, schools and public
facilities and was accorded a social status commensurate
with his economic class. Politically the Chicano was
excluded from meaningful participation altogether.

In New Mexico, the situation again differed somewhat.

Here there were two patterns. In "Little Texas" (the eastern and southeastern parts of the state), the pattern that had occurred in Texas was pretty much duplicated. The "Lincoln County" wars essentially duplicated the range wars that had occurred in Texas.

In northern New Mexico, the large concentration of Mexicans, the fact that the evolving pattern of new stages of civilization (the patron as a large scale rancher and farmer), the fact that most of the land had been divided into community and proprietory land grants, and the fact that Mexicans in New Mexico had been engaged in an enterprise of self-government (due to the benign neglect of Mexico) all created a unique political evolution in that state. The most significant fact was that the Mexicans in New Mexico had developed a class structure with an elite group that not only had ruled, but was capable and interested in retaining their power and influence. General Kearny very perceptively chose to secure the collaboration of some of the major Mexican influentials in the state in the new government, by appointing Donaciano Vigil as the first Territorial secretary to the first military governor, William Bent. Vigil became Governor upon Bent's assassination in the Taos revolt of 1847. Thus although there were several

instances of minor rebellion against the American government in New Mexico, the fact that Mexican leaders had been
included in the government, as they continued to be in the
territorial government, and territorial legislatures,
tended to create a source of legitimacy for American government from the start. At the same time the participation of
Mexicans in government helped initiate a pattern of political
participation in New Mexico not duplicated in any other
southwestern state.

Chicanos in New Mexico, as will be shown later, have
participated more, more consistently and effectively than
their counterparts in any other state. However, in spite
of higher levels of participation and greater levels of
political effectiveness, the economic plight of the Chicano
in New Mexico was essentially the same as that of his
counterpart elsewhere. Here also the Mexican American lost
much of his land, and entered the ranks of the unskilled
laborer and came to occupy the lowest rungs of the social
ladder. This in spite of proportionally larger numbers
and greater political sophistication.[8]

Summary

This chapter has provided a brief demographic sketch
of the Chicanos, including population characteristics,

numbers, socio-economic standing, and regional (state to state) patterns. From the standpoint of the making of the Mexican American minority we have described the factors and forces that led to the political, social and economic position which Chicanos find themselves in today. Already some of the "political" consequences of the Mexican American's historical experience have become evident. The following chapter will address in greater depth some of those consequences of the Mexican immigrant, minority and subordinate experience.

NOTES

[1]Tom Pino and Daniel Valdez "Ethnic Labels in Majority-Minority Relations", Journal of Mexican American Studies V. I, No. 1 (Fall, 1970), 16-30.

[2]Matt S. Meier and Feliciano Rivera, The Chicanos (New York: Hill and Wang, 1972), 8.

[3]U.S. Bureau of the Census, Census of Population: Persons of Spanish Surname, (Washington: U.S. Superintendent of Documents, 1970), vii.

[4]U.S. Bureau of the Census, Current Population Reports, Population Characteristics: Persons of Spanish Origin in the United States (Washington: U.S. Superintendent of Documents, 1972).

[5]New Mexico unemployment hovers above average," Las Vegas Daily Optic, March 18, 1975. This article based on a report published by the Bureau of Business Research, University of New Mexico. In addition to Mora County, similar deplorable depressed conditions exist in San Miguel, Taos, Rio Arriba, and Guadalupe Counties all with substantial Chicano populations.

[6]Joan Moore, The Mexican Americans (Englewood Cliffs, N.J.: Prentice Hall, 1970), 11-20. The Moore text has been used to extract this broad and general outline or historical profile of the Chicano.

[7]Paul Taylor, An American-Mexican Frontier (Chapel Hill, N.C.: University of North Carolina Press, 1934), 294.

[8]Moore, op. cit.

FURTHER SUGGESTED READING

Rodolfo Acuna. Occupied America: The Chicanos Struggle
    Toward Liberation. San Francisco: Canfield Press, 1972.

Nancie Gonzales. The Spanish Americans of New Mexico: A
    Heritage of Pride. Albuquerque: University of New
    Mexico Press, 1967.

Carey McWilliams. North From Mexico: The Spanish-Speaking
    People of the United States. New York: Greenwood
    Press, 1968.

Matt Meier and Feliciano Rivera. The Chicanos: A History
    of Mexican Americans. New York: Hill and Wang, 1972.

Joan Moore with Alfredo Cuellar. Mexican Americans.
    Englewood Cliffs, New Jersey: Prentice Hall, 1971.

Armando Rendon. Chicano Manifesto: The History and
    Aspirations of the Second Largest Minority in America.
    New York: Collier Books, 1971.

CHAPTER III

THE POLITICAL CULTURE OF THE MEXICAN-AMERICAN PEOPLE

The emerging nations are presented with two
different models of the modern participatory state,
the democratic and the totalitarian. The democratic state offers the ordinary man the opportunity
to take part in the political decision-making process
as an influential citizen; the totalitarian offers
him the role of the participant subject. . .If the
democratic model of the participating state is to
develop in these new nations, it will require more
than the formal institutions of democracy - universal suffrage, the political party, the elective
legislature. These in fact are also part of the
totalitarian participation policies in a formal if
not functional sense. A democratic form of participating political system requires as well a
political culture consistent with it.*

Gabriel Almond, 1963

Political Culture

A comparatively new and provocative area of study in

political science is the concept of political culture.

Though most often employed in studies of comparative politics,

for example, in comparing degrees of popular participation

in different democratic polities[1] (as in modern and develop-

ing countries), the concept can be employed in studying

particular political characteristics or orientations of

minority groups in a given polity. Political culture has

been defined by Professor Martin Needler as the "totality

*Gabriel Almond and Sydney Verba. The Civic Culture
(Boston: Little Brown, 1965), 3.

of the factors, not themselves political, which determine
the environment in which political processes operate: the
traditions, attitudes, or normal patterns of behavior and
thought that condition political action."[2] The concept of
political culture is often tied to notions of national
character in considering its impact on particular societies
as Almond and Verba have done in The Civil Culture. Here
they uncovered different political orientations ranging
from "participant" to "subject" to "parochial" among the
citizens of the United States, Great Britain, Germany,
Italy and Mexico.

Minority Political Culture

Although the assumption of the close relationship
between national character and political culture is valid
in considering comparatively homogenous societies and
closed political systems, this diminishes as one considers
pluralistic societies with open political systems as in the
case of the United States. Thus while a single political
culture can be said to exist in Mexico, it is less likely
that a single political culture has existed in American
society, especially among American minority groups. The
case of the Native Americans who have not only remained
segregated (both by choice and by the reservation system)

but retained many elements of their antecedent culture
(language, religion, ceremonies), including their own
political culture while existing under the American polity
is an example. It is argued that in American society
because of its diversity and pluralism, and because of the
openness of the system, a dominant political culture has
existed, but in addition a number of peripheral "political
cultures" have influenced the political orientations of
minority groups, the Chicano being one of those groups.

Synthesis of Chicano Political Culture: A Model

Part of the problem which some minorities (especially
ethnic minorities such as Chicanos and Native Americans)
have experienced in American life is perhaps the result
of "practicing" one political culture and existing in another. Especially, would this be a problem if the two
political cultures (the American and the minority) are
incongruent as in the situation where in the dominant
society the norm is for a "participant" orientation and that
of the minority is a "subject" orientation. What is being
suggested here is that just as a minority group brings into the American milieu a distinct cultural orientation which
might resist a process toward acculturation or assimilation
into the American mould, so also could this exist as far

as "political" orientations are concerned. Thus a minority group in becoming "politically acculturated" can not reasonably be expected to assume a new political culture readily, especially when there are a number of other variables militating against the process. Chart B is designed to depict the hypothetical process which the Chicano has experienced in arriving at what might be termed its contemporary political culture.

The minority group, in this case the Chicano, brings into the new political milieu (the American polity) a distinct political culture with explicit political orientations toward the regime and his role _vis_ _a_ _vis_ the regime. The Chicano having emerged primarily from the pattern of hierarchial political rule (initially Spain and later Mexico) is characterized by "subject" political orientations, as Almond and Verba have observed about the Mexican citizen.[3] The subject orientation is characterized by a passive attitude towards politics, a feeling that little can be done to influence government in the input process (low political efficacy) and an unchallenging acceptance of the outputs (policies) of government. Thus what might be mistaken by some as the non-existence of a Chicano political culture, is probably a distinct and coherent pattern of political

CHART B

THE POLITICAL CULTURE OF THE MINORITY GROUP

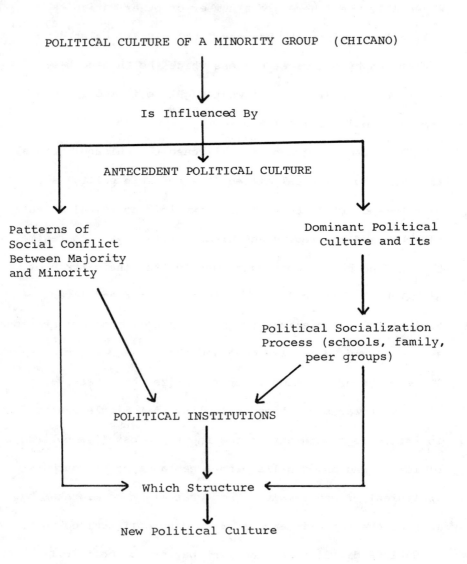

POLITICAL CULTURE OF A MINORITY GROUP   (CHICANO)

Is Influenced By

ANTECEDENT POLITICAL CULTURE

Patterns of
Social Conflict
Between Majority
and Minority

Dominant Political
Culture and Its

Political Socialization
Process (schools, family,
peer groups)

POLITICAL INSTITUTIONS

Which Structure

New Political Culture

orientations that happen to be anti-thetical to American political institutions.

The antecedent political culture, contrary to what some have argued, does not preclude the group from altering its political culture, since the political culture is a dynamic, evolving pattern of orientations. The Chicano's traditional "subject" orientation does not necessarily mean he cannot become a highly effective and participant citizen. There are a number of conditions that the Chicano (and other minority groups) encounters in the American political milieu that will either encourage his integration into the new polity or that will preclude it. Some of these the Chicano has no control over. Probably the most important is the relationship (race relations) between majority and minority as Professor Guzman has observed.[4] Some patterns of social contact might be, for example, mutual views of the groups (stereotypes, etc.) of each other, ideological congruence or competition, and so on. If the patterns of contact are favorable, the political acculturation (or socialization process) of the minority group proceeds systematically as the minority becomes inbued with the norms, values, benefits, and patterns of behavior of the

dominant political culture as transmitted by the socializing agencies, the schools, the family, peer group associations and secondary associations. The political institutions will respond by clearing away legal obstacles
that would militate against the group such as the elimination of "costs" to voting. Political parties - the main
institution that in the American urban setting has worked
to "politicize" minorities - would contribute greatly to
the political integration of the minority group.

On the other hand if the patterns of social contact
are abrasive it is more likely that the processes will
militate against the political integration of the minority,
engendering an alternate political culture characterized
perhaps by "subject" orientations that manifest themselves
in apolitical behavior, or political apathy and isolation,
or perhaps alienation, separatism or radicalism.

The Chicano has experienced a number of obstacles in
his path to political integration in the American polity.
He began with an antecedent political culture inconsistent
with the American polity. His cultural integration or pattern
of racial contact in the American environment was highly
abrasive and conflict ridden. In every sphere of social
and economic and consequently political life, the dominant

society's structures militated against Chicano integration
into the polity. In California, legislation adopted in 1894
making the ability to read and write English a standing
requirement for voter registration, discriminated against
Mexican Americans. In Texas, the poll tax, and usually
restrictive registration procedures (annual registration,
short registration periods) also inhibited participation
among a group to whom the salience of politics was already
limited.[5] Often, intimidation (in Texas, much Klu Klux Klan
activity was directed against Chicanos) proved a valuable
way of discouraging Chicano political participation. The
political parties unlike the pattern in most American cities
chose to ignore the Chicano in spite of its potentially
important cohesive vote. Political socialization patterns
and influences to which the Chicano became exposed did often
build, as Professor Chris Garcia has observed, support for
the regime, but often it was support built on the antecedent
culture subject orientation and not on an efficacious
participant one. Thus to Chicanos, there has been some
question as to whether the American polity was as democratic as it claimed to be as Professor Garcia's study
has observed.[6] Rather than encouraging the political
integration of the Chicano group, the structures often
served to reinforce the antecedent "subject" orientation

and possibly even contributed to political alienation and radicalism that would emerge in the 1960's as part of the reaction against the political system.

The present Chicano political culture is thus a reflection of this entire process. First of all, large numbers of Chicanos (outside of New Mexico) remain unpoliticized and not registered to vote. As a result much of the group exists in a politically isolated situation very much like that of a "subject" orientation. Political alienation from the system has given rise to a number of radical groups especially among the young Chicanos. At the same time, a separate third party movement appealing to the unpoliticized Chicano community remains a very distinct and potentially viable force. The political culture of the Chicanos has of course been subject to regional variations resulting from the different experiences and patterns of social contact, and in this the Chicano in New Mexico has been the most notable exception. The political experience of New Mexico's Mexican Americans has in several ways been different than their counterparts in other states, and has manifested itself in greater political participation. These differences will be explored later. For now it is appropriate to focus on general patterns applicable more or less to the whole group.

The leading features of Chicano political culture that are considered here are the evolutionary patterns of the political culture based on the Chicano political experience or heritage (this can be called political development), some manifestations of Chicano ideology or philosophy that are tied to the political culture, and the effects of the political culture on the contemporary political orientation of the Chicano group. We have already suggested in the previous pages the most significant political effects - apolitics, isolation, alienation, and radicalism, and these manifestations will be outlined in later chapters. The concern here will be on the two former manifestations of Chicano political culture.

The Political Development of the Mexican American People

The study of the political development - essentially the evolution of a group of people or polity from one level to another - of the Chicano can be useful in describing, analyzing and explaining significant events or factors that may have influenced and moulded the current political orientations of the group. Since we've suggested that the political development of the Chicano at least up to now has not led toward effective participation in the traditional pattern of American politics, it is useful to see where the evolution toward that pattern became sidetracked.[7]

The study of the political development of the Chicano must begin with at least a brief view of the elements that created the Chicano's antecedent political culture. Like the Mexican and other Latin American peoples the Mexican-American's political culture was strongly tinged by the Spanish colonial heritage. This was a political heritage characterized initially by the absolute monarchy of the Catholic monarchs of Spain in the fifteenth and sixteenth century, and after the independence period by continued authoritarian domestic dictatorships. Combined with the strict hierarchical authoritarian rule, Mexican political culture was influenced by the highly stratified class structure, by the primacy of the Catholic Church over religious and some non-religious matters, and by the systems of authority that combined civil and military authority in a single leader (adelantado), thus military force was a characteristic source of a government's legitimacy.[8] This background was not the most ideal from which to forge a new political culture based on citizen participation, but that was nevertheless the political culture of the Mexican when the American occupation engulfed the South-west. The political socialization process that ensued

among the Mexican Americans following the occupation by
the United States government followed a general pattern to
which New Mexico was the only exception. The pattern has
been well outlined by Alfredo Cuellar,[9] who argued that
the political development of the Chicanos can be divided
into four distinct periods, and that the political activity
of each period was manifest in the form of organizational
activity and the patterns of contact between the minority
and the dominant society.

The first period outlined by Cuellar is called the
period of "conflict and apolitics." Spanning from the
1840's or the period of initial American occupation up
until about 1920, it was a period that characterized a
bitter conflict over land and water and a more profound
clash of cultures and economic systems. The conflict
between Mexican and American was initially manifested over
land, water, and grazing privileges. In Texas, the armed
raids of Mexican chieftains such as Juan Cortina and Juan
Flores Salinas against the Texas Rangers, have served to
illustrate the bitter wars between the Texas authorities
and die-hard Mexican resistance. In California, Tiburcio
Vasquez and Joaquin Murietta have been depicted as leaders
of Mexican resistance to American colonization. The later

manifestation of conflict were the clashes between Mexican laborers and management in the railroads, in the mines and in the fields that began in the early 1900's. In the Southwest as Carey McWilliams has observed, Mexican laborers served as the vanguard for the labor movement. Throughout the three generations of the first period, the Mexican was systematically excluded from politics in all but New Mexico. The process was relatively simple, the prominent position of previous Mexican leaders was undermined by eliminating their titles and land and livestock holdings, and superimposing American authority. The Mexican campesino to whom politics was not overly compelling anyway, simply accepted the change of command which could not be prevented anyway. Mexican organizations of the period were essentially mutual aid societies such as the Alianza Hispano-Americana, La Liga Protectora, La Sociedad Espanola de Benificiencia Mutua, and lay brotherhoods such as the Sociedad de Nuestro Padre Jesus Nazareno or Penitentes as they were better known, which essentially reflected the isolation, the turning inward of the group as a result of the abrasive external social environment. The organizations not only provided mutual protection and benefit, but served as social outlets for members, and instruments for the preservation of the hispanic culture, language and traditions, and generally the welding of the Mexican American into a closely knit group.[11]

The second period, "the politics of accommodation," lasted from approximately 1920 until World War II and was a by-product of the earlier period of conflict. The Mexican American was viewed with suspicion and hostility because of his retention of Spanish culture and language. Life for the Mexican-American in the United States became harsher as he fell victim to economic subordination and consequently racial segregation, discrimination and prejudice. It was an era in which the Mexican American suffered the indignities of mass deportations as law enforcement authorities sided with management in labor-management confrontations. The Mexican-American (especially the middle-class) sought to accommodate themselves to live in a hostile environment, by asserting their loyalty to the United States government. The organizations such as La Orden Hijos de America (Order Sons of the Americas), and the most important, League of Latin American Citizens emerged during this period. Both organizations asserted their loyalty to the United States, stated as their objectives the making of good American citizens, employed the use of English language as their official language, and excluded non-United States citizens from participation.

The political significance of this period was the severing of bonds between Mexican-Americans and Mexico, and the beginning of their total commitment to securing a better life in American society. Like the accommodative temper of Black leader Booker T. Washington, these organizations were willing to accept - at least temporarily - second class American citizenship, as a necessary pre-condition to entering the mainstream of American life. The Mexican-American sought acceptance by the Anglo-American society, of his status as an American citizen and of his loyalty to the American government, even if it meant foregoing the basic American privileges of popular political partici-pation and suffering the indignities of discrimination and second class status.

The third period, "the politicization period" was the dramatic result of the combined changes wrought on the Mexican American community by the second World War. The period began in the 1940's and continued until recent years and was characterized by the beginnings of continued polit-ical activity among the Mexican American community. For the first time, Mexican Americans began to appreciate the importance of group solidarity in the American political game, as efforts to increase Chicano voter registration which would improve chances of gaining elective or appointive political office became more prominent. World War II drastically altered the situation of Mexican Americans in the United States in several ways. First, the need for manpower in the cities to man the American war machine resulted in the urbanization of the Chicano population. The urban areas which were much more politicized, and harsher on the minority in socio-economic problems necessitated the beginnings of political consciousness as a way of attempting to alleviate their harsh situation. Secondly, the entry of hundreds of thousands of Mexican Americans into the Armed Forces in World War II, served to break the racial barriers that had separated the group. Chicanos found themselves as equals to their Anglo peers in uniform, and the exposure to new parts and elements of American life meant that they could not and would not return to or tolerate the patterns of life (segregation and discrimination) which they had left. Mexican Americans would no longer be suspect, since their participation in the war effort had been considerable, as documented by Raul Morin's book, Among the Valiant. Finally, the adoption of the G.I. Bill afforded thousands of Mexican Americans educational opportunities which were heretofore unavailable, and which resulted in the entry of Chicanos into the professions and skilled trades. Once again the Mexican American organizations reflected the mood of the period. The Community Service Organizations (CSO) that emerged in California cities following the war were the first of the Chicano "political" organizations. The CSO was made up of local barrio neighborhood chapters of Chicanos who banded together in efforts to deal with common problems of the Mexican American Community. The CSO was sponsored for a time by Saul Alinsky's Industrial Areas Foundation which supported community organizers such as Fred Ross who entered barrio communities and laid the groundwork for permanent organizations and united ethnic community endeavors. The CSO was instrumental in initiating the politicization of the Mexican American community by launching the first voter registration drives, and by recruiting leaders of the likes of Cesar Chavez and Dolores Huerta who later went on to organize the farm workers, and Edward Roybal who later served as an organizer of the Mexican American Political Association (MAPA) and went on to become the most successful Chicano politician in California history as Congressman from a district in Los Angeles. The demise

of the CSO in the 1950's combined with the disenchantment

of many members with Democratic Party politics in the state

of California gave rise to the Mexican American Political

Association (MAPA) which actively has professed the "ethnic

politics" idea. MAPA not only has advocated Chicano-

oriented issues such as the East Los Angeles incorporation

movement of the 1960's, but has consistently encouraged

Chicano candidacies in either major party and launched

Mexican American voter registration drives.

In Texas, the post World War II politicization of

Chicanos was manifested in the growing activism of LULAC

which reoriented its priorities toward greater politicization

of the Chicano community. LULAC, became the Chicano counter-

part of the Black NAACP, by sponsoring litigation designed

to test Texas school segregation laws. The American G.I.

Forum probably reflected the new post war activist mood

more than any other organization. It emerged in 1948 under

the leadership of Dr. Hector Garcia, a Corpus Christi

physician, as a result of the furor created by the refusal

of the funeral home in Three Rivers, Texas to conduct

funeral services for Felix Longoria a Mexican American

who had died in the Battle of the Phillipines. The specific

crisis was resolved when Senator Lyndon Johnson intervened

on behalf of Longoria and arranged for a hero's burial at
Arlington National Cemetery, but not before a human rights
commission (The Texas Good Neighbor Commission) had been
created, and the ground laid for a stronger civic action
organization in the G.I. Forum. The Forum continued to
pursue Chicano Civil Rights in the 1950's and 1960's. As
in California the early "quasi-political" organization gave
rise to the strictly political groups. In 1960, Dr. Garcia
who had become closely associated with the reform activities
of the G.I. Forum was among the organizers of the "Viva
Kennedy" clubs designed to consolidate the Mexican American
vote for the candidacy of John F. Kennedy. With the
culmination of the 1960 election the Viva-Kennedy clubs
were transformed into the Political Association of Spanish-
speaking Organizations (PASO) which continued efforts to
politicize Chicanos through voter registration drives, and
by encouraging Chicano candidacies, mainly within the framework of the Texas Democratic Party.

In Arizona, the MAPA-PASSO counterpart has been the
American Coordinating Council for Political Education
(ACCPE) which made impressive progress in securing members,
registering voters and participating in some county
elections.[12]

Although a significant beginning was made by the various organizations in politicizing some segments of the Mexican American community during this third period, the progress has been far from overwhelming, as the most recent studies of Chicano voting behavior have manifested, with large percentages of Mexican Americans remaining outside of the domain of American politics.

The fourth period of the political development of the Mexican American people has overlapped the latter stages of the politicization phase and largely coopted it. This period has come to be known as the Chicano movement, and it to date has been the most activist phase. Whether this movement was inspired by the radical politics of Reies Lopez Tijerina, the fiery Chicano land grant leader from New Mexico, or the charismatic leadership of Cesar Chavez, the organizer of the farm workers, has been a point of debate among Chicano scholars. Quite probably the simultaneous emergence of these two leaders and their respective causes together were the catalytic force that inspired the movement. The Chicano movement, has grown beyond the particular struggles led by Chavez and Tijerina, and beyond even the urban civic action efforts of Rodolfo "Corky" Gonzales and the third party leadership of Jose Angel Gutierrez (who together with the former have come to be known as the big four of the activist Chicano leaders), but has encompassed a broader more pervasive struggle.

The Chicano movement today represents a diverse multi-pronged attack on many fronts by many groups and individuals in an effort to uplift the Chicano from his subordinate political, social and economic status. Chicanismo - as the movement can be called since it has become synonymous with the contemporary movement - encompasses Tijerina and the land grant question, Chavez and the struggle of the farm workers; Gonzales and the plight of the urban Mexican American; Gutierrez and the La Unida Party Movement; but it also encompasses the Chicano student's efforts to reform educational processes and curriculum discrimination to Chicanos; the effort of various civic action organizations to eliminate discrimination in housing, employment, law enforcement and education, and the efforts of Chicano scholars, primarily social scientists, and their battle against the traditional social science distortion of Mexican American history and culture, and their pursuit of a reinterpretation of Chicano culture, history and politics.

The strategies and tactics of the movement have encompassed the legal battles, the intellectual rewriting of history and cultural interpretation, the voter registration drives, as well as the violent confrontations, the protests, the boycotts and the demonstrations. As such the Chicano movement has touched and affected all Chicanos, young or old, middle or lower class, conservative and liberal, it has crossed regional boundaries. Just how this most recent phase in the political development will influence the Chicano socialization and political culture is difficult to say, at this point, but the growing evidence of Chicano political activity described in the following chapters may be an indicator.

Chicano Ideology

The previous pages have outlined the historical forces, especially those relating to the Mexican American experience in the United States which influenced the development of contemporary Chicano political culture. The next area of concern is the subject of Chicano ideology or philosophy and its relationship to contemporary Chicano political culture. Chicano ideology must not be confused with Chicanismo, or the Chicano movement, the most recent phase of Chicano political development described above. Chicano ideology, probably gave rise to the various manifestations of the Chicano movement, but as conceptualized here it encompasses the more profound elements of Chicano character and identity.

Needless to say, assertions about "character" and "identity" are the most speculative any scholar must make, especially if such assertions are to be related to particular political orientations. Such speculations, however, must be made because of the profound importance of these phenomena to particular political attitudes that are part of the political culture of the group.

Ralph Guzman[13] has contributed a very provocative essay on the main elements of contemporary Chicano ideology and their historical origins, thus the following speculation relies heavily on Guzman's observations.

Of several possible approaches and possible themes that could be discussed in relation to Chicano ideology, probably four themes stand as constituting primary importance. The four are the concept of la raza, the concept of historical primacy, the Mexican American's culture, and Chicano stereotypes. These four elements have most influenced Chicano political ideology. Just how these elements became part of Chicano ideology is most difficult to outline, because they were elements that developed as a result of the evolving Chicano experience. The origins of the first three are traceable at least to some Mexican and Mexican American writers, so it can be assumed that in some way these written or oral expressions of Chicano ideology found their way into the belief systems of the Chicano community and were transmitted through oral histories. The origin of Chicano stereotypes is attributable more to the dominant society's popular perception of the Chicano in written literature.

The concept of la raza (the race) is probably the central element in Chicano identity. It is the concept or idea that has moulded an ethnic group into a "racial" group. The connotation of la raza is that mestizo (the mixture of Spanish and Indian) represented a distinct race. Jose Vasconcelos may have been the first proponent if not the originator of the term "la raza" and the conceptualization attached to it. Vasconcelos' theory was that the mestizo, "la raza cosmica" was genetically destined to become a super race. Citing the writings of European elitist writers Ashley Montesquieu, Arthur de Gabineau, and Frederick Teggart, Vasconcelos integrated their elitist notions into a systematic argument stating that the combined elements, climate, biological genetic selection, and racial mixture were present in the emergence of la raza. The concept was a defensive ideology (reflecting Vasconcelos' own experience as a Mexican in the United States), and in a sense a state-

ment condemning assumptions of Anglo-Nordic superiority,
and consequently the racial inferiority of the Mexican
American.[14] Although the Vasconcelos conceptualization
has been criticized effectively in scholarly circles, it
goes far in describing the profound significance of the
term to Chicanos. The term "la raza" is embraced by the
overwhelming majority of Mexican Americans, and implies
as powerful an association as racial identity. The
concept embodies also a sense of pride in mestizaje and
the Mexican American culture so closely tied to it. Thus
the element of ethnic awareness and consciousness gives
rise to symbolism attached to "la raza." A less visible
aspect of the concept is the anti-Anglo connotation.
There is a distrust, fear, and suspicion of the Anglo
among the Mexican Americans that often serves as a wall
for cross-cultural understanding. Guzman has shown, for
example, how Chicanos responded to the Anglo's negative
perceptions of Chicanos with reverse negative stereotypes.
These were manifested in pejorative in-group referrants
to Anglos as gringos, bolillos, gueros, and in in-group
ditties such as "gringo salado. . . ." and "chile con carne,
pan con jamon. . . ." Thus, the concept of la raza embraces
an enthnocentrism, a pride in racial and cultural superiority,

and at the same time a hostility toward the presumed antag-
onist, the Anglo. The manifestations of "la raza" in
Chicano ideology are explicit in the symbolism of the contemporary Chicano movement, as they have been manifest in
other ways in the past. The exhortations of "la raza," the
retention of Mexican cultural traditions - language,
ceremonies, songs, family - in spite of American assimilationist patterns, the demand among Chicanos for a retention
of their racial and cultural distinctiveness, the spiritual
sense of community, are all manifestations of the continued
importance of the concept.

The second theme, that of historical primacy embodies
several ideas that are consistent with the first theme of
la raza. The theme like the first was probably ingrained
in Chicano ideology long ago, but was probably first articulated in recent years by George I. Sanchez in his work,
Forgotten People: A Study of New Mexicans. The notion of
historical primacy is the feeling that Mexican Americans
were here long before the Anglo-American, who is viewed
as the intruder, the interloper. The Mexican American by
his Indian origins was here from time immemorial, and even
from his Spanish origins was here long before English
colonization in America.[15] It is from this backdrop of

historical primacy that the Chicano's claim to his distinct
racial and cultural heritage is made. Mexican Americans,
for example, reject most Anglo-American interpretations of
Mexican-American history and culture as "distorted."
Mexican Americans feel they have been a forgotten people
because American historical accounts have not only ignored
and neglected Mexican Americans, but those that have
existed have maligned and disparaged the group. The
Mexican American, in other words, has challenged the
imposition of external standards in evaluating the group
and its worthiness to become Americans. Perhaps like the
Indian, the Mexican American has used the notion of historical primacy as an argument on behalf of cultural
distinctiveness. The manifestations of this mood are
reflected in the resentment against the Anglo for the loss
of the land, and for the social, political and economic
subordination. Rigid adherence to the traditional Mexican
American culture, and the demands for its legitimization
(as bi-lingual, bi-cultural education) in the curriculum
of public schools, is of course the most obvious manifestation in most recent years. Reinterpretations of Mexican
American history and culture and concomitant anthropological
and sociological stereotypes have become the main bone of
contention by Chicano scholars. A more profound political

consequence of this mood may have been a subtle rejection of the American political process on questions of legitimacy, just as has occurred with the Native Americans.

The third theme in Chicano ideology is Chicano culture itself. It is unavoidable that the non-political elements of Chicano culture would influence Chicano political ideology. Here again it is quite difficult to speculate on the exact meaning or impact that this has had on Chicano political orientations, but citing some questions might help make the point.

Chicano culture has been described as highly individualized or introverted. How and why has this affected the political integration of the group? Has the patron system, patriarchal tradition and the extended family (all well documented characteristics of Mexican Americans) and perhaps the breakup of these elements in Chicano culture had consequences on the political orientations of Chicanos, since they were basic political components of the antecedent culture? What has been the political effect of the divergent value systems of the Anglo-American and Mexican American cultures? The Anglo materialistic culture with its fetish for economic acquisition, and "success" as measured by political position, professional attainment, wealth, has been found to be inconsistent with Mexican cultural value orientations. What have been the "political" consequences of these cultural differences?

It seems possible to say, as Arthur Campa has maintained, that the Chicano's culture militated against his assimilation into American life, and it can be assumed that in the same way certain cultural attributes were inconducive to the political integration of the group.

Chicano ideology has also unavoidably been influenced by assumptions or stereotypes generated about the group by the dominant society, or what Guzman calls "majority" ideologies. Majority ideologies had an important impact upon the Mexican American political culture, because they were more widely disseminated in the existing literature which formed the basic knowledge on the Chicano. By and large, majority ideologies presented a negative characterization of Mexican American political behavior. Mexican Americans were felt to be submissive and incapable of independent political activity, being the captives of a "semi-feudal" colonial system run by benevolent patrones and priests. The Mexican American value system was foreign and not consonant with the democratic participatory process of American politics. The Mexican Americans

were possessed of cultural characteristics such as individual-
ism which made it difficult for the group to achieve cohesion
and envidia (envy) which led to members of the group to
suspect aspiring and successful group members and to undermine by deceit or rumor their position.[16]

In light of such assessments mainly by social scientists,
it is not surprising to encounter frequent reference in the
literature on Chicano politics, to the "apathy" the "apolitics"
the "lethargy" the "docility," of the Mexican American group
which has kept the group from political integration.

It has been assumed that the failure of Chicanos,
politically, is the result of a racially or culturally based
apathy and apolitical nature; and consequently this nature
has kept Chicanos from coalescing into a strong, viable
political group that would enhance its political power which
would serve as a basis for altering its socio-economically
deprived condition.

One of the more important problems resulting from
limited knowledge - especially when that knowledge is
negative - according to Guzman is "the creation of an
ideology within which social judgements are made by the
minority group to find his own identity vis a vis the larger
society."[17]

Thus an important manifestation of negative images perpetrated by the majority against the minority is their appearance in minority ideologies. In the case of the Mexican American, one example is the trait which Guzman calls "self-derogation," Arthur Campa calls "negative self-assertiveness," and Raul Morin a "vacilada" (self-derision). A vacilada is a self-group "put-down," such as that frequent heard phrase of hopeless frustration "a que mi raza," which defies correct translation except that it exudes at the same time some frustration, disgust, and derision.

The point Guzman makes is that once ingrained in minority ideology, certain negative assumptions take the form of reality as a result of self-fulfilling prophecies. The group may, for example, see itself as incapable of achieving ethnic unity because of peculiar ethnocentric traits that militate against unity. The common reference by Mexican Americans to the effect that "nosotros la raza no somos unidos" (we of la raza are not united) implies two things. First, that non-Chicanos _are_ united; and secondly that the Chicanos are _not_, because they _are_ Chicanos. This writer has pointed out elsewhere that the great body of literature on the American public by sociologists seriously contradicts the assumption that Americans

are "joiners," and shows that Americans in fact only
sporadically join formal organizations and participate
actively, and do not manifest group cohesion.[18] Thus in
reality frustration by leaders of Chicano conferences over
inability to achieve "like-minded" agreement on all issues
is perhaps based on an unrealistic expectation (an expectation that cannot reasonably be held since Chicanos are a
diverse people with different ideas, motives and aspirations)
that stems from ideological belief patterns.

Another trait often referred to is the notion of
envidia (envy) and is well illustrated by a story included
by Guzman:

> If a Mexican and an Anglo were both trying to
> climb greased poles with prizes at the top, the
> Anglo would clap when the Anglo reached the top,
> but when the Mexican got near the prize, the
> other Mexicans would pull the fellow down by
> his breeches.[19]

The story again implies two things: that the Mexican
American holds the negative trait of envy and that he holds
a premium on that characteristic which is not prevalent
among other groups. The manifestation of envy in Chicano
ideology may be illustrated by phrases such as "orgulloso"
(conceited) or "vendido" (sellout) in reference to aspiring
Chicanos who have "made it" and abandoned their group. Again
the trait is not itself uncommon, but it becomes unfavorable

when it is assumed that it is peculiar only to the Chicano
group.

Guzman says that the product of self-derogation, is
that it becomes ". . .a process that leads to the articulation
of defeat by a minority.../it becomes/ the final creed, the
final ideology of a people who can find no other explanation
for their condition of social disadvantage."[20]

The implication is therefore that the Chicano is in
his present condition of socio-economic deprivation and
political subordination primarily as a result of certain
cultural attributes peculiar to the group which preclude
ethnic unity and cohesion because of their diversive nature.
Since such characteristics are "cultural or racial" and not
easily remediable, the group is more or less "doomed" to
its present fate.

Summary

This chapter has introduced the concept of political
culture, essentially those factors such as history, tradition,
attitudes, themselves not political, which influence political
attitudes and orientations, and applied it to the case of
the Chicano. A model depicting the evolutionary process
and development of Chicano political culture was offered to
help explain the particular pattern which Chicano political

has taken. Central to the process are the antecedent culture, the patterns of contact, the role of the institutions and the socialization process. Although the process can lead to political integration of the minority group into the dominant political culture, in the case of the Chicano the overwhelming forces militated against that integration, creating instead an alternative political culture. The political development of the Mexican American people was outlined in order to underscore the main political orientations of the antecedent Chicano political culture, and how some of the events in the Chicano experience as a minority in the United States might have influenced that development. Essentially, the political experience of the Chicano was abrasive, contributing to political exclusion, subordination and even a measure of alienation and radicalism. Finally, an effort was made to outline the main elements of Chicano ideology or character that have developed as part of the Mexican American experience. Among the important elements discussed were the concept of "la raza," the notions of historical primacy, the importance of Mexican American culture, and Chicano stereotypes. It was briefly shown how these among other elements have found their way into the belief patterns that have become part of Chicano political culture and thus influenced Chicano political orientations.

One central point that emerges from this entire discussion is that Chicano political behavior (orientations) are not solely the product of "racial" and "cultural" characteristics of the group. While Chicano political culture was subjective oriented, there were a number of forces and events in the political experience of the Chicano in the United States that contributed to his present political orientation.

NOTES

[1] See Almond and Verba, The Civic Culture, op. cit.

[2] Martin Needler, Latin American Politics in Perspective (New York: Van Nostrand Reinhold Co., 1968), 6.

[3] Almond and Verba, The Civic Culture, 310-311.

[4] Ralph Guzman, "The Political Socialization of the Mexican American People" Unpublished Ph.D. Dissertation (University of California, Los Angeles, 1970), 6.

[5] Armando Rendon, Chicano Manifesto (New York: Collier Books, 1971), 250-251.

[6] F. Chris Garcia, "The Political Socialization of Mexican American Children: The Development of Political System Values," paper presented at the 26th Annual Meeting of the Western Political Science Association, March 23-25, 1972.

[7] Political development is a very subjective term implying movement from one state or level to another. In this case the subjective standard would be a hypothetical movement toward integration in the American polity as an effective, supportive, participant, citizen.

[8] See Needler, op. cit., Chapter 1.

[9] See Chapter 8, 137-156, in Moore, op. cit.

[10] Lynn I. Perrigo, The American Southwest: Its Peoples and Cultures (New York: Holt, Rinehart and Winston, 1971), 167-168.

[11] For further elaboration see Maurilio Vigil, "Ethnic Organizations Among the Mexican Americans of New Mexico: A Political Perspective," Unpublished Ph.D. Dissertation (Albuquerque: University of New Mexico, 1974), 66-70.

[12] For further description of these four periods and the main organizations of each see Cuellar, op. cit., Guzman, "The Political Socialization of the Mexican American People," op. cit., and Vigil, "Ethnic Organizations Among the Mexican Americans of New Mexico. . ." op. cit.

[13] Guzman, "The Political Socialization of the Mexican American People," Chapter 5. See also Octavio Romano V, "The Historical and Intellectual Presence of Mexican-Americans" in <u>Voices</u>: <u>Readings</u> <u>from</u> <u>El</u> <u>Grito</u>, (Berkeley: Quinto Sol, 1971), 76-90.

[14] Guzman, <u>op</u>. <u>cit</u>.

[15] <u>Ibid</u>.

[16] <u>Ibid</u>., Chapter 4.

[17] <u>Ibid</u>., 52.

[18] See Vigil, "Ethnic Organizations Among the Mexican Americans. . .", 53-59.

[19] Guzman, <u>op</u>. <u>cit</u>., 175.

[20] <u>Ibid</u>., 176.

FURTHER SUGGESTED READING

Gabriel Almond and Sydney Verba. The Civic Culture: Political Attitudes and Democracy in Five Nations. Boston: Little, Brown, 1965.

Arthur Campa. "The Mexican American in Historical Perspective in Chicano: The Evolution of a People. Minneapolis: Winston Press, 1973.

Alfredo Cuellar. "The Political Development of the Mexican American People" in Moore, Mexican Americans. Englewood Cliffs, New Jersey: Prentice Hall, 1971.

Ralph Guzman. "The Political Socialization of the Mexican American People". Unpublished Ph.D. Dissertation, University of California, Los Angeles, 1970.

Octavio Paz. The Labyrinth of Solitude: Life and Thought in Mexico. New York: Grove Press, Inc., 1961.

Octavio Romano V. "The Anthropology and Sociology of the Mexican Americans" and "The Historical and Intellectual Presence of the Mexican Americans" in Voices: Readings from El Grito, Berkeley: Quinto Sol Publications, Inc., 1971.

Maurilio E. Vigil. "Ethnic Organizations Among the Mexican Americans of New Mexico: A Political Perspective." Unpublished Ph.D. Dissertation, University of New Mexico, 1974.

CHAPTER IV

MEXICAN AMERICAN ORGANIZATIONS

An organized interest group may be said to
represent a concentration of power. It is a means
by which individual units of power may be maximized
to exert an impact greater than the sum total of
such units acting separately. A group that is
organized has, on the whole, a tremendous advantage
over comparable unorganized groups. . .It focuses
the energies and political resources of the membership more efficiently behind these interests which
they have in common. . .Organization then provides
a tool for articulating and focusing a group's claim
upon society. The second advantage of organization
is that it establishes an accessible source from
which politicians, government and other interest
groups may seek support for their own endeavors. . .
when all is said and done, organization in politics
remains a sine qua non for effective action.*

Abraham Holtzman, 1966

The Importance of Mexican American Organizations

The paradigm developed in Chapter I suggested that

organizations, in this case ethnic organizations, are basic

to the success of an ethnic group in American politics.

This theme has been the view of Edgar Litt in referring to

the importance of organizations generally in American ethnic

politics. Litt says:

The persistence of American ethnic politics can
be traced, in part, to the activities of organizations capable of mobilizing ethnic sentiments for

*Abraham Holtzman, Interest Groups and Lobbying
(London: Collier-Macmillan Ltd., 1966), 4-5.

political objectives. Indeed, without the
existence of ethnic-based organizations, it is
doubtful that ethnic politics, as we know it,
would have been with us for so many years.[1]

Litt goes on to show how ethnic organizations, "by providing identification, political styles and core values,"[2]
contributed to group cohesion by enhancing the ethnic group
member's subjective identification with the group.

Traditionally, studies of Mexican American voluntary
organizations have noted the failure of the group to form
viable organizations.[3] Miguel Tirado, whose work on Chicano
organizations has been exhaustive, reflects the theme:

When compared with the organizational participation
in politics of other segments of the society, the
Mexican American's ability to organize effectively
into voluntary political association has been dis-
appointing.[4]

Perhaps such assessments failed to consider the
symbolic or subtle importance of ethnic organizations in
creating a more consolidated Chicano community, or perhaps
their assessments of the failure of Mexican American organizations were based on comparisons with inflated assumptions
of the participatory behavior patterns of Americans as a
whole.

Considering the fact that, in spite of the observations
of Tocquevelle and Bryce, Americans are not joiners and do
not actively participate in voluntary associations (political

or otherwise) perhaps observers have held expectations of the Mexican Americans that could not have reasonably been held of Americans as a whole. It is on this moderate but realistic perspective that the possible importance and viability of Mexican American organizations must be considered.

Adapting further the model outlined in Chart A, it is possible to speculate on how the Mexican American organization has served in a crucial role for the ethnic group.

In Chart B, the pre-figure illustrates the typical array of associations possible for a Mexican American. Ethnic identification can be enhanced by two distinct variables that are classified by Litt as "individual bases", and "organizational bases". In terms of the individual bases, ethnicity is enhanced by natural properties such as the salience or visibility of the ethnic factor (such as Spanish surname) and by man's propensity to rely on traditional loyalties (such as ethnicity) in making political choices. In addition, ethnicity may be enhanced by explicit practical incentives including material rewards (jobs, patronage), psychic rewards (recognition), and social mobility.

The ethnic organization contributes to the "natural" drives toward ethnicity by reemphasizing ethnic core values

CHART B

**A MODEL DEPICTING THE PRESUMED EFFECTS OF MEXICAN AMERICAN ORGANIZATIONS
ON ETHNIC IDENTIFICATION AND SERVICE TO THE ETHNIC GROUP**

THE INDIVIDUAL

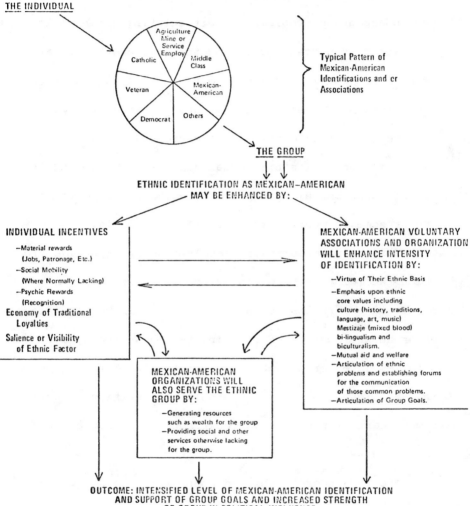

Typical Pattern of
Mexican-American
Identifications and or
Associations

THE GROUP

ETHNIC IDENTIFICATION AS MEXICAN–AMERICAN
MAY BE ENHANCED BY:

INDIVIDUAL INCENTIVES

—Material rewards
(Jobs, Patronage, Etc.)
—Social Mobility
(Where Normally Lacking)
—Psychic Rewards
(Recognition)
Economy of Traditional
Loyalties

Salience or Visibility
of Ethnic Factor

MEXICAN-AMERICAN VOLUNTARY
ASSOCIATIONS AND ORGANIZATION
WILL ENHANCE INTENSITY
OF IDENTIFICATION BY:
—Virtue of Their Ethnic Basis
—Emphasis upon ethnic
core values including
culture (history, traditions,
language, art, music)
Mestizaje (mixed blood)
bi-lingualism and
biculturalism.
—Mutual aid and welfare
—Articulation of ethnic
problems and establishing forums
for the communication
of those common problems.
—Articulation of Group Goals.

MEXICAN-AMERICAN
ORGANIZATIONS WILL
ALSO SERVE THE ETHNIC
GROUP BY:
—Generating resources
such as wealth for the group
—Providing social and other
services otherwise lacking
for the group.

OUTCOME: INTENSIFIED LEVEL OF MEXICAN-AMERICAN IDENTIFICATION
AND SUPPORT OF GROUP GOALS AND INCREASED STRENGTH
OF GROUP IN POLITICAL INFLUENCE.

(history, traditions, culture) through symbolism (la raza),
by encouraging mutual assistance through concerted community
action, by generating forums and communication for discussion of group problems, by articulating group goals, by
generating resources and laying the groundwork for strategies
of action. As will be shown, often ethnic organizations
themselves may develop programs and services that will
improve the lot of members of the group.

While not all ethnic organizations are involved in
all of these pursuits and activities, their involvement in
one or some is contributory toward group goals.

It should be borne in mind that the perspective from
which the role of the organization is viewed here is a
practical and realistic one. First of all, the significance
of organizations can be contemplated by analyzing its
parallel (i.e. organization and/or the lack of it). Viewed
in this light, any level of ethnic organization is politically
significant, since it will contribute to ethnic group
cohesiveness.

The remainder of this chapter will consider various
categories and types of Chicano organizations with emphasis
on their objectives, activities, strategies, and importance
to the Chicano as a whole. Since an undertaking to study

all the Chicano organizations throughout the southwest would

require a separate treatise, in itself, this chapter will

concentrate on the most important national organizations

as well as the localized organizations that exist in New

Mexico, a subject with which this author is most familiar.

The emphasis is on the political dimension - even if by

inference - of the consequences of organizational activity.

Later chapters will be devoted to considering political

parties, and quasi-party political organizations as well

as the organizations led by charismatic Chicano leaders. In

reality all of these organizations political or not, are

included in the references to ethnic organizations made in

the model at the beginning of this chapter; however, for

purposes of in-depth analysis, this division is made at this

point. The order in which the categories of organizations

is taken up has no special significance, but essentially

follows the order in which they were discussed in this

writer's dissertation.

Some General Characteristics of Mexican American Organizations

It is possible and perhaps desirable at this point to

make certain statements about assumptions relating to

Mexican American organizations. These assumptions, sum-

marized most effectively by Tirado,[5] can serve as points of departure for the categorization of such organizations.

Three characteristics seem to suffice in describing
what is currently known about Mexican-American organizations.
These can be summarized as (1) multi-functionalism, (2)
appeals to ethnicity or symbolism, and (3) small active,
sometimes quasi-personalist leadership.

The first characteristic, the multi-functional nature
of Mexican-American organizations is well described by
Tirado who argues that the Mexican Americans have been
criticized for their inability to form viable political
organizations by observers who overlooked the multi-
functional nature of Mexican-American organizations, a multi-
functionality that encompassed political concerns. This
error is due, according to Tirado, to ill founded comparisons
with Anglo organizations. He says:

> Unlike the Anglo-American, the Mexican-American
> traditionally has not developed highly specialized
> organizations for the sole purpose of political
> action. Rather, he has preferred to establish multi-
> purpose organizations which will serve not only his
> political needs but also his economic, social, and
> cultural ones as well.[6]

Tirado goes on to emphasize the reticence of Mexican
Americans to use the term "political" in their titles of
organization, or statements of purpose, perhaps because of
a fear of sanctions from the dominant society, or perhaps
potential members would shun affiliation with a "political"

organization. Notwithstanding this, however, the Mexican American organizations have, according to Tirado, been quite political in actuality.

A corollary to Tirado's observation is that when such organizations have adopted and emphasized the political approach, they have not restricted their activity strictly to political affairs, but have ventured into matters of economics, civil rights, and so on as will be illustrated later when discussing La Raza Unida Party.

As to the explanation for the multi-functionality of such organizations, this can probably be most correctly attributed to the low socio-economic and deprived condition of the minority. That is, the same conditions that created mutual aid and benefit associations and which continued to emphasize the mutual benefit nature of any ethnic organization.

What is the result of this multi-functionality? The most obvious result is that the organizations are not strictly political, not strictly economic, not strictly social, but respond to all kinds of problems, perhaps to the extent of deflating at times their effectiveness in any single area. Normally the response of such an organization is what Tirado calls the "crisis issue" approach, which means that at any single point in time the organization is involved with a single issue which has reached crisis proportions.

While Tirado's point - that such diffusion in organizational activity and that failure of concentration in a single area robs the organization of the expertise and effectiveness it would otherwise have - is well taken, the underlying effects of such organizational activity, based on mutual aid may by establishing a greater "sense of ethnic community", outweigh the losses.[7]

The second characteristic of Mexican American organizations is their appeal to ethnic loyalty by means of ethnic symbols. Since such organizations are based on their ethnic identification, it is most appropriate that membership recruitment, goal articulation, strategies for action, appeals for loyalty and cohesion, be consistent with ethnic group aspirations and methods. Perhaps the most profound ethnic symbol that has permeated the Mexican American community is that of race in the form of "la raza" (the race).

To the Mexican American, his brown skin, a product of his mestizage, serves as the most visible manifestation of his ethnicity, and has served as a source of pride instead of shame to the Mexican American. From this ethnic symbol flow others. Mexican Americans, for example, identify with the religious symbols of the Mexican peasant such as Nuestra Señora de Guadalupe (Our Lady of Guadalupe), who appeared to Juan Diego, symbolizing the concern of God for all peasants. Pictures of Nuestra Senora, in addition to adorning the homes of many Mexican families in early years, have also been carried in banners by Mexican Americans in protest marches. In addition, the retention of the Spanish language (in archaic form) in everyday conversation has served to weld Mexican Americans to their Spanish past. Furthermore, Mexican corridos (songs) such as "Adelita" (the song of the Mexican Revolution), cuentos or dichos (verse or proverbs), dress (such as the colorful fiesta dress), food (such well known dishes as enchiladas, chile, tacos, frijoles, rellenos, posole, tortillas, etc.), fiestas and funciones (community celebrations such as those celebrating conquest, colonization, independence, or a religious patron saint), are all still part of Mexican American culture.

Finally, the Mexican American in his subordinate position in the United States, has found historical refuge in the spirit and ideology of the Mexican Revolution of 1910 and its cry of "tierra y libertad" (land and liberty), and symbolic leadership in its peasant leaders such as Emiliano Zapata and Doroteo Arango (Pancho Villa).

To these historical cultural symbols, the contemporary Mexican American has contributed his own. One is the bold red flag created by Cesar Chavez' United Farm Workers

Organizing Committee (UFWOC), depicting a black Aztec eagle on a background of a white circle, which has been used by other Mexican American groups. Another is the Alianza Federal de Pueblos Libres' (Federal Alliance of Free City States) three headed mural of the Indo-Hispano which depicts a profile of an Indian woman on the left, a profile of a Spanish soldier on the right, and the full face of the Mestizo (Mexican American) depicting the product in the cross-breeding of Spanish and Indian. Still another symbol is the current concept of AZTLAN which connotes a spiritual nationhood of Mexican Americans in the American Southwest. The concept, pronounced by the Rodolfo "Corky" Gonzales led "Crusade for Justice" of Denver and the National Chicano Youth Liberation Conference of 1969, which the Crusade sponsored, calls for a spiritual "nationalistic" union of all Mexican Americans in the United States in language, culture, ideals, and hopes.

Needless to say, the ethnic symbolism portrayed in the above examples and in the vast array of those inferred, is a basic element of Mexican American organizations.

A third and final characteristic of Mexican American organizations is that of a small activist and sometimes quasi-personalist leadership. The first phenomenon - that of a small activist leadership - is a well known axiom of organizations. Much of the current available literature on the properties of small formal groupings seems to confirm the well known premise of Robert Michels about the "iron law of oligarchy". While no effort is made here to confirm or reject the wisdom of the assumptions of elitism, it does seem that Mexican American organizations do conform to the pattern of leadership by a small group that has been discerned in previous studies. That is, organizations within the Mexican American community, rather than being mass grass-root organization movements, are more likely to be inspired and led by a small cadre of interested and active leaders. Quite often, there has been a tendency for a quasi-personalist type of leadership in Mexican American organizations. The quasi-personalist designation is appropriate because although such organizations are very much subject to the influence of a charismatic leader and his particular ideology and concerns, the organization does not usually serve solely the autonomous will of the leader and quite often supercedes his own particular concerns. The ethnic leader quite often develops an ideology that will appeal to that constituency he wishes to serve, and the ideology changes as the needs of the group change. It is after the formative period that the charisma of the leader and the ideology become synchronized in the organization that the

personalist influence emerges. Perhaps this personalist
tendency is a product of the Hispanic political cultural
influences in the Mexican American past, since similar
characteristics have existed among Latin American populations.

A Definition and Classification of Mexican American Organizations

The first surprise that encounters the would be re-
searcher about Chicano organizations is the great number
and variety of such organizations. Because of this, it is
necessary at the outset to provide an operational definition
that can encompass the various categories that need be
established to systematically describe and analyze them.
A Chicano organization is defined as any voluntary organization whose principal ethnic composition (a majority)
consists of Mexican Americans, and in some way is involved
in activities that directly or indirectly foster the ethnic
group's position in American society. As stated before, the
Chicano political organizations and charismatic leader organizations will be described in later chapters because of
their special importance to the topic of Chicano politics.
The other organizations are included among the categories
that follow.

The Chicano Student Organizations

If leaders and organizations like Reies Lopez Tijerina

and the Alianza have been the vanguard of the new Chicano

movement, then Chicano students have been its most consistent

shock troops.[8] Chicano students have not only provided much

of the support for the main Chicano organizations such as

the Alianza and the United Farm Workers, but they have

formed their own organizations with specific objectives

related to their particular concern, education. The

spontaneous Chicano student movement that emerged in the

late 1960s and spilled over into the 1970s can be credited

with providing the movement a continuing drive and probably

its greatest tangible gains thus far.

The Chicano student leaders of today are the product

of abrasive conditions of social contact between the dominant

society and the subordinate Mexican American minority, and

a product of an age of protest in American society.

Quite naturally, the student in venting his protest,

attacks the establishment institution closest to him, the

institution that represents the most important socializing

instrument, the school.

The school, symptomatic of the White Anglo-Saxon Protes-

tant (WASP) dominant society, first in the philosophical

orientation, aimed at socializing students into that WASP

cultural milieu, becomes in reality a "symbol" of that which the Chicano student objects to, and thereof are a target of his protest. Moreover, the school in its "physical" presence including a predominance of Anglo teachers, Anglo control of schools, WASP-oriented courses, especially in history and social sciences, defacto-segregation, presents a picture of basic problems the Chicano faces in American society, thus the school becomes a symbol and target of protest. Moreover, as the schools have come to play an increasingly important role in the political socialization of its citizens and in the transmission of the system's cultural and normative value system, change in this institution, has become a primary concern of all minorities.

Two Levels of Student Protest

Two distinct levels of Chicano student protest can be discerned in relation to academic level and strategy, although the basic underlying objective of making schools more responsive to the Chicano, remains the same. These include the secondary school student movement that has employed the "blowout" or walk-out as the main means of protest and the university student movement, which has relied on mass demonstrations, sit-in occupations and other means to secure its objectives. The dual movements are in fact complementary to each other. The students in the secondary schools are principally concerned with three problems relative to the schools: the high drop-out ratio of Chicano students which is probably attributable in part to the failure of the schools to cope with the particular educational and language problems of Chicanos and the lack of relevancy of social science courses to the Chicano, and finally, the paucity of Chicano teachers with whom Chicano students could better identify. The students in the college level, on the other hand, have been concerned with the failure of universities to train teachers to deal with particular problems of Chicano students as in bilingual, bicultural education. They have also been concerned with the problem of drop-out ratios of Chicano students in the universities, working for the establishment of tutorial and counseling services that would improve the situation. In addition, the university students have strived to increase Chicano representation in the university faculties, especially in the social sciences, as a way of providing a scholarly Chicano perspective in traditional courses.

The Secondary School Movement

The pattern of the secondary school protest was set by the blowouts at Wilson High School, located in the East

Los Angeles barrio area on March 1, 1968. The Wilson High
School walkout soon spread to other schools in Los Angeles.
The school authorities responded by calling the police who
invaded the barrio schools, breaking up protest meetings,
conducting mass arrests, and blockading the East Los Angeles
neighborhoods. The Board, after continued confrontations,
eventually agreed to discuss and remedy some of the problems
cited by the protesters.[9]

The pattern established by the Los Angeles blowouts
soon spread to other cities in the Southwest with similar
problems. In the spring of 1968, students at a Denver
high school, demanding that a teacher who had made a racial
slur be transferred, attempted to occupy the principal's
office. The melee that followed as police intervened soon
turned into a riot in which Chicanos were beaten, maced
and tear-gassed. Eventually 34 Chicanos were arrested.[10]

In Texas, the secondary school student protest evolved
around the Mexican American Youth Organization (MAYO),
centered in the Rio Grande Valley of South Texas. Advocating
the familiar objectives cited before, MAYO helped sponsor a
student walkout at Burbank High School in San Antonio, Texas,
in the spring of 1968 which ultimately succeeded in curriculum
changes that would help channel more Mexican American students
toward college preparation instead of the traditional voca-

tional education programs. In the spring and late fall of 1969, MAYO initiated and led the walkouts of Crystal City, Texas, which resulted in the eventual takeover of the Crystal City School Board by La Raza Unida Party which was in essence launched by MAYO.[11]

New Mexico has also had its share of secondary school student protest since the 1968 Los Angeles blowouts. School systems in the state which have experienced problems include Albuquerque, Las Cruces, Las Vegas, Española, Portales, Roswell, and Santa Rosa.

Three organizations were behind the student demonstrations and walkouts in Albuquerque, Las Cruces, and Roswell. These include the Brown Berets, a para-military type of Chicano youth organization, the Black Berets, a similar group restricted to Albuquerque (both of these will be discussed in greater detail later), and an organization known as the Chicano Youth Association (CYA), made up largely of secondary school students. The CYA's primary function evolved around basic issues involving the schools. The organization organized and carried out student walkouts in Roswell and in Albuquerque schools. In March, 1971, for example, CYA organized walkouts involving 300 students from Rio Grande, Sandia, Del Norte, West Mesa, and Albuquerque High Schools, and Washington, Hayes, and Lincoln Junior high schools, in Albuquerque.

The student protest activity has been an important factor in the introduction of Chicano culture related courses in Albuquerque junior and senior high schools, and bilingual programs in the elementary levels, especially in the valley areas where the bulk of the Chicano population is concentrated. In February, 1972, Chicano student walk-outs and protests forced the resignation of the Anglo high school principle in Santa Rosa high school, for alleged prejudicial attitudes. The Las Vegas protest demonstrations occurred in 1972 (forcing injection of Chicano culture courses in the curriculum) and in 1973 when a newly hired Anglo Superintendent of Schools was forced to resign. Protestors objected to the hiring of an "outsider" who was not aware of the special educational problems of Hispanic students.

In addition to the curriculum, program, and staff policy changes directly attributable to the specific pro-tests, the various protests served as an impetus for other school systems to adopt similar programs. Many schools in New Mexico not subject to protests, have adopted ethnic culture courses and policies that include ethnic minority teacher recruitment, cultural awareness programs to sen-sitize school staffs, and remedial or compensatory education for minority students.

University Chicano Student Movement

More pervasive and successful than the secondary school protests have been the many Chicano student organizations that have developed in the colleges and universities in the Southwest. One of the earliest of such organizations was the United Mexican American Students (UMAS) which developed at the University of California at Los Angeles in 1968 and soon spread to other campuses in California and elsewhere in the Southwest.

In addition to UMAS, other organizations developed in 1968 and 1969 in California colleges under different designations. The Mexican American Students Association (MASA) was concentrated in southern California, eventually coming under the umbrella of UMAS. Another organization, the Mexican American Student Confederation (MASC), was concentrated in the San Francisco Bay area, and another group known as Committee for the Advancement of Mexican-Americans (CAMA) also developed.[12]

In 1969, a movement was initiated at a conference at the University of California at Santa Barbara to bring all university groups under the banner of a new name, Movimiento Estudantil Chicano de Aztlan (MECHA). Since then, about 80% of the Chicano student organizations in California have adopted the new designation, while other chapters retained previous names.

Under the new organizational arrangement each MECHA chapter is an independent entity. The common designation helps achieve cross-campus dialogue and if necessary, collaboration in local struggles. MECHA has spread to campuses in other southwestern states, and as such is probably the most common name, but other designations for campus Chicano organizations are common. In New Mexico, for example, UMAS was instrumental in securing the establishment of a Chicano studies program in 1969, and in applying pressure for the hiring of more Chicano professors. At Highlands University in Las Vegas, New Mexico, the Spanish American Students Organization (SASO) and later Chicano Associated Students Organization (CASO) applied pressure that culminated in the hiring of the first Chicano university President in the country and a redirection of the University's objectives to allow for a multi-cultural orientation. As a result many innovative programs in multi-cultural education have been attempted at the University.

Although the objectives of Chicano student organizations have been quite variable, there are some basic similarities. These have involved efforts to establish ethnic studies programs which make it possible for students to study an ethnic group as a major or minor field of study. Included are courses on a particular group that can be taken in different departments - History, Political Science, Sociology, Language, and so on- and together constitute a field of study. Where such an objective cannot be achieved, the organizations seek the introduction of specific courses - history, politics, sociology which treat the particular ethnic group. The objective of these programs is to allow interested students to "specialize" in such fields and thus develop a competence for teaching them in elementary and secondary schools as the need arises. In addition to curriculum changes, the organizations generally attempt to lobby for the hiring of qualified Chicanos for faculty positions, especially if their field of competence includes ethnic studies. The objective being to provide the "chicano-perspective" in traditional courses. In some cases, these organizations have sought appointment of Chicano university administrators as a way of generating more profound changes in the philosophical directions of universities.

Furthermore, the organizations strive to secure alteration of teacher-training programs so that these allow for specific problems of teaching Mexican Americans. Included are bilingual and bicultural education teacher training and counseling programs. Some organizations have become involved in changes in counseling and tutorial services for Chicano college students as a way of increasing their retention in college.

The strategies employed to secure the above objectives can generally be classified as protest strategies. Students have conducted mass student protest demonstrations, including marches and rallies. They have staged occupations of buildings, thus halting or interrupting normal business. Occasionally, they have gained control of University Student Senates using them as instruments for making demands upon university administrations. Infrequently, they have resorted to more violent and illegal methods of protest.

Chicano Community Self-help Social Service Organizations in New Mexico: A Case Study

An important new development in Chicano organizations has been the emergence of the Chicano community self-help organization.[13] The main difference between this and other ethnic organizations is its entry into "administrative politics", in organizing the minority community for providing social services to the minority community.

The domain of community organizing is a relatively new one in American politics, stemming principally from the Economic Opportunity Act of 1965, the most important of the Johnson "Great Society" programs. John C. Donovan in The Politics of Poverty,[14] speculated on the community organizing aspect of the E.O.A.:

> ...community action as it appears in Title II of
> the Economic Opportunity Act, provides not only
> the largest single program in the Johnson anti-
> poverty attack, but also represents an innovation
> of surpassing importance. Title II also has a
> direct impact upon urban politics in this country
> ...in the section which stipulates maximum feasible
> participation of the poor (although it does not
> read the poor) and thereby stipulates a process
> of major social change...community action is a
> technique for mobilizing the resources of the whole
> community to respond to families and individuals
> as full human beings.../and is based on/ a belief
> that a program which would effectively attack
> deeply rooted economic and social inequities must
> necessarily involve the development of groups
> among the poor capable of exerting substantial
> political pressure on existing institutions.[15]

Although studies analyzing the impact of community

action endeavors have resulted in mixed interpretations,

some favorable and others not, the experience of community

organizing among the Mexican Americans in New Mexico provides

some insight as to one potential strategy for social change

among the Mexican Americans.

Following in the tradition of the mutual aid societies

of the 19th century, a group of self-help organizations has

emerged among Chicanos in New Mexico. These innovative

organizations have responded to the social-economic problems

of the Chicano community by encouraging self-help or endem-

ically generated efforts at dealing with the problems in-

stead of relying on external sources such as governmental

agencies to provide such remedies and services.

The effort is a reflection of either the failure of existing institutional services in correcting the problems, or the failure of such services to reach the ethnic group in the first place. The self-help organizational activity may involve the sponsorship of supplemental or compensatory services to parallel existing institutional services which have not reached the ethnic group, or the creation of corporate entities which will seek external funding (whether governmental or foundational philanthropic) and sponsor the lacking professionalized services. It is appropriate therefore to distinguish between the two categories - self-help compensatory and self-help corporative compensatory organizations. Most at one time or another strive to perform some compensatory service role.

A Self-help Compensatory Organization: La Gente

"La Gente" (The People), an organization made up of mostly young Chicano barrio residents in Santa Fe, New Mexico, and organized in 1970 represents a category of Chicano organizations that essentially address themselves toward resolving the socio-economic problems of the group by generating those services from within the community.

The initial stimuli for the organizational effort

was the desire to create a pressure group made up of barrio

residents which could speak for the residents of the barrio

in relation to local governmental agencies such as the Model

Cities Program responsible for expenditure of vast sums of

federal funds. Their desire was to increase Chicano barrio

input into the decision-making behind such programs and at

the same time, expose inequities that developed in such

programs. However, there was from the start, a desire that

the organization, in addition to acting as such a pressure

group, should itself formulate endemic programs and services

to benefit the people of the barrio.

At early organizational meetings in the latter part of

1970 and early 1971, the name of "La Gente" was adopted and

a structural organization resembling that of the Black

Panthers was adopted.[16] Five ministries - culture, informa-

tion, education, service, and justice - were established.

The Ministry of Culture was made responsible for sponsoring

cultural activities that would emphasize the Mexican culture

and help instill ethnic pride within the barrios. One of

its early efforts was the organization of a "Teatro de la

calle" or (street theatre group) geared to perform mainly

for barrio children. The Ministry of Education was respon-

sible for providing compensatory education, especially the

area of ethnic studies. It began work on initiating a

Chicano school in the barrios. The Ministry of Justice was made responsible for exploring solutions with respect to legal aid as well as problems with the police. The Service Ministry was to undertake feasability studies toward the development of a health clinic and a food cooperative to serve the barrios. The Ministry of Information was set up to coordinate all news and publicity in relation to the organization.

The first activity of La Gente was directed against the Santa Fe Model Cities Program, being largely administered by the Santa Fe Urban Renewal Agency. La Gente became a vehement critic of the Santa Fe Model Cities Program and was instrumental in making the agency more responsive to the interests of the barrio people being served. The organization, having legitimized itself in the eyes of the community and the barrio as an organization representing Chicanos from the barrio, thereafter relaxed its pressure on the whole Model Cities Program, devoting its efforts more toward its "service" function to barrio people.[17]

The group decided initially to concentrate on three activities organized by the Ministries of Culture, Justice, and Services. The Ministry of Culture coordinated the revival of street fiestas in barrios which had been customary in Santa Fe. The Ministry of Justice concentrated its efforts on police relationship with barrio residents, especially youth, in an effort to prevent future instances of police brutality which had been reported.

The main efforts of the organization were directed toward the establishment of "La Clinica de la Gente" (The People's Clinic) a free health clinic located in the barrios of Santa Fe. This has been the most durable accomplishment of the organization.[18]

Self-help Corporative Compensatory Organizations

Another category of organizations that has emerged to provide services that would compensate for the dearth of such services available to the Mexican American community, are a group here labelled "self-help corporative compensatory service organizations." The distinction between these organizations and the aforementioned category of La Gente is that this category represents a corporation consisting of non-professional barrio Chicanos who design and administer programs funded both by private and governmental sources, but principally from governmental sources. Two prominent examples of this category of organization are Nosotros in Las Vegas and COPAS in Santa Fe.

Nosotros, Incorporated

In 1971, a group of barrio Chicano residents in West

Las Vegas, New Mexico, interested in addressing themselves
to some of the problems of the underprivileged and elderly
in the town, launched a new organization called <u>NOSOTROS</u>
(Us).[19] The 40 people who attended the meeting adopted a
proposed corporate charter for the organization and selected
a board of directors consisting of six members.

According to the charter, Nosotros was "a community
corporation," private and non-profit in nature. The charter
provided that the board of directors manage and govern the
organization, and that all members participated in the
selection of the board. The board itself assumed a dual
function, as a plural executive, and as individual administrators of specific programs.

Nosotros was based as the name itself implies (we, us,
ourselves), on the concept of self-help, and aside from the
external funding received for its projects, the effort was
to generate social services from within the barrio community
as much as possible. Programs were planned, organized,
staffed, directed, coordinated, and administered by non-
professional barrio residents, the "potential beneficiaries
because they best know their needs." The organization
received its funding for its various social service programs
from Title IV of the Social Security Act through a contract
with the New Mexico Health and Social Services Department.

Local (including private funds) and state funds were matched by proportional federal contributions.

A very important facet of Nosotros was the pedagogical experience which the board and the membership were part of. The experience, based on the fact that "la gente pobre" (the poor people) can plan, set up, and administer their own social service programs and effectively deal with their own problems democratically through their own organizations, was underscored in its statement of purpose:

> --Nosotros is a dream--A dream for unity and self development among Chicanos in northern New Mexico. A dream for power, economic, and political autonomy, to be able to work for social change and a better quality of life for our people. Toward this end, we are seeking funds, to create more jobs, and independent, non-governmental sources of income. However, the Nosotros philosophy believes that it is not enough to merely feed more people or increase their incomes. We believe that How people are helped is just as important. Nosotros seeks to restore traditional values of cooperative hiring and socializing common to our people by creating economic ventures and employment opportunities that enhance these values.[20]

To implement the ambitious objectives, Nosotros initiated a comprehensive social service program including services for the elderly, day care centers, home and family counseling, mental helath, criminal rehabilitation, and youth services.

Nosotros at its height maintained a staff of 52 full-time and 11 part-time employees in its various programs.

Because the employees were "non-professionals", their moderate salary made it possible for the program to benefit employable community residents who in turn helped the needy in the community.

In addition to the broad range of programs sponsored by Nosotros itself, the organization was instrumental in generating other community services for the disadvantaged of the community. Nosotros lobbied and laid plans and ground work for the location of an office of JUNTOS (together), a state rehabilitative organization and program for ex-convicts.

Nosotros was also instrumental in securing the location of an office of the New Mexico Rural Legal Services (NMRLS) in West Las Vegas.

Nosotros was disbanded in 1974 after its contract for funds with the New Mexico Health and Social Services was curtailed. Since that time efforts to revive the much needed programs have been continued.

Corporacion Organizada Para Accion Servidora

A second example of the self-help corporative compensatory organization is Corporacion Organizada Para Accion Servidora (known by the acronym, COPAS (cups), of Santa Fe.[21] COPAS, unlike its Las Vegas counterpart Nosotros, did not receive its initial impetus from grass-roots community meetings, but instead developed from city governmental initiative.

In mid-1970, as the city of Santa Fe launched its Model Cities and Community Action Programs, administrators involved in the program, as is customary, sought the participation of residents of the urban ghetto environment which was to benefit from the program. The Model Cities administrators in line with standard practice in other communities, sponsored a "pro forma" election in the barrios for the selection of a board of directors from among the poor to administer the broad social service program. It was expected that the board after its formation, would select an executive director - a professional administrator of such programs - to administer the programs and fade to the back ground as the bureaucracy took over, thus having presented the facade of barrio community leadership. Spurred by a group of community organizers known as the Center for Community Action (CCA) who promised technical advise and assistance, the newly elected board of directors broke precedent by refusing to hire a single professional executive director and instead appointed themselves jointly as full-time executive directors of the private people's corporation they called COPAS.

Operating under a comprehensive CCA plan, the COPAS

board secured funding contract approval from the New Mexico
Health and Social Services Department which administered
U.S. Department of Health, Education, and Welfare funds
from the Santa Fe Model Cities program administering U.S.
Department of Housing and Urban Development funds, and from
the New Mexico Department of Hospitals and Institutions.

Probably the main reason for the receptiveness of the
funding agencies to the people's corporation idea was the
novel or fresh approach toward the problems of the poor.

The organizational concept is similar to that of its
Las Vegas counterpart, Nosotros. The board of directors,
acting jointly as the plural executive, direct and coordinate
the planning, staffing, policy-making and budgeting. At
the same time, each board member is administratively responsible for a specific program.

COPAS has administered five social service programs
including a mental health program, an arts and crafts program, a drug abuse program, a cultural awareness program
designed to enhance Mexican American cultural awareness in
the residents of the Santa Fe Model Neighborhood area, and
finally, a program to assist the recovery for former
alcoholics.

COPAS has not been without its problems since its
inception. Efforts by and failure of Santa Fe Model Cities

officials to secure control of COPAS funding (and the jobs
provided), resulted in the cutoff of COPAS funds, forcing
the organization to go to private sources for their local
share of in-kind contribution. COPAS has continued operation
in spite of this financial problem.

In a very important way the efforts of La Gente, COPAS,
and Nosotros represent perhaps a new approach to the problems
of the poor, dispossessed, isolated minorities in American
society.

Probably the most significant aspect of the self-help
community organization is that it represents an effort
among people in one of those minority groups to deal with
their own problems. It engenders a feeling of pride among
ethnics in the barrio that they can, by ethnic community
mobilization, influence and perhaps manipulate their own
socio-economic environment.

Chicano Community Service Organizations

The pattern of segregation in which the Mexican American
has lived in the United States made it necessary for the
group to develop parallel structures often emulating those
of the dominant society. Thus, often Mexican American ethnic
organizations have essentially been the product of efforts
among Mexican Americans to form their own groups to compensate

for their exclusion from organizations of the dominant
society. The organizations here labeled "community service
organizations" are examples of this pattern. The League
of United Latin American Citizens (LULAC) and the American
G.I. Forum are categorized as community service organizations
because of their similarity - in activities (civic service
while providing a social outlet for members), organizational
structure (voluntary membership with decentralized local,
state, national organization), and leadership patterns
(popularly elected short-term leaders) - with the typical
American community service or fraternal club, Kiwanas,
Rotary, Elks, Lions and so on. The unique feature of
Chicano community service clubs has been their ethnic
basis (created because of the exclusion of Chicanos from
Anglo service clubs), and the nature of their community
service, which of course has involved problems such as civil
rights and political, social and economic reform. Aside
from this, however, LULAC and G.I. Forum have been very much
like the typical American service club, attracting mainly
middle and lower middle class membership, serving as an
important social outlet for the members, and duplicating
the organizational structure as well.

This summary will attempt to outline the origin and
development of the LULAC and G.I. Forum, their accomplishments

and their importance to the Mexican American community.
It will also speculate on factors that have limited the
effectiveness of these organizations in relation to social
reform on behalf of the group. It is suggested here that
regional variations in the social milieu, combined with the
problematic organizational structure, leadership recruitment,
and ambivalence over organizational objectives, have minimized the potential importance of these organizations.[22]

First of all, the dual function of the Chicano service
clubs - "service" and "social" - have created a question as
to which objective was to have priority. The question is,
how effective can a service club which is socially oriented
be, in resolving complex social problems of an ethnic minority? The answer is probably, only partially successful,
depending upon specific variables such as its commitment
and its leadership, at a given time.

Moreover, since the purely ethnic community service
clubs were emulative of such groups in the dominant society,
they were more prevalent and strongest in areas where Chicano
isolation was greatest and most persistent (i.e. Texas),
and less prevalent where ethnic isolation was not as great
or as persistent. In New Mexico, where the conditions leading
the continued social isolation of at least the middle class
sector of the minority group were promptly being reduced,

the development of these Chicano service clubs was adversely affected. Thus in New Mexico the earlier "parallel" Chicano community service club organizations which were introduced - namely, LULAC and the G.I. Forum - prospered in the 1940s and 1950s but tended to decline by the 1960s as the avenues for membership in the traditional service clubs - Kiwanas, Rotary, etc., - were opened.[23]

The decentralized organizational structure of both LULAC and G.I. Forum has largely been imitative of the service clubs they were patterned after, thus the organizational pattern left the local chapters pretty much to their own initiatives and concerns, including determining which - service or social - was to be the main priority.

The organizational problem is compounded by the leadership problem such organizations have faced. Again, patterned after the service clubs, the tradition in both LULAC and G.I. Forum has been that of selecting local, state, and national officers for a single one-year term. By thus rotating leadership positions, they have minimized the possibility for sustained, effective leadership.

The overall effect of these combined problems - regional variations, ambivalence over goals, organizational and leadership problems - seem to result in a highly variable pattern of organizational effectiveness in terms of region and time among both LULAC and G.I. Forum. Local chapters of the organizations are often very active in social reform efforts, especially if they come up with a particularly able leader. However, as often happens, the local chapters may rarely meet and or engage in little or no social or reformist activity. Nationally, therefore, they are comparatively large organizations with large memberships and impressive organizational structures. In reality, however, more often the bulk of the membership is rarely involved in everyday organizational activity, and often many of the numerous local chapters are dormant. The sustained activity of the organization is carried on by a loyal group of involved leaders and a select group of local chapters.

The League of United Latin American Citizens - LULAC

As mentioned before, LULAC emerged as one of the first Mexican American organizations during the "accomodative" period of Mexican American political development. In fact the early history of LULAC was tied closely to La Orden Hijos de America (Order Sons of the Americas) the accommodative organization that preceded it in 1921. The origin of LULAC stems to a meeting in Harlingen, Texas in August, 1927, when a new Mexican American organization called League of Latin American Citizens was formed. The sponsors of the

meeting seeking to integrate the Order had invited the
participation of the older organization, but those members
refused, insisting that the new group should be a new
chapter of the Order. In 1929 efforts to unify the two
groups and a third new organization, the Order Knights of
America, resulted in the calling of a meeting by the San
Antonio Council of the Order. The meeting held in the
Salon de Obreros (Workers Hall) in Corpus Christi, Texas,
resulted in the creation of the League of United Latin
American Citizens.

The constitution and by laws adopted by the new organization emulated those of the Order, in asserting loyalty
to the United States government and to the principles of
good American citizenship and in restricting membership to
American citizens, thus excluding Mexican nationals. English
was the official language, and LULAC pledged to encourage
members to become supportive of the American system.

The organization's first priorities were mutual assistance based on ethnic brotherhood, (the by-laws also stressed
pride in ethnic origins), but stressed that these were in
the context of American life. The local chapters became a
major social outlet for members and their families, since
the organization was viewed as acceptable and not as a
threat by the Anglo dominant society. The overly accommodative

temper of the organization understandable in light of the harsh social environment of the period - enabled the organization to grow rapidly, as new councils were founded in other Texas cities. By the 1930s, the organization became truly national as local chapters were founded in Arizona, Colorado, California and New Mexico, and as a national organizational structure headed by a national chairman was established.

In 1938 the first non-Texan was elected national chairman of LULAC. Also by this time a women's auxilary and Junior LULAC (for young Mexican Americans) had been organized making the LULAC a family membership endeavor.[24]

The second world war had a profound impact upon LULAC and its membership, thousands of whom participated in the war effort. The accomodative and non-political orientation gave way to a more activist political orientation in the 1940s. With its counterpart among the black community, the NAACP, LULAC became involved in the civil rights litigation struggle in the courts. LULAC sponsored litigation in state and federal courts in Texas and California challenging school segregation policies successfully, and foreshadowing the success of the NAACP in the Brown decision of 1954. LULAC later initiated their famous "Little Schools of 400" which were pre-school programs manned by LULAC

volunteers designed to teach Mexican American 400 basic
words in English before entering first grade. These schools
laid the basic framework for the philosophy of the federal
government's "Operation Headstart" program.

In the 1940s, LULAC was instrumental in securing passage
of the Fair Employment Practices Act by the New Mexico
legislature. The law did much to remove discriminatory
employment practices against Mexican Americans.

With the G. I. Forum, LULAC assumed in the 1950s and
1960s the foremost advocate of the Mexican American community
in civil rights matters. The two organizations initiated
litigation in the courts, lobbied in state legislatures
and petitioned for the removal of discriminatory barriers
against Mexican Americans in education, employment, and
public facilities.

At the present time, LULAC is the largest and oldest
Mexican American organization in the United States with an
estimated membership of well over 250,000. The national
organization consists of national officers selected for one-
year terms at an annual convention. The organization is
further subdivided into three major regions: the Midwest
(including all Midwestern and Eastern states); the Far West;
and the Southwest (including Texas, New Mexico, Colorado,
Oklahoma, Kansas, Louisiana, and Arkansas). Each region

also holds conventions and elects officers. The state organization likewise holds conventions subdivided into districts, and both levels elect officers. The local council is the basic cog in the highly decentralized administrative structure, and thus exercises great discretion in the extent or nature of its participation in organizational matters. The official newsletter of LULAC is the LULAC News, a monthly newsletter (usually about four pages) printed in Paramount, California, which communicates to members ongoing activities of the national officers and matters of national LULAC policy, news of respective regional state or local interest, and social notices relating to conventions, etc.[25]

On a national basis, the LULAC has been involved in an effort to create progress for the Mexican American, simultaneously and alternately, through civil rights, education, job training, housing and economic development projects. Some of its most important current projects include joint sponsorship with the G. I. Forum of Project SER (or Jobs for Progress) a manpower development training and referral program for Mexican Americans; sponsorship of low-income housing in Mexican American barrios of southwestern cities; the LULAC Economic Development Association (LEDA) which is an effort to encourage economic development within the minority by assisting minority business development; the educational referral program, wherein LULAC helps place Mexican American students in colleges and trade schools and helps secure financial assistance. LULAC has also supported other Chicano organizations in their respective struggles, such as the farm worker's boycotts and the G. I. Forum's boycott on Coors.

While the objectives, concerns, and activities of the national organization have been quite consistent, this has not always been the case in the respective state and local chapters which have varied in the extent of activity and involvement either in national LULAC projects or in local problems.

The American G.I. Forum

As has been emphasized before, World War II wrought very significant changes in the conditions of Mexican Americans, especially those young men who found themselves in military service. Having returned from service to their country where they had been treated as equals, Mexican American veterans found themselves returning to the same pattern of segregation, discrimination, and prejudice which they had left prior to the war. Especially in the more abrasive settings of Texas, California, Arizona, and little Texas in New Mexico, Mexican American veterans found the schools still segregated, public accommodations still closed to Hispanos, and especially the familiar discriminatory practices in employment. As the returning veterans applied for membership in the traditional veterans groups, they were often refused membership or encouraged to form their own separate chapters. These conditions were severely resented by Hispano veterans. This was the situation in 1948, in Texas when the Longoria controversy stimulated the emergence of the American G. I. Forum.

The furor created by the incident climaxed the anguish of Mexican American veterans in south Texas who united behind the leadership of Dr. Hector Garcia, a Corpus Christi physician who had served as an officer in the Infantry, Engineer, and Medical Corps. Garcia founded the initial chapter of the American G. I. Forum in Corpus Christi on March 26, 1948. The Corpus Christi chapter waged a nation-wide campaign which publicized the inequities and indignities returning Mexican American veterans were facing, as visibly dramatized by the Three Rivers, Texas incident. In view of the publicity generated by the incident, the Texas State Legislature appointed a committee which formed the Texas Good Neighbor Commission which investigated the allegations and reported that the funeral director's actions were indeed discriminatory. The matter of Longoria's burial was resolved when then Senator Lyndon B. Johnson intervened and arranged for Longoria's burial at Arlington National Cemetary with full military honors.

The burial of Longoria, however, did not bring an end to the Forum. Spurred on by the fiery leader who used the patriotic organization as his platform and base of support, the G.I. Forum, overnight, became the champion of civil rights for the Mexican Americans in Texas. Dr. Garcia, in public meetings, legislative hearings, court cases, and whatever forum available, was critical of, and presented facts and statistics relating to widespread discrimination against Mexican Americans in Texas - ranging from discrimination in employment (hiring, firing, wages, working conditions), to education (continuing school segregation policies, sub-standard schools, teaching, and curriculum), to public facilities (housing, restaurants, barber shops, swimming pools which were barred to Chicanos), to health (in which Garcia presented shocking statistics about high incidence of infant mortality, tuberculosis, and other diseases).

The G.I. Forum, though veiled in the guise of a veterans group extolling the virtues of patriotism, citizenship, military service, sacrifice for country, became primarily a Mexican American civil rights organization. The organi-zation grew rapidly, expanding to over 100 chapters in Texas by the end of 1949. By 1951, the forum was national in scope, having formed chapters in New Mexico, California, and other states.[26] The growth of the organization tapered off since then.

Part of the success of the Forum, both in attracting adherents and in maintaining its legitimacy with American society was that its leaders successfully emphasized American symbolism emulative of such groups as the American Legion and the Veterans of Foreign Wars. Aside from its symbolic designation, the forum adopted an emblem consisting of a shield emblazened in red, white, and blue, with 13 stars and stripes depicting the original colonies. The Forum uniform consisted of a blue and red "overseas" cap and a blue blazer, both with the Forum insignia. The local chapter was identified by a patch on the right hand side of the cap. Moreover, the Forum constantly reminds its members and the public of the heroism and patriotism manifested in time of war by Mexican American servicemen. It was this facade which allowed the Forum to serve as perhaps the most effective Chicano organization in the transitional period between World War II and the onset of the Chicano movement.[27]

By the 1950s, the primarily social action activities of the Forum had given way to greater political activism. The individual Forum chapters, especially in Texas and

California, launched registration, "get out the vote", and "pay your poll tax," drives and members were encouraged to run for office. Dr. Garcia, who went on to become the first National Chairman of the Forum, later served as National Coordinator and organizer of the "Viva Kennedy" clubs which sought to secure the Mexican American vote for John F. Kennedy in 1960, and later served as National President of PASO from 1960 to 1964.

Although the Forum developed and admittedly was the most successful of the Chicano social reform organizations in the late 1940s and 1950s, it has, like its counterpart LULAC, experienced problems in the 1960s that derive partially from its organizational and leadership structure. It is this evolution of the organization, over time toward social concerns, which justifies in the present study, its characterization as a Chicano community service organization.

Presently, the Forum maintains chapters in 23 states with an estimated membership of 20,000. At the top of the highly decentralized organizational structure are the national officers headed by the National Chairman, selected at the annual national convention. Each state sends delegations to the national convention. The leadership structure and tenure of offices is duplicated in the local forums. Essentially what results is a highly variable pattern of

activity relating to participation in civic affairs. The
national officers are usually quite involved in selected
national Forum programs. The local chapters may or may
not be active in pursuing national and/or local projects,
or may be merely social clubs. Like LULAC, ongoing concerns
of the active chapters are scholarship drives, low cost
housing, employment training and referral services, boycotts of discriminatory businesses, and so on. The local
forums serve the social needs of traditional service clubs
by sponsoring dances, picnics, queen contests, and so on.
Like LULAC, the Forum maintains sponsorship of a women's
auxiliary and a youth counterpart. At the national level
the Forum has devoted much of its efforts to Project SER,
an ambitious job training and referral program with offices
in 39 major cities in the United States serving mainly
Mexican American clientile. In 1973 the National G. I. Forum
also initiated a "Veterans Outreach Program" designed to
help returning veterans in readjustment to civilian life by
providing educational and employment counseling and referral.

Since 1968, the Forum also sponsored the boycott against
Coors Beer because of alleged discriminatory hiring practices
by the Coors Brewery in Colorado.

The short tenure of the Forum's officers at all levels,
needless to say, has limited the long-range effectiveness of

the organization as a social action group. During Garcia's
leadership, the Forum reached its height of success. Garcia
continues to serve in the Forum's Board of Directors, and
as its founder and greatest leader, is appropriately granted
continuous prestigious accolade in the _Forumeer_, the four
page newsletter of the Forum, and in such events as the
annual Founders Day Banquet in Corpus Christi. Dr. Garcia
is still quite active as a spokesman for Chicanos in civil
rights matters.[28]

In retrospect, the LULAC and G. I. Forum certainly
rate among the most important organizations as far as contributions to the Chicano community are concerned, and the
critical outlook has not been intended to challenge their
significant contribution. Instead, the effort has been to
suggest possible factors that have tended to limit the long-
range importance of these organizations. Certainly being
the largest of Chicano organizations in membership, they will
continue to play an instrumental role in the future development of the monority group.

Chicano Business and Professional Associations

It was perhaps inevitable that the Chicano movement
would begin to generate more specialized organizations that
would deal with the particular problems of certain segments

of the Chicano community.

Just as a natural outgrowth of societal evolution toward more complicated forms is the development of more complex and differentiated organizations, so also would it seem natural that the evolution of a social movement from the general to the specific, would lead to the development of concern for more specialized and specific problems that would affect particular segments of an ethnic group, and thus to the formation of specialized organizations that would address themselves to those problems. Such an evolution to such complicated forms of organization, it would seem, manifests the organizational sophistication that an ethnic group has reached, and is an indication of the "maturation" of a social movement.

The next discussion will illustrate how some segments of the Mexican American community in the southwest and particularly in New Mexico have generated several examples of what are herein classified as specialized organizations. These organizations may be broadly categorized as "business" and "professional" associations because each category serves a particular clientele, each possesses distinct objectives and performs distinct functions, although both are essentially ethnically based. Because of these distinct functional properties, the two categories will be considered separately.

Minority Business Organizations

The evolution of the American capitalistic system from
the simple to the complex, and from a laissez fairre economic
doctrine toward a Keynesian doctrine of a government reg-
ulated economic system, has resulted in the proliferation
of a whole array of heterogeneous business associations in
American society. Not only do general business associations
such as the U.S. Chamber of Commerce and the National Association of Manufacturers continually protect, preserve, and
foster the interests of business in the Congress, the courts,
or the executive agencies, but also trade associations
reflecting particular business and industrial concerns and
private corporations, are actively engaged in the ongoing
arena of government policy formulation. Whether business
associations have emerged in response to external threats
(for example, that of labor) or to help establish internal
codes of fair competition (as the trade associations) or
simply to foster a more favorable climate for private
business enterprise, there is little doubt that business
associations are inextricably intertwined in the ongoing
process of government policy formulation.

This setting of business involvement in the policy
process has enhanced the importance of those resources -
primarily money or capital - which are employed by business

groups in securing their influence. Money, whether employed
in the form of legal campaign contributions or illicit kick-
backs and bribes, is an important if not the most important,
resource for political influence; possession of this resource, needless to say, will vastly improve a group's
political influence. It is axiomatic that a minority group,
traditionally exempted from political access, would almost
necessarily be characterized by its lack of capital resources, and that perhaps its minority status is directly
or indirectly a reflection of such a lack of capital.

Recognizing this problem, ethnic minority leaders have
long argued that the most plausible approach to resolving
ethnic minority problems is by generating the capital
necessary to enhance the economic development of the minority
group. Reflecting this general thinking, there has been a
marked effort in the late 1960s and early 1970s to implement
programs that would do just that. The impetus for such
efforts have been ethnic minority business organizations and
interestingly, one agency of the federal government, perhaps
responding to the traditional pressures of other ethnic
organizations. The most recent trend, therefore, in the
long line of business organizations is the minority business
association which serves its own minority constituency,
which has as its objective generating capital for the

minority, and which serves as the clientele and supporter
of a distinct federal agency, the Office of Minority Business Enterprise (OMBE).

Needless to say, the main impetus for minority business
associations came initially from the Black community. But
in recent years, the Mexican American minority has responded
positively. The Office of Minority Business Enterprise was
created within the U.S. Department of Commerce in 1969 as
a result of a Presidential Executive Order. The agency has
become a "major catalyst in both the federal and private
sectors in developing and coordinating opportunities for
qualified members of minority groups to engage or participate in profitable business enterprises."[29] The creation
of OMBE has, consequently, fostered the growth of minority
business associations among all of the ethnic groups by
providing capital resources which were traditionally lacking.
Reflective of the growing trend of Mexican American minority
business initiatives, former President Nixon appointed in
1973, a Chicano, Alex Armendaris, as the Director of the
Office of Minority Business Enterprise.

CAMBIO: A New Mexico Chicano Business Association

It was shown in the previous chapter how Chicano
organizations, namely LULAC and the American G.I. Forum,

recognized the need for internal economic developmental efforts that would improve the condition of the Mexican American minority, and how these organizations responded with programs such as LEDA and SER, designed to provide some remedy. Traditionally, however, such programs floundered because neither organization had the capital to finance either the projects generated or the operation itself. The creation of OMBE has remedied the problem of capital and has thus enhanced the development of such organizations.

In New Mexico, the most prominent Chicano minority business organization is the Corporation in Action for Minority Business and Industrial Opportunity, or as it is commonly referred to by its acronym, CAMBIO, the Spanish word for Change. CAMBIO was established and incorporated as a private, non-profit, statewide, economic development cor-poration in 1970. From an initial membership of twenty, the corporation had risen to a membership of over 1,500 by January, 1973.[30]

The organization is governed by a 25 member, non-paid Board of Directors, some of whom are elected by the entire membership. The CAMBIO rules provide that the president of the local chapters also serve on the Board of Directors and allow for each chapter to select one additional representative to serve on the State Board. As of January, 1973, local CAMBIO chapters have been established in Española, Las Vegas, Albuquerque, and Santa Fe. Its membership is primarily, but not legally, confined to Mexican Americans, and consists of individuals who presently operate a business or who are engaged in business related careers. Members are required to submit a formal application for membership along with a minimum contribution of $10.00, which is deposited in capital account and used for development enterprises.

In April, 1972, CAMBIO was funded by the Four Corners Regional Commission for $49,400 which financed administrative offices in Albuquerque and Espanola. During this first year, CAMBIO helped clients secure some $310,000 in federal loans. Upon expiration of this contract, CAMBIO was awarded federal funding through a contract with the OMBE. In fiscal year 1972-1973, the contract called for $205,752, most of which was used to finance administrative offices in Española, Las Vegas, Roswell, Las Cruces, and Grants. Each CAMBIO office is headed by an area deputy administrator who is assisted by an administrative assistant/secretary. The Las Vegas office is also assisted by an economic development specialist provided by Highlands University through

separate funding. The office staffs are supplemented by
Vista Action Program volunteers who may provide extra legal,
accounting, marketing, or other expertise depending upon the
volunteer's own field of interest.

The CAMBIO concept embodies a philosophy committed to
bringing about economic change within the minority segment
of New Mexico's population by encouraging and assisting
them "to partake of the free enterprise system." The concept
includes both general and specific objectives and goals
aimed toward improving the plight of the minorities (primarily the Mexican American) by attacking the economic
problems which, it is felt, are at the base of the minority
group's ills. In general terms, CAMBIO's purpose is to
"promote economic development on a statewide basis" by
generating "venture capital to establish or assist new or
existing minority businesses," and by providing "technical
and managerial assistance."[31] By its emphasis upon economic
development through business enterprise, CAMBIO:

> . . .recognizes the needs of residents in many
> New Mexico communities for jobs, education, health
> assistance and other matters that serve to provide
> a better life for all. In its efforts to address
> these broad human needs, CAMBIO assumed an econo-
> mic approach to its program of service to the
> community. The simplified theory is that if there
> are sufficient jobs that pay a just wage for a man's
> labor, each person will be able on his own to care
> for himself and his family. CAMBIO set out to

create jobs for New Mexico residents by developing
business enterprises. Some enterprises have been
fairly common business, while others have been
innovative and experimental.[32]

In more specific terms, CAMBIO provides technical and

professional managerial service for potential and existing

minority businessmen. For the person desiring to initiate

a business, CAMBIO will assist in conducting a feasibility

study to ascertain the proposed business's potential, will

advise the client about capital investment requirements,

and sources of financing needed to start a business, and

provide ongoing and follow-up advise on procedures, account-

ing, and other technical matters. For the person already

in business, CAMBIO will provide technical advise on solving

specific business problems, operating more efficiently,

and where appropriate, secure additional funding for expansion

of operations.

The CAMBIO concept is based on the assumption that the

Mexican American community has traditionally faced problems

because of the self-perpetuating economic cycle which has

maintained the group in its subordinate status. Mexican

Americans, CAMBIO argues, have been unable to initiate

business endeavors due to lack of capital. Conventional

lenders cite insufficient experience and collateral for

loan application rejection. Yet, without the capital, the

experience cannot be had. The question of lack of experience involving such technical matters of initiating a
business such as feasibility studies, prospectus, bookkeeping, tax structures, and so on, result in the labeling
of the Mexican American as a "bad credit risk". Thus,
according to CAMBIO:

> The potential Mexican American entrepreneur
> is sometimes discouraged because he sees himself
> as others see him: limited in business and
> economic skills. . .all of the above feed on each
> other, worsening the economic situation of the
> Mexican American community. . .[33]

In an important way, CAMBIO feels it must alter existing attitudes and images held by the dominant society about
the business potential of Mexican Americans, while enhancing
the self-image of the individual Mexican American about his
own business ability. To accomplish this, CAMBIO hopes to
establish a "risk capital fund" which along with federal
small business loans could help get a business off the
ground. CAMBIO will itself provide the needed technical
advise and assistance to the novice businessman. The
positive results will be, according to CAMBIO, that:

> As Mexican Americans find themselves competing
> successfully on an equal basis, their own sense of
> worth and ability will be greatly enhanced. . .As
> self-image and outmoded attitudes are changed, a
> new cycle will emerge that is the reverse of the
> current trend.[34]

CAMBIO's main objective is to generate new minority
businesses and to expand existing ones, and the main part
of its effects have been in this area, described by CAMBIO
as "loan packaging" or acquiring various forms of loans
from commercial banks, from the Small Business Administration, from other SBA guaranteed loans, and from other
agencies. In 1972-1973, for example, CAMBIO helped prepare
and submitted 91 loan requests of which only five were
rejected for an approval percentage of 94.5%. The loans
approved totaled over $1,579,032. In addition, CAMBIO has
assisted in loans totalling $2,543,000 which are currently
pending approval. In relation to the types of businesses
which serve as CAMBIO clients, 48.4% are service type
businesses; 28% are retail outlets; 12.4% are construction
firms; 3% are manufacturing; 2.5% are wholesale; and 5.6%
are miscellaneous businesses. In addition to conventional
retail outlets such as "Paul's Men's Shop" in Taos, CAMBIO
has helped such unique ventures as Apodaca Brothers Chile
Products firm in Bernalillo, New Mexico, and Evergreen
Products, Inc., a Christmas ornaments firm begun in Las
Vegas, New Mexico.[35]

However, CAMBIO activities have not been restricted to
loan packaging functions. In the course of normal operations
in its local offices, CAMBIO has identified other needs and

problems confronting all small businessmen and has acted
to provide help in other areas.

One problem CAMBIO recognized was the lack of local
small business participation in government contracting for
goods and services. Local businesses, potentially eligible
to bid for supplying goods and services to the federal government, were not doing so because they were not registered,
licensed, or bonded with the Small Business Administration.
Thus, one early project of CAMBIO was to assist local businesses desirous of such service to get appropriately certified and submit bids for providing such goods and services.
As a result, in fiscal year 1972-1973, CAMBIO assisted in
securing $395,000 in such procurement of contracts.

Another project of CAMBIO involves offering seminars
on taxation and bookkeeping for small businessmen. The
objective of the seminars being to provide them with full
information regarding full tax credits for operating expenses,
business improvements which are available to all business
concerns. In addition, a free tax assistance program for
individuals was undertaken by CAMBIO in 1972 to assist
individuals in CAMBIO's service area to benefit from federal
and state low income tax credits. In all, CAMBIO staff
members helped prepare 820 individual and small business
returns. Another supplementary project of CAMBIO chapters

has been to provide outreach services. The Grants office,
for example, assisted flood victims in Gallup, New Mexico,
in securing some $308,000 in disaster relief loans. The
Las Vegas chapter has assisted a local organization,
Montezuma Unidos, prepare proposals, plan meetings, etc.,
in their effort to secure local control over the Montezuma
Seminary facility for the operation of a Veterans Home in
the site.

Of particular importance in relation to CAMBIO's recent
activities is its willingness to provide assistance to
"service type" businesses such as electricians, plumbers,
carpenters, oil and gas maintenance firms, and gas station
operation, in addition to business outlets which provide
goods, since more minority members are probably engaged in
service type businesses than otherwise, and since these
firms rarely have outside help in dealing with their everyday business problems.

Although CAMBIO is still in its organizing and growth
stage, its organizational expansion in the span of four years
has been impressive. Whether the organization will reach
its goal of 10,000 members and chapters and offices in most
of the smaller, predominantly Hispanic communities in
northern New Mexico remains to be seen. Future CAMBIO
plans, in addition to expanding its membership, include the

creation of a Minority Enterprise Small Business Investment Corporation (MESBIC), which would allow CAMBIO itself to maintain its own investment fund in which it could provide loans to small businesses.[36]

The National Economic Development Association (NEDA)

Another organization which has made an important imprint in its efforts "to become a force in the involvement of Spanish-speaking Americans in the free enterprise system,"[37] is a national organization, the National Economic Development Association (NEDA). NEDA is undoubtedly the most important and successful national Chicano organization in the area of Chicano business enterprise. According to its own annual report:

> NEDA is a private, non-profit corporation whose primary objective is to foster the free enterprise system among Spanish-speaking people by providing the following forms of management and technical assistance:
> (1) Preparation of Financial Assistance Proposals for potential and existing businesses;
> (2) A continuing source of management assistance to these businesses;
> (3) Identification and development of business opportunities;
> (4) Serving as a source of information on economic development matters.
> NEDA's service line includes debt and equity financing, securing of government and private contracts; use of government guaranteed programs such as construction, bonding, leases, and lines of credit, formation of local development corporations, and information on education and housing.[38]

Formed in June, 1970, NEDA grew to a total of 21 offices in 11 states by 1973, with a total annual budget exceeding two million dollars, and total national staff of 118 persons.

NEDA is headed by an 18-member national Board of Directors which represents a broad regional cross-section of the United States. The corporation is administered by an Executive Vice President and an administrative staff headquartered in Los Angeles, California, and regional vice presidents who may be responsible for operations in one or more states, and area vice presidents, responsible for particular offices. NEDA operations are funded through contracts with national and state agencies including the Office of Minority Business Enterprises, the Economic Development Administration, both of the U.S. Department of Commerce, the Small Business Administration, the U. S. Office of Economic Opportunity, and the California Job Development Corporation.

The success of NEDA in generating expansion of minority business enterprises is reflected in their Annual Report of 1973 which showed that in 1973 alone, NEDA-sponsored Financial Assistance Proposals totaled 2,510, involving over $90 million. This brought the total NEDA assistance figures to over 4,000 proposals approved, involving over

$162 million.[39]

In comparative terms in New Mexico, NEDA has been more successful than CAMBIO in terms of loan proposals approved and total funding generated for new or existing small businesses. Since its inception on July 1, 1970, through November 30, 1973, for example, the Albuquerque NEDA office had 278 proposals approved, totaling minority business loans of $11,859,472. The Santa Fe office since opening on August 2, 1971, through November 30, 1973, secured approval for 199 proposals totaling $5,475,424. Thus, up to November 30, 1973, NEDA offices in New Mexico have had 477 proposals approved, totaling $17,310,896, in capital for minority businesses.[40]

However, in terms of technical and managerial services, outreach services to individuals and businesses in the more impoverished northern New Mexico communities, and general community economic development assistance, CAMBIO has probably been more involved and impressive in those areas. It seems, therefore, that the two organizations have complemented instead of duplicated each other's services in New Mexico.

Other Minority Business Enterprise Efforts

More limited in scope than CAMBIO or NEDA in the area

of Chicano business enterprise in New Mexico have been the aforementioned short-lived efforts of LULAC's, LEDA, and the more recent efforts of the Southwest Council of La Raza and its affiliate in New Mexico, the Home Education Livelihood Program, (HELP).

Although involved in a variety of problem areas including education, housing, and employment, some of the most important efforts of the council (which was organized in 1968), have been in the area of economic development. The council established the La Raza Investment Corp. (LRIC), which was the first Chicano Minority Enterprise Small Business Investment Corp. (MESBIC).

Like other existing MESBIC's, the LRIC is designed to generate a capital fund of its own which is thereupon used to provide loans to small businesses instead of depending upon capital from commercial banks or federal lending agencies. In New Mexico, the LRIC has been principally sponsored by HELP, thus it has served as a third, though more limited source of Mexican American small business enterprise initiatives.[41]

Mexican American Business Organizations: Prospects

All present indications point to the fact that the

CAMBIO/NEDA concept is an idea whose time has arrived for the Mexican American people. The early 1970s has witnessed an unprecedented business expansion within the Mexican American community that goes beyond simply business ventures into ventures in banking and finance.

The effort to stimulate new businesses wrought by minority enterprise organizations such as CAMBIO, and the difficulty of securing loans from existing banking institutions - which are often quite conservative in their lending practices - has underscored among minority entrepreneurs, a realization of the need for minority owned and operated outlets which are willing to gamble and invest in minority businesses.

In 1971, for example, although minority bank assets totaled only $600 million as compared to majority bank totals of $700 billion, the minority banks provided $60 million out of the total $150 million, or 33% of all minority business loans.[42] This situation which has traditionally been reflected in New Mexico, has stimulated the creation in recent years of several banks and savings and loan associations in New Mexico.

The typical pattern is reflected in the formation of the Coronado Savings and Loan Association in Albuquerque, New Mexico. Incorporated in 1971 under the leadership of

Mike Alarid, supermarket owner and operator, and former
State Legislator; G.P. Reyes, manager of a large shopping
center and former city commissioner; Robert Torrez,
architect; Art Trujillo, President of the firm; Benigno
Hernandez and Fernando C De Baca, the firm is located in
the valley area and has served a primarily Mexican American
clientele. By December 31, 1973, Coronado Savings and Loan
reported assets totaling $3,374,223.66.

In addition, the Sentinel Bank in Taos, El Valle State
Bank and Plaza del Sol Bank, both located in Albuquerque's
valley area (where the Chicano population is concentrated),
Española's Pueblo State Bank, and Santa Fe's, United Southwest National Bank, are viable going banking enterprises
among the Mexican American group. Chicano businessmen are
also prominent stock holders in many non-minority controlled
banks. Several other minority banking ventures are still
in the planning stages.

Although it would be problematic to suggest a long-
range impact of these recent business and banking initiatives
within the Hispano community, such as inferring an ultimate
monetary self-sufficiency for the group, the prospects for
political and social change do seem favorable in light of these
developments, especially considering the paucity of such

activity in the past.

Although speculative, several possible beneficial effects to the Chicano community can be suggested from these trends. The first is obviously the personal advantage to an Hispano of being able to conduct financial transactions (loans, mortgages), with his own people. Although Anglo bankers have not always discriminated against Hispanos (because of ethincity) they often have, as inequitable standards have existed in qualifying for loans.

Another possible benefit, especially in economically depressed areas such as northern New Mexico, is that minority banks will help encourage economic development ventures by helping finance new industries, especially labor-intensive industries which could provide jobs in the high unemployment region. Often, existing banks in northern New Mexico communities have been conservative, limited development oriented, and this has been discouraging to potential business investors.

In terms of strictly political benefits, the availability of more "business" or "banking" money for Hispano candidates who have had to rely on other sources to finance political campaigns probably will increase the number and caliber of Hispano aspirants for public office.

Chicano Professional Organizations

Another genre of specialized Chicano organizations are
the group of organizations that have developed among Chicanos
in particular occupational fields. Again originating from
an ethnic basis, these organizations generally seek to
create an altogether more favorable environment for the
ethnic in the particular occupation by encouraging Chicanos
to enter and participate in the professions, by lobbying
for more favorable and equitable policies relating to li-
censing, hiring, wages, training and promotions of Chicanos
in the professions. The organizations also often strive to
improve the services provided by or in relations of
certain occupations to the Mexican American community.

Although these occupational organizations present
unique dimensions, they do not represent the first time
Mexican Americans have developed organizations related to
occupations and employment. Carey McWilliams has correctly
shattered the "myth of the docility of Mexican labor" and
credited the Mexican American group with being at the vanguard of the labor movement in the Southwest in the early
part of the 20th century.

McWilliams describes how Mexican Americans developed
their own labor organizations such as the Confederacion de
Uniones Obreros Mexicanos (CUOM, Confederation of Mexican

Labor Unions) formed in southern California in 1927, and
La Liga Obrera de Habla Espanol (the Spanish-speaking
Labor League), formed in New Mexico in the 1930s, and
also participated in the traditional labor unions such as
the United Mine Workers, the Mine, Mill, Smelter Workers
Union, among others.[43]

The Mexican American Legal Defense and Education Fund (MALDEF)

The Mexican American Legal Defense and Education Fund
is a private, non-profit organization founded in 1967 by
a small group of Hispano attorneys who sought to create an
instrument to protect by "legal action and legal education"
the constitutional rights of Mexican Americans. From a
single office, the organization has expanded to include a
national office in San Francisco, California, and four
regional offices in Los Angeles, Denver, San Antonio, and
Albuquerque. Future offices are planned for the Midwest
and East Coast regions. The organization consists of and
is administered by a 35-member Board of Directors, mostly
Chicanos, which includes attorneys, law professors, law
school deans, and other community leaders.[44]

Although MALDEF maintains its staff of attorneys in
each regional office, these are supplemented by members of
the organization and by "a national network of referral

lawyers."

The main objectives and rationale for MALDEF are set

down in one of their publications:

> Discrimination and segregation have long been
> suffered by Mexican Americans, but, until recently,
> their poverty, lack of education, and traditional
> suspicion of the legal processes combined to keep
> them from attacking these injustices in the courts.
> Above all, there has been no cadre of Mexican
> American lawyers trained to handle civil rights
> cases as Black lawyers have done over the past
> quarter century. . .Today the Mexican American
> Legal Defense and Educational Fund is fighting
> the Mexican American's court battles against dis-
> crimination in the Southwest almost singlehandedly
> . . .Litigation is an effective tool to correct
> these gross injustices. It must be used vigorously
> and without delay.[45]

MALDEF has employed several strategies in its effort

to accomplish its ambitious goals. The most important of

which is a "litigation program," which is designed to implement

legal action to eliminate discriminatory practices. The

procedural strategy has been to initiate "class action"

suits involving numerous Mexican Americans, especially

those which promise to set important precedents. In terms

of substantive cases, the MALDEF objective is to select

cases directed at traditional barriers to the Mexican

American minority such as abridgment of civil rights, in-

equalities in educational opportunities, discrimination in

employment, police brutality, antiquated penal conditions,

and inequities in public services.

The list of cases which MALDEF currently sponsors is quite lengthy and is normally included in its "Docket Report" as part of its annual report. Normally included are cases involving discrimination in education, employment, "abuses of authority," "participatory rights," "consumer protection," and "administrative cases."[46]

No less important than its litigation program is MALDEF's "Educational Grants Program" which is aimed at correcting the dire shortage of Chicano lawyers by providing scholarships as financial assistance to Chicano law students. Noting that out of 350,000 lawyers in the United States only 700 are Chicano and that only one out of 380 Federal District Judges is a Chicano, MALDEF has been able to negotiate financial assistance agreements with 24 law schools whereby MALDEF will provide an annual stipend, usually $1,000, which is matched by the participating law school for the law student. Since its inception in 1969, the program has provided financial assistance for some 230 Chicano law students of which 85 were three year grants. MALDEF scholarship grants are made with the understanding that recipients will do some work on behalf of the Mexican American upon completion of law school.[47]

A third program is the "referral attorney program" by which MALDEF provides outreach legal service and information through attorneys who although not themselves on the MALDEF staff, agree to represent Mexican American clients on MALDEF related cases. By this program, MALDEF vastly extends its service beyond those handled by its own staff in the regional offices. In a given period, probably more than half of MALDEF related cases are handled by other than MALDEF attorneys.[48]

The "Brief Bank and Information Center" program, sponsored by MALDEF, is designed to provide lawyers involved in cases regarding Mexican American issues with readily accessible briefs, law review articles, cases, sociological and statistical data which can be used in arguing cases or preparing arguments in specific cases. The objective of the program is to avoid duplication in research effort and to maintain consistent reliable, up-to-date information. The brief bank and information center is contained in two MALDEF libraries in San Francisco, California, and San Antonio, Texas. This program is also charged with responsibility for publishing the MALDEF monthly newsletter which describes MALDEF activities including reports on pending litigation, scholarship reports, and so on.

MALDEF has also sponsored national and regional seminars in various parts of the Southwest designed to interest and attract attorneys to the MALDEF program and to update information on Civil Rights cases.[49]

Mexican American Law Students Association (MALSA)

An organization which has worked closely with MALDEF
and has itself pursued an objective of increasing Chicano
representation in the legal profession is the Mexican American Law Students Association (MALSA). MALSA was organized
to promote the academic, social, and cultural welfare of
Chicano law students. It is affiliated with the La Raza
National Law Students Association which maintains chapters
in 28 law schools in the United States.

The principal objective of MALSA seems to involve the
increasing of the number of Chicano lawyers by encouraging Chicanos to attend law school. MALSA has conducted recruitment
drives and "recruitment programs" at universities where
current law students provide information regarding application to law schools, information on preparation for and
taking of The Law School Admission Test, information on financial assistance available to Chicanos including the MALDEF
scholarship program and the Council on Legal Education
Opportunity (CLEO) program which is also designed to help
defray minority law students' legal expenses, as well as provide information on special benefits offered by schools.

The recruitment efforts conducted by MALSA are followed

up by their on-campus efforts to ensure the retention of law students in the program. Not only does MALSA provide an immediate source of tutoring and counseling help for new students, but course outlines and general academic information is provided to them.

A less publicized, but no less important effort of MALSA has been that of attempting to generate law school curriculum reform which would include introduction of law courses which would prepare Chicano lawyers to better cope with peculiar legal problems of the Chicano community.

Needless to say, the active effort to recruit potential law students into the legal profession inspired principally by MALDEF with the support of groups such as MALSA, will probably result in a marked increased in the number of Chicanos pursuing a legal career, and an increase in the number of Chicano lawyers in tune with efforts to bring about legal reform and protection of constitutional rights and privileges of the Mexican American. The experience of the Black Civil Rights Movement and the vanguard role of the NAACP in its sponsorship of litigation in the courts resulting in such milestone cases such as Brown v. Topeka Board of Education certainly underscores the importance of similar efforts by MALDEF for the Chicano community.

Ecclesiastical Chicano Organizations

It is estimated that 95% of all the Mexican Americans in the United States are Roman Catholics and that one out of every four Catholics in the United States is Mexican American. Despite the great concentration of Hispanos in the Catholic Church "the ruling spirits of the Roman Catholic Church," says Joan Moore, "have been reluctant to take the ideological lead in any of the important issues of past or present for Mexican Americans."[50]

It is not surprising, therefore, in view of this situation, that the Church itself has been the setting or target for contrived changes sought by religious groups.

Padres

The most important of these groups is Padres Asociados Para Derechos Religiosos Educativos y Sociales (Associated Priests for Religious, Educational, and Social Rights) or PADRES, the Spanish word for priests. PADRES was organized by a group of Hispano priests in San Antonio, Texas.

Although PADRES is a national organization and the great majority of native Hispano priests are members, the organization is not subdivided into state or local chapters. The only sub-national entity are the six regional convocations. The organization has attracted a wide cross section

of Chicano priests as evidenced by its leadership. The
present national chairman is Bishop Patrick Flores of San
Antonio, the highest ranking native Hispano clergyman in
the United States.[51]

Aside from the underlying objective of altering the
traditional posture of the Church - from its overriding
Irish orientation, and the ignoring of the Hispano -
PADRES has sought more substantive changes relating to
the Chicano clergy. It has sought greater representation
of Hispanos in the Church hierarchy where Church policy
is determined. Pointing out that Hispanos had held only
two (Bishop Flores and Bishop Juan Arzuke of Los Angeles)
of 280 Bishop positions in the United States, PADRES has
hoped for selection of Hispanos to at least the sixteen
sees with large concentrations of Hispano population.[52]
Its greatest accomplishment in this effort was in lobbying
for and securing the selection of Rev. Robert Sanchez
as Archbishop of the Archdiocese of New Mexico. The
selection of Archbishop Sanchez, itself a precedent,
also set precedent in that for the first time a committee
of native clergy and laymen participated in the selection
process, and in the fact that Rev. Sanchez was elevated
to the high position from his role as parish priest

without having served in intervening positions as is customary. Archibishop Sanchez has decidedly undertaken to improve
the Church's posture relative to New Mexico's Hispanos. The
organization has also lobbied for a vacancy in the Browns-
ville, Texas, Bishopric. In addition, efforts have been
made to increase the selection of Hispanos as pastors in
parishes with a large concentration of Hispano parishoners.

PADRES has also sought to increase recruitment of
young Hispanos for the priesthood, while attempting to
alter traditional training practices which tend to "educate
a Chicano's inborn culture out of him." At the same time,
the organization has sought to "sensitize" non-Spanish
priests to the problems and needs of the Hispanic community.

In regard to the aforementioned first objective, PADRES
is committed to a "cultural pluralistic" philosophy wherein
cultural differences can be recognized, engendered, and
accepted by the Church. PADRES hopes to:

> . . .involve the Church not only in revising
> those of its own structures and policies which are
> impeding equality and full participation for the
> Hispanos, but also to take part in broader social
> action. The Hispanic leaders want the Church to
> accept a bigger role in ending police brutality
> against minorities, to work for reforms in public
> education, and to raise the economic level of the
> poor.[53]

One of the first priorities of PADRES regarding education is the introduction of bilingual, bicultural programs

and new testing procedures in Catholic parochial schools
serving Hispanic children.

PADRES has, in its short tenure, seen some changes
despite the traditional conservative temper of the Church.
In addition to influencing the selection of the two Bishops,
and increases in lower echelon appointments such as pastors
and in assignment of Hispanic priests, it has been instrumental in sponsoring a national and a Southwest region
"encuentro" (encounter), or convocation of Hispano Church
leaders to discuss needed policy changes and strategies for
accomplishing the objectives cited by PADRES.

PADRES, under the leadership of Bishop Flores, established the Mexican American Cultural Center in San Antonio, which
is designed to serve as a resource center for preservation
of the Chicano culture.

Although it is understandably difficult to foresee the
political importance of what essentially are internal short
term changes in Catholic Church policies and procedures, it
is important to point out that these short-term internal
changes could foreshadow long-term changes in the posture
of the Catholic Church regarding social change for the
Mexican American group. The churches in American society
have traditionally been and continue to be important political institutions, even though American churches have not

always actively pursued political issues.

The church, as Litt points out, was important as a "conduit" for "ethnic political claims" involving civil rights in the sixties, and the National Council of Churches has been a powerful pressure group in legislation involving "economic reform, social justice, and civil rights."[54]

That such long term objectives are undoubtedly in the minds of the leaders who are at the vanguard of the PADRES movement is clear in a communication to all PADRES member priests from PADRES National Executive Director, Rev. Juan Romero:

> Dear Father: May God abundantly bless you for your continuing support of PADRES! Because of our imput /sic/ and your support, the consciousness of the Hispanic Church in this country has been heightened, and the whole Church seems more ready than ever to direct energy and resources to meet our particular needs. Many groups are echoing with us our priorities, and are trying to bring them about: 1) grass roots formation of the Spanish-speaking poor to have control over their own destiny; 2) coordinated efforts to effectively overcome those forces which are at the root of oppression; 3) multiplication of efforts to provide the kind of information necessary for those engaged in Hispanic ministry; and 4) Native Spanish speaking leadership within every level of the Church in this country.[55]

This argument becomes more plausible when one considers the fact that part of the Church's response to the demands of PADRES and the Mexican American in recent matters is due

to the challenge placed on it by various Protestant sects
that by responding to Hispano problems have cut into the
normally unflagging Mexican American allegiance to the
Catholic Church.

Las Hermanas

Paralleling the organization of Chicano priests into
PADRES has been a more recent movement of Mexican American
nuns or missionary sisters into an organization known as
Las Hermanas (the sisters). Las Hermanas is a group of
"religious women of Hispanic origin. . .interested in
bringing about social change on behalf of the Spanish-
speaking people."[56]

Recognizing that the Catholic Church "has not often
responded" to the needs of the Spanish-speaking population,
Las Hermanas whose motto is "unidas en accion y oración"
(united in action and prayer), hopes to take an active role
in the future development of Hispanic people in the United
States. Carrying forth the spirit of the Papal Encyclical
"On the Development of Peoples," the group hopes to further
the concept of "Christian humanism", a doctrine which re-
emphasizes the importance of Christian brotherhood and
mutual aid to supplement the Church's spiritual message.

Members of Las Hermanas see themselves as a compatible

and complementary religious organization to PADRES in their
mutual efforts to "humanize" the Catholic Church, and to
an affiliate lay women's organization known as Mujeres
Unidas en Jesus Efectivas con la Raza Ejemplares y Sensibles
(United Women in Christ for La Raza), or MUJERES (women),
itself an organization made up of former nuns dedicated to
service in the Spanish-speaking communities.[57]

Miscellaneous Chicano Occupational Organizations and Their Functions

In addition to the organizations in the legal and religious categories whose importance, as indicated, may transcend
the particular profession, Chicanos have formed numerous
occupational organizations which vary in the extent of
formality in organization, and vary in the extent of purposive
activity regarding such matters as minority recruitment,
improving working conditions and benefits, and their service
to the minority as a whole. The summary of these is given
to illustrate the proliferation of this kind of organization
among Chicanos whose problems stem from their minority and
subordinate status.

The Chicano Police Officers Association (CPOA)

In 1973, an organization known as the Chicano Police
Officers Association was organized by a group of Mexican

Americans in the Albuquerque Police Department. The organization was "designed to protect and advance Chicano police officers within the Albuquerque Police Department."[58]

Operating from the assumption that a police department should approximate the general ethnic composition of the city population, and that disproportionate percentages are related to inequities in law enforcement, the CPOA has urged greater Chicano recruitment, and open avenues for promotion. The main efforts of the association have been to remove alleged discriminatory testing and educational procedures in hiring and promotions which have reduced the number of Chicano police officers and the advancement of Chicano officers in rank within the Department.

The CPOA filed suits in February and June, 1973, in U.S. District Court alleging discrimination in promotion standards. The suits were ultimately dismissed in January, 1973, by U.S. District Judge Edwin Mechem. He did recommend that the Police Department review its recruiting and promotional procedures and remove potentially discriminatory procedures that could create future problems. Accordingly, in February, 1974, Albuquerque Police Chief Bob Stover announced that although there were no prior conscious prejudicial procedures in promotions and hiring, he promised review of procedures.[59]

Incorporated <u>Mexican</u> <u>American</u> <u>Government</u> Employees (IMAGE)

Still another national occupational Chicano organization
is the Incorporated Mexican American Government Employees
(IMAGE). Launched in February, 1973, the organization is
made up of principally Spanish-speaking federal government
employees. By the summer of 1973, the organization had
grown to 22 chapters in 12 states. The main objective of
the organization is to ensure that the Spanish-speaking
"share equitably" in government employment. The specific
objective of IMAGE is to secure the support of leading
Congressmen, especially influential Hispanos, in implementing
and solidifying "President Nixon's 16-point plan for the
Spanish-speaking." IMAGE feels that by placing more Hispanos
in more and key government positions, the whole Spanish-
speaking group will benefit since officials might express
greater sympathy and understanding for the needs, wants, and
problems of the Chicano group.[60]

Chicano Educators Organizations in New Mexico

Chicano college professors have also inclined toward
some form of ethnic association, even though the extent of
activity and formality has varied. At the University of
New Mexico, a group of Chicanos organized sometime in 1971
under the designation, "<u>Los</u> <u>Profesores</u>" (the Professors).

Made up of representatives from several departments, the
group's major objective was to encourage recruitment of
Hispanos for faculty and staff positions.

Chicano teachers in some "public, private, and parochial
schools in New Mexico" formed an organization known as New
Mexico Raza Educators. The most active affiliate is the
Albuquerque Raza Educators Association, made up of "bilingual,
bi-cultural" teachers organized for the purpose of "improving
the quality of learning for the Spanish-speaking population
and to support efforts which provide equal educational opportunities for all." It is also committed to the teaching of
"bilingual, multi-cultural education."

National Chicano Health Organization (NCHO)

Although Chicanos are poorly represented in most of the
professions, nowhere is the lack of Chicanos more pronounced
than in the health care professions. According to recent
statistics, it is estimated that there are 250 Mexican
American doctors in the United States or comparatively,
seven Mexican American doctors to every 10,000 doctors.
Moreover, statistics foreshadow a gloomy picture, for out of
some 47,000 medical students in the U.S. in 1973, only 351,
less than 1%, were Chicanos. This for a population that
makes up close to 5% of the national population.

This is an especially acute problem when one considers
the tremendous health problems of the Hispano community.
This paucity of Chicanos in health careers is the primary
motivation which led to the creation of an organization
known as the National Chicano Health Organization.

The organization was launched in 1972 by young Chicano
medical students, barrio community health workers, and
health professionals who were concerned over Chicano health
problems. A pamphlet published by NCHO states its purpose
and goals:

> The deplorable state of health conditions in
> the Mexican American communities of this country
> is well known to those who work in area of commu-
> nity health. This situation is further aggravated
> by the absence of Chicanos within the health pro-
> fessions. . .The primary goal of the National
> Chicano Health Organization is to ensure first
> class health care for the Chicano community. To
> accomplish this objective, NCHO has identified as
> a major priority, a substantial increase in the
> number of Chicano health professionals.[61]

The organization is administered by a national Board
of Directors and maintains regional offices in Oakland,
Chicago, Denver, Albuquerque, San Antonio, and Los Angeles,
which also is the main NCHO office. Each regional office
has two main objectives, initiating "cluster group"
programs in high schools designed to counsel, encourage,
and recruit Chicano students into health careers, and
secondly, generating chapters in the various state

universities which themselves will serve as bases for recruitment of Chicanos for health fields. Subsidiary functions
include establishment of a "registrant bank" of potential
health science school applicants, development of a central-
ized financial aids directory, assisting in campus medical
school minority recruiting, and development of summer health
jobs and placements.

Chicano "Militant" Organizations

The designation, "militant", which is applied to certain organizations that have emerged primarily among young
Chicanos is in a way a misnomer because it yields the im-
pression of groups that are in the least, violence-prone
and at worst, are revolutionary. The Chicano organizations
usually labeled militant have been neither violence prone
nor revolutionary. It is noteworthy that the Chicano movement has not generated any organization which has openly
proclaimed and advocated violence or revolution as a primary
strategy or tactic for social change. That is to say, no
Chicano organization has as yet employed urban guerilla
tactics such as use of snipers, kidnapping, or terror,
comparable to such organizations as the Black Panthers, the
Symbionese Liberation Army, and ideological groups such as
the Weathermen, the Minutemen, Students for a Democratic

Society, and so on.

Perhaps a more correct categorization for Chicano groups formerly labeled "militant" would be "defensive" for this is the posture such organizations have taken. Although the ministerial organizational structure, the quasi-military disciplinary structure, and the extra-legal procedures sometimes employed by these organizations creates a feeling of militaristic intent, they maintain it is defensive in nature. In most instances, the Brown Berets and the Black Berets see themselves as "shock troops" of the Chicano movement. This mood is reflected by David Sanchez, founder of the Black Berets:

> We're not a violent or a non-violent organiza-
> tion. . .we are an emergency organization. . .if we
> see a cop beating up a Chicano, we move in and stop
> the cop, we try to be ready for every emergency.[62]

The Berets see themselves as the buffer between the dominant society and the Chicanos. Because the activity of these organizations has sharply declined in recent years, references will be made in the past tense, with the notation made that some chapters of the organization remain active.

The Brown Berets

The best known of the Chicano defensive organizations has been the Brown Berets, a paramilitary organization of young Chicanos which emerged originally in Los Angeles and expanded into 27 other Southwestern cities. Because the main Brown Beret activity has been concentrated in California cities, especially in East Los Angeles, it is appropriate to discuss the origin and nature of the organization there, as a basis for comparison with its activities elsewhere and with other similar groups.

The name "Brown Berets" is derived from the brown colored berets (the color of a Chicano's skin) the members wear which contains an insignia of crossed rifles and a cross, and is the most distinct part of their uniform; and secondly, from the symbolic similarity to the famous Green Beret fighting force of the Vietnam War era.

Rona Fields and Charles Fox who studied the organization more extensively than anyone else, maintain that the Berets represented a "reconstitution of all of the old gangs /commonly prevalent in the urban ghetto environment/, but with political content and strong emphasis on Mexican American identity."[63] Thus, according to Fox and Fields, one important function of the Berets was to channel the aimless violence of Chicano "batos locos" (crazy guys) to meaningful efforts for the Chicano group.

The Berets were characterized by an extremely loosely defined national organization with little formal organizational contact, and communication among the various chapters

in Southwestern cities. Each chapter was an entity in itself, while adhering to the basic dress, code of conduct,
and philosophy of the parent California organization. The
membership of the chapters was highly variable, reaching a
peak during recruitment efforts and sometimes reducing to
as few as a handful of members, and sometimes becoming
dormant.

The influence of the Black Panthers (whom Beret members
interacted with during the organizing stages) is clearly
evident in the ministerial structure (Prime Minister,
Ministers of Defense, Justice, Information, Discipline, and
so on), the uniform (beret), the discipline-building drills
which were part of the daily regimen of members, and in the
"defensive functions" performed by the Berets. The Brown
Berets saw themselves as an alternative for young Chicanos
(between the ages of 14-35 from which the membership is
drawn), that of committment and service to the Chicano
community rather than the traditional drug and crime scene.
The Beret manual stressed the personal leadership and
example of cleanliness, self-discipline, abstention from
drugs and excessive drinking which the Berets are sworn to
because it signified their organizational and ethnic pride.[64]

The activities of the Berets took four general forms:
that of protest activities against the schools; confrontation

between Chicano students and school authorities over issues involving school curricula, bilingual education, and Hispano teachers. School authorities charged, after the Los Angeles school "blowouts", that Berets were among the "outside agitators" of the walkouts. In those walkouts, the shock troop function of the Berets was manifested as it has been in similar Chicano protest demonstrations since. This practice involved the Berets placing themselves between the police authorities and demonstrators and thereby receiving the brunt of the physical punishment and arrest. The activity brought the Berets into direct confrontation with the police, however, in their effort to stop alleged incidents of police brutality against Chicano youth. The Berets also instituted "community patrols" which "shadowed" police cars patrolling in barrio neighborhoods and intervened in confrontations between authorities and Chicanos. This "shock troop" orientation was also manifest in the common Beret practice of providing security for other Chicano organizations in public demonstrations, marches and boycotts. When authorities intervened, generally the clash was with the Berets providing security. The most important community service program of the Berets was the establishment of a free health clinic in the East Los Angeles barrio.[65]

In November, 1972, newspapers carried a story attributed to David Sanchez, Prime Minister of the Berets, announcing that the Beret organization was being disbanded. Whether the story was true, whether it hinted of intra-organizational conflict, or whether it indeed spelled the end of Brown Berets, remains unclear. What is known is that scattered examples of Beret activity have occurred since the announcement, but the organization has declined in its activity.

The Black Berets of New Mexico

Although the Brown Beret activity in New Mexico has been sporadic in nature, this has not been the case with the Black Berets, a similar organization that emerged in 1969 among young Chicanos in the barrios of Albuquerque to "commit itself to the service, education, and defense of La Santa Raza, the Mexican American race."[66] The organization, though never larger than 25 active members, has been quite persistent in the Albuquerque scene, perhaps because of a highly committed and consistent leadership.

The organization, for unknown reasons, chose to disassociate itself from the Brown Beret organization despite the fact that remaining members of the Albuquerque Brown Berets joined the new group, and despite the similarity in organizational structure and objectives of the two organizations.

The Black Berets operate under a similar ministerial structure. The two organizations were also similar in their "shock troop" or "defensive" orientation whereby members see themselves as a buffer between the law enforcement authorities and the Chicano community. The rules of the Black Berets also stressed personal discipline among the membership including abstention from narcotics, opposition to using violence against La Raza, or other minorities, and stressing codes of honesty and self-improvement.

The formal objectives of the Black Berets contained in a "21 point" program and platform, include broad philosophical statements rather than specific objectives. Included are statements of "opposition to capitalism", and "alliances with treacherous politicos", "self-determination and liberation for la raza and Third World people," and "an end to oppression." Also contained in the platform is a statement relating to self-defense and violence:

> We believe armed defense and armed struggle
> are the only means to liberation. . .we are
> against violence, the violence of illiteracy,
> the violence of diseased old people, and the
> violence of poverty and profit. . .we have to
> arm ourselves now to protect ourselves and the
> people from the oppressions perpetrated by the
> businessmen, government, and the police.[67]

Despite such open flaunting of a violent tendency, the organization was not tied to any incident involving violence.

It is likely that the extra-legal tendencies of the Berets has made them especially vulnerable to scrutiny, harassment, and possibly violence by police. One incident involved the shooting of the two Berets, who were burglarizing a construction site.

The early activities of the Berets brought them in conflict with the police. From their initial appearance, the Berets were publicly critical of police brutality against Chicanos and actively lobbied in the press and in council meetings for the creation of a "citizens review" board to monitor activities of the Albuquerque Police Department.

In conjunction with their shock troop policy of placing themselves between the authorities and the protestors, the Berets participated in the student walkouts in Albuquerque Public Schools in 1970 and 1971, and in the major civil disturbances that occurred in the city in the summer of 1971. In both cases, they were considered instigators of the disturbances. They were probably among the agitators which inspired the student walkouts, but their role in the civil disturbances probably was greatest after the initial outbreak of violence at Roosevelt Park, and after the rioting and looting had taken place in downtown Albuquerque.

Quite aside from their association or inclination toward militance which, as stated, has been an incidental and not primary focus, the Black Berets have involved themselves in community service functions designed to benefit the Chicano community in the barrios of Albuquerque. One of their first projects was the establishment of the "El Mestizo Recreation Center" for south valley youths.

Later projects included the sponsoring of a daily breakfast program for needy children in the recreation center. The Berets also operated a "clothing bank" for families who needed clothing either because of poverty conditions or disasters such as fires.

Probably the most important continuing project which the Black Berets have sponsored is the "Bobby Garcia Memorial Clinic". The clinic was named after a former Beret member who had been killed under mysterious circumstances. The clinic is directed by the Black Berets' Minister of Health.

The Berets coordinated the activities which included securing a South Broadway Blvd. site from the Catholic church, securing of equipment and supplies, enlisting the support of volunteer doctors from various Albuquerque hospitals, and enlisting volunteers who would assist in nursing services, clerical and administrative work, and maintenance for the facility.

The clinic is strictly a donation-funded operation, deriving funds from contributions of private foundations, and the "pay-what-you-can kitty" located in the clinic. No federal funds are used or sought for the operation of the clinic which averages approximately $1,500 per month.[68]

As the clinic itself is the most notable endeavor and accomplishment of the Black Berets, it is this accomplishment the Berets can stand on, notwithstanding the more militant reputation of the group.

In addition to serving a genuine and needed service for the Chicano community, the clinic has served to channel the efforts of young Chicanos (including the Berets) into constructive ways of serving their community. In this way, the Berets have shown that an organization - even if it is militant and made up of the more alienated of the minority group - can channel the basic motivations of ethnic pride and community toward humanitarian efforts to help fellow ethnics, and thus indirectly serve as a rehabilitative instrument for young Chicanos whose background would probably foreshadow a dismal future.

Miscellaneous Chicano Organizations

There are organizations among the Mexican American

community that for one reason or another do not fit into any of the previous categories. For want of a more appropriate categorization which would apply to all the remaining organizations the following summary is intended as a "catch-all" for these groups. It should be borne in mind that many Chicano organizations have been excluded from this summary out of the necessity for brevity, so this list is not exhaustive, though it does consider the most unique and potentially important organizations.

The Chicano Welfare Rights Organization

The typical Chicano family on welfare in New Mexico has to be among the poorest of the poor in the state. The State Department of Health and Social Services' standards for qualification for relief and assistance are designed to exclude all but the most destitute of the population. It is among this group of Chicanos that one of the more recent Chicano organizations has emerged.

The inordinately high incidence of Chicanos on the welfare rolls of New Mexico gave rise in November, 1973, to the Chicano Welfare Rights Organization (CWRO). The main impetus for organization was the leadership of Clemencia Martinez Jabbs who had been an active participant in the efforts of the National Welfare Rights Organization (NWRO), the national organization with over 125,000 members, representing welfare recipients across the country.

In November, 1973, a group of activist Chicanos met in Las Vegas and founded the first state chapter of the Chicano Welfare Rights Organization which soon qualified as a chapter of the National Welfare Rights Organization. By the summer of 1974, the local chapter reported total membership at about 2,110 in New Mexico.

The activism of the CWRO and its parent affiliate, NWRO, is based upon a unique but practical view of the philosophy behind public welfare and assistance to the indigent. Their philosophy is that the need for public welfare is a natural outgrowth of a democratic and capitalistic society. The emergence of the modern corporation with its capitalist class has inevitably led to inequities in the distribution of wealth, and the sources of that wealth - land and natural resources. Thus, just as capitalism has created a wealthy class, so also has it created an indigent class. The democratic society, however, unlike the fascist or totalitarian society, is based upon ideals of humanitarianism, fraternity, and equality, hence "pacification" measures in the form of public assistance, public housing, and so on, are devised to ameliorate the normal disaffection that would emanate from the group which is the byproduct.

It is from this perspective, that American society is responsible for the indigent and for his welfare, and not from a perspective that the government is responding due to altruistic, beneficent, humanitarian motives, that these organizations operate.

The CWRO has thus emerged as a new form of pressure group for the poor Chicano. Working from the assumption that Chicanos that join the welfare rolls do so because of economic necessity - primarily their inability to locate gainful employment - CWRO seeks to foster the interests of and protect this group from the unnecessary harassment that normally befalls such dependent groups. The organization feels that the indignity such people endure in obtaining such benefits - considered handouts by most - should not be compounded by capricious, insensitive, tactless bureaucrats and bureaucratic policies, that view the welfare recipient with contempt or distain. The CWRO thus provides a source of support for the welfare client in dealings with welfare agencies. CWRO has also lobbied in the state legislature and state agencies for increases in public assistance allowances and other benefits such as higher clothing allowances, while pursuing more favorable adminstrative policies for its clientele.[69]

To the American normally inclined to view public welfare as a necessary but evil phenomenon, the thought of pressure groups representing people on welfare is outrageous. The trained social scientist, however, is inclined to see the emergence of pressure groups for the poor as a natural outgrowth of the same forces that create pressure groups which represent other aggregates in American society, even if the philosophical motivations are poles apart from each other.

La Academia de La Nueva Raza: A Chicano Literary and Cultural Organization

Considering that some aspects of the Chicano movement have taken the form of challenges to or reactions against traditional American institutions and the body of knowledge about the Chicano transmitted by these institutions, and considering that at least part of the thrust of efforts for change are addressed at these institutions and that knowledge, there has emerged an awareness among certain Chicanos of the need for a body of knowledge which would supplant or supplement that which is the target of the reaction.

One organization which emerged in response to this particular challenge is La Academia de La Nueva Raza (the academy for the new Chicano race). La Academia (the shortened common euphemism) was founded in November, 1969, initially

under the designation of "La Academia de Aztlan," by a group
of New Mexico Chicanos. The headquarters of La Academia is
located in Dixon, New Mexico, a small, obscure village
located in the foothills of Truchas Peak in Taos County,
and significantly for the purposes of La Academia in the
epicenter of the Chicano population's historical concentration in northern New Mexico. In January, 1970 a group of
Chicanos from Texas, California, and New Mexico, met and
decided to make the organization national in scope.

La Academia's philosophical objectives are well portrayed
in its symbolic byword, "El Oro del Barrio," (the gold of
the community). La Academia views the barrio - the Chicano
neighborhood as the last "bastion of community" for the
Chicano. The Chicano rural barrio, isolated as it was from
the dominant system, served to insulate the Chicano culture
and preserve it from the normal assimilation process which
would tend to undermine it. "Oro" (literally gold), the
symbolic gold which is contained in "the lore, oral history"
and represents the remnants of Chicano culture and "its
spirit and its wisdom." La Academia sees as its purpose
". . .the self-imposed task /of/ mining el oro del barrio,
refining it through dialogue, discussion, symposia, and
seminar and relating it. . .through La Academia's organ:
El Cuaderno de vez en cuando (the occasional journal). . .

From El Oro del Barrio, La Academia proposed to bring together a philosophy that comes from our own experience."

La Academia is convinced that the antecedent culture of the Chicano, that of the Mexican in New Mexico in the 19th century is a viable alternative for the Chicano to the confusion, isolation, alienation, and failure which he experiences in modern American society. La Academia's "meta" (method) is to create an atmosphere where the Chicano can find self-identity through cultural awareness.

The strategy of action involves three phases or factors. The first is the process of "discovery or rediscovery" by which La Academia returns to the colonia, the barrios, and mines "el oro" by rediscovering the lore. The main source of this lore has been in the oral history that remains in the memory of the elders in the villages. The objective here is to rescue this often unwritten lore which contains the cultural and philosophical bases of the Chicano. The second involves a process of analysis, both through reflection and educational dialogue in seminars and symposia of the most important and consistent philosophical currents. Finally, the writing of scholarly essays and papers which would reflect the rediscovered ideas and thoughts and which would add to the developing body of knowledge.

La Academia publishes El Cuaderno de Vez en Cuando

(The Occasional Journal) which contains articles on Chicano politics, philosophy, sociology, anthropology, and literature. Interspersed among the articles are Spanish poems, stories, proverbs, riddles, that focus on the Chicano life, culture, and experience. La Academia has also published "La Madrugada" (the awakening), a periodic newsletter to members and interested readers of La Academia activities. Finally, La Academia has published a small monograph, <u>Entre Verde y Seco</u> which contains examples of the oral lore which La Academia has uncovered in its visits with Chicano old timers.

Members of La Academia feel that the paucity of Chicano organizations, concerned primarily with these literary and philosophical questions, will ultimately yield to La Academia that legitimacy it now lacks, and in thus receiving legitimacy its contribution toward Chicano cultural awareness will be felt. Moreover, by establishing a systematic, viable, body of knowledge to supplement or supplant existing knowledge about the Chicano, La Academia feels it is contributing to the tenacity of the Chicano movement.[70]

Although the Chicano organizations described and contained in this final section on "Miscellaneous Chicano Organizations" have little or no relationship to each other, they should provide the reader with an idea of the highly specialized nature of such organizations, and also make one aware of the possibility that this summary does not include all of the Chicano organizations, in view of the proliferation of those and in view of the fact that new organizations are constantly emerging.

Summary

This chapter has provided a greatly abbreviated outline of the most important, viable, and unique ethnic organizations that exist among the Mexican American community. The emphasis was on the "political" importance of such organizations, and this perspective was outlined in the model presented at the outset. A general definition and description of Chicano organizations was then provided. The summary then proceeded with the various categories of organizations, student, self-help, community service, business and professional and concluding with the miscellaneous category. It is felt that the organizations studied in this chapter reflect not only a comprehensive view of Chicano organizations and the nature, goals, activities, strategies, accomplishment, and failures of such organizations, but also the diversity and specialized nature to which Chicano organizations have evolved, and the ultimate importance of those organizations with respect to the Chicano in American society.

NOTES

[1]Edgar Litt, *Ethnic Politics in America* (Glenview, Ill.: Scott, Foresman and Co., 1970), 42.

[2]*Ibid.*, 59.

[3]For a complete discussion of this theme see Vigil, "Ethnic Organizations Among the Mexican Americans of New Mexico. . .", 46-59.

[4]Miguel Tirado, "The Mexican American's Participation in Voluntary Political Associations" (unpublished Ph.D. dissertation, Claremont University, 1970), abstract of dissertation.

[5]Miguel Tirado, "Mexican American Community Political Organization: The Key to Chicano Political Power," *AZTLAN* (Spring, 1970), 53-78.

[6]*Ibid.*, 72.

[7]*Ibid.*, 72-75.

[8]Vigil, Chapter 8.

[9]Dial Torgerson, "Brown Power Unity Seen Behind School Disorders" *Mexican Americans in the United States* (Cambridge: Schenckman Publishing Co., 1970), 272-288.

[10]Ruth Lamb, *Mexican Americans: Sons of the Southwest* (Claremont, California: Ocelot Press, 1970), 130.

[11]*Ibid.*, 123-140.

[12]*Ibid.*, 124.

[13]Vigil, Chapter 10.

[14]John C. Donovan, *The Politics of Poverty* (New York: Pegasus, 1964).

[15]*Ibid.*, 39-43.

[16]Much of the information on La Gente was derived from publications of the organization as well as two student papers: Hilario Rubio, "The Development of La Gente," a graduate research paper presented in the course, Interest Groups (New Mexico Highlands University, Las Vegas, New Mexico, May, 1973), and Eugene Garcia, "La Gente, The People," a paper presented in the course, Chicano Politics" (New Mexico Highlands University, Las Vegas, New Mexico, February, 1973).

[17]Rubio, op. cit.

[18]Rubio and Garcia, op. cit.

[19]Most of the information on NOSOTROS is taken from publications of the organization, news articles on the group in the Las Vegas Daily Optic, and personal observation.

[20]"What is NOSOTROS", mimeographed pamphlet distributed by NOSOTROS, Inc., 1971.

[21]Most of the information on COPAS was taken from pamphlets printed and disseminated by COPAS.

[22]Vigil, Chapter 10.

[23]In New Mexico membership rolls of these traditional service clubs and those of veterans organizations such as American Legion and VFW indicate high Mexican American memberships, thus these kinds of groups have attracted Mexican Americans more than ethnic service clubs.

[24]See O. Douglas Weeks, "The League of Latin American Citizens: A Texas Mexican Civic Organization," The Southwestern Political and Social Science Quarterly, X (December, 1929), 260 and Edward D. Garza, LULAC: League of United Latin American Citizens," (M.A. Thesis, Southwest Texas State Teachers College, 1951), reprinted by Rand Research Associates, San Francisco, 1972), 4-13.

[25]Garza, op. cit., 9-10, 16-17.

[26]See Tirado, op. cit., 65-66 and Guzman, op. cit., 205-210, 269-270.

[27]Ibid.

[28]See The Forumeer, May, 1973; January, February, 1973.

[29]Office of Minority Business Enterprise, Directory of Private Programs Assisting Minority Business, 1970 (Washington: U.S. Government Printing Office, 1970), ii.

[30]CAMBIO, "CAMBIO Gives People the Chance to Try," (pamphlet, 1973).

[31]CAMBIO, CAMBIO: Yesterday-Today-Tomorrow, Annual Report, 1972-1973, (a pamphlet), 3; also CAMBIO, "Economic Progress" (a pamphlet), 1973.

[32]"CAMBIO Gives People a Chance to Try."

[33]Ibid.

[34]Ibid.

[35]CAMBIO, Annual Report, 1972-1973.

[36]Ibid.

[37]National Economic Development Association, Annual Report, 1972-73, 1.

[38]Ibid., 8.

[39]Ibid.

[40]Letter from Anna Muller, NEDA Area Vice President, Albuquerque, New Mexico, January 17, 1974.

[41]Southwest Council of La Raza, (a pamphlet describing the organization and HELP).

[42]"Intelligence Report" Parade Magazine (Dec. 23, 1973).

[43]Carey McWilliams, North From Mexico: The Spanish Speaking People of the United States (New York: Greenwood Press, 1968), 188-194.

[44]MALDEF "The Mexican American Legal Defense and Education Fund" (a pamphlet), 2-3.

[45]Ibid.

[46]Ibid.

[47]Ibid.

[48]Ibid.

[49]Ibid.

[50]Moore, op. cit., 88.

[51]"Los PADRES, Hispano Priests Organize," La Luz V, No. 2 (May, 1973), 6-9.

[52]"PADRES Seeks to Improve Spanish American Status," Albuquerque Journal, March 26, 1971.

[53]"Hispanic Agenda Convocation," The Catholic Communicato: IV, No. 13 (Jan. 6, 1974), 1.

[54]Litt, op. cit., 49.

[55]Letter to Hispano priests from Rev. Juan Romero, PADRES Exec. Director, July 16, 1973.

[56]"Los Hermanas: Who Are We?", a mimeographed pamphlet published (no date) by Las Hermanas.

[57]Ibid.

[58]Albuquerque Journal, July 22, 1974.

[59]"APD to Revise Policies on Recruiting, Promotions," Albuquerque Journal, Jeb. 10, 1974.

[60]IMAGE Rapidly Growing Group" AGENDA: Monthly News-letter of National Council of La Raza, III, No. 3 (May, 1972), 12.

[61]National Chicano Health Organization, NCHO Newsletter, III (January, 1974), 1.

[62]Lamb, op. cit., 125-126.

[63]Rona Fields and Charles Fox, "The Brown Berets," The Black Politician, III (July, 1971), 58.

[64]Lamb, op. cit., 125-128.

[65]Ibid.

[66]"Black Berets Pledged to Help Raza" Albuquerque Journal, Dec. 20, 1970.

[67]Ibid.

[68]"Garcia Clinic Serving Health Care Need," Albuquerque Journal, April 24, 1973.

[69]Personal interview with Clemencia Martinez Jabbs, head of CWRO, April 25, 1974.

[70]Tomas Atencio, "La Academia de la Nueva Raza: La Historia," El Academia de Vez en Cuando I, No. 1 (Dixon, New Mexico: Academia de la Nueva Raza, 1971), 4-5.

195

FURTHER SUGGESTED READINGS

Kaye Briegel, "The Development of Mexican American Organizations" in The Mexican Americans: An Awakening Minority, Manuel Sernn, ed. Beverly Hills: Glencoe Press, 1970.

Rona Fields and Charles Fox. "The Brown Berets," The Black Politician, III (July, 1971), 53-63.

Edward Garza, "LULAC: League of United Latin American Citizens". Unpublished M.A. Thesis, Texas State Teachers College, 1951.

Ruth Lamb, Mexican Americans: Sons of the Southwest. Claremont, California: Ocelot Press, 1970.

Paul Sheldon. "Mexican American Formal Organizations," in Mexican Americans in the United States: A Reader, John H. Burma, ed. Cambridge: Schenchman Publ. Co., 1970.

Miguel David Tirado. "Mexican American Community Political Organization: The Key to Chicano Political Power," AZTLAN (Spring, 1970), 53-78.

O. Douglas Weeks. "The League of Latin American Citizens: A Texas-Mexican Civic Organization," The Southwestern Political and Social Science Quarterly, X (December, 1929), 257-278.

In addition newsletters, circulars, pamphlets and other publications of the various organizations are quite useful in describing their nature, objectives and activities.

CHAPTER V

MEXICAN-AMERICAN POLITICAL PARTY AND QUASI-PARTY ORGANIZATIONS

> No America without democracy, no democracy
> without politics, no politics without parties,
> no parties without compromise and moderation.*
> Clinton Rossiter, 1960

American political parties - although among the most

criticized American political institutions because of their

decentralized, undisciplined, non-doctrinaire nature - are

still the most important of American political institutions.

Political parties serve a very crucial role in the conflict

process of American politics described earlier. Clinton

Rossiter has spoken of that function when he said:

> The primary function of a political party
> in a democracy such as ours is to control and
> direct the struggle for power. . .It is the
> great purpose of political parties, the hand-
> maidens of democracy to bring the struggle
> under control; to institutionalize it with
> organization, to channel it through nomination
> and elections, to publicize it by means of
> platform and appeals, above all to stabilize
> it in the form of the Ins and Outs.[1]

In light of the central importance of political parties

in the policy making process - both in formulating policies

and recruiting and electing the implementors of policy -

it is incumbent on groups seeking to improve their benefits

---

*Clinton Rossiter, _Parties_ _and_ _Politics_ _in_ _America_
(Ithaca, New York: Cornell University Press), 1.

from public policy to participate in political party
activity. The record of the Mexican American community's
efforts to compete effectively in American party politics
is - outside of New Mexico - a poor one, but as the present
chapter will show, the poor record is more a reflection of
the failure of American parties, than that of the minority
group itself. As in other forms of organizations, the
Mexican American in the southwest was excluded from active
participation in political parties, in spite of an aggressive
and sustained effort. Political parties in California,
Texas, Arizona, and Colorado not only did not attempt to
politicize Mexican Americans as was traditionally the case
of minorities in the American cities, but they systematically
worked to exclude the group from participation. The main
result of this condition was that Mexican Americans as in
the case of ethnic organizations developed their own
political organizations, paralleling those of the dominant
group. The main thrust of Chicano political organization,
it should be noted, has occurred since World War II, because
the socio-political environment of the two early periods
of Chicano political development naturally excluded
political activity. The pattern that this form of political organization has taken recently are here described as
the quasi-party political organization, and the separate

ethnic minority political party.

Quasi-Party Political Organizations

The earliest political organizations among the Mexican American community in the modern period can be called quasi-party organizations because they participated in most of the activities - voter registration drives, candidate recruitment, get out the vote drives, policy formulation - that are the purview of the modern political party, however, these organizations eschewed the designation of political party and instead chose to work outside of but with the major parties.

The main reason for the emergence of the Chicano political organizations needless to say was the failure of the major political parties to respond to the needs and problems of the Mexican American community.

The Community Service Organization (CSO)

The first of these quasi-party political organizations that emerged within the Mexican American community was the Community Service Organization (CSO) in Southern California. The CSO was the off-spring of the Civic Unity Leagues which had been organized in California during World War II by Ignacio Lopez, editor of El Espectador, a Spanish language newspaper in the Pomona Valley, and Fred Ross, a community

organizer. The purpose of the Leagues was to organize the
Mexican Americans and equip them with the political skills -
voter registration, bloc voting, and so on - by which they
could resolve their own local problems. Meetings to plan
mass action took place in homes, churches, and public
facilities, and these served as forums where neighborhood
and community problems, ranging from police brutality to
health to employment, were aired and discussed. The Leagues
enjoyed minor success in securing community cooperation for
solving of local problems.

By the mid-1940s, a second current was leading to the
formation of CSO. This was inspired by Saul Alinsky, the
self-inspired social reformer who had founded the Industrial
Areas Foundation in Chicago as a vehicle for sponsoring
community organizing efforts. The effort in Chicago
successfully accomplished, Alinsky looked toward new areas.
The opportunity came from Los Angeles in 1947 where a group
known first as the Community Political Organization (CPO)
and later as Community Service Organization, had been
established. Because CSO was basically a grass roots
organization focusing upon neighborhood organization and
mobilization as a way of resolving local problems, the CSO
soon embraced the Industrial Areas Foundation sponsorship.

In addition to young Mexican American leaders, the

main organizers in the new CSO were Fred Ross and Father William Barry. The organization formally adopted a constitution and bylaws dedicated to "guard and further our democratic rights; to become aware of our responsibilities as citizens; to better discharge our civic duties; to coordinate our efforts for the common good of the community; to encourage active participation of our neighbors to civic life. . ."[2]

The CSO, directed its efforts at organizing chapters which would then hold meetings where all kinds of problems - health, police, employment, were discussed. The means for community action normally centered on the establishing of voting blocs. Thus, CSO became actively engaged in voter registration drives. In 1950, for example, CSO sponsored 112 volunteer voter registrars who in a three month period registered some 32,000 new Spanish-surnamed voters. CSO registration drives were so successful during this period that Republican party officials applied threats and intimidation forcing CSO to initiate its "flying squads" of security men who circulated around polling places to protect Mexican American voters. So intense was the CSO voter registration activity that it resulted in the election of its first chairman, Edward Roybal, to the Los Angeles City Council.

The CSO continued to increase its strength through
the early 1950s as new chapters were formed in other cities
and new leaders such as Cesar Chavez were brought in, but
it declined by the late 1950s largely as a result of the
withdrawal of funding by the Industrial Areas Foundation.
The significance of CSO lay in its massive voter registration drives which not only introduced thousands of new
voters (mostly Democrats) to the American political system,
but it indicated (in Roybal's and other electoral victories)
what could be accomplished. It also set the stage and
provided the basis for the emergence of the next quasi-
party organization.[3]

The Mexican American Political Association (MAPA)

The Mexican American Political Association (MAPA) was
organized in April, 1960, in Fresno, California, by some of
the more activist former members of CSO. The impetus for
the formation of MAPA lay in an accumulated series of
grievances Chicano leaders had against the Democratic Party
in California (such as the defeat of Edward Roybal for Lt.
Governor in 1954), which were climaxed by the defeat of
Democrat Henry Lopez, a young Chicano attorney, for Secretary of State, in a year which otherwise produced a Democratic Party landslide. The Chicanos felt that the Democratic Party had not fully supported Lopez and became

convinced that the unequivocal allegiance of the group to the party of Roosevelt was resulting in their being taken for granted, without receiving a fair share of the spoils. The need for a political organization that would advance solely the interests of the Mexican American in California was deemed essential.[4]

The Fresno Conference therefore, adopted as its objectives the following:

(1) To seek the social, economic, cultural, and civic betterment of Mexican Americans and other persons sympathetic to their aims.

(2) To take stands on political issues and present and endorse candidates for public office.

(3) To launch voter registration drives throughout California.

(4) To encourage increased activity within the political parties.[5]

Thus, while CSO had been an ethnic interest group functioning within the Democratic Party for Hispanos, MAPA declared its independence of both major parties, but did not carry the independence as far as creating a new party, but instead established itself as a political interest group working for Mexican Americans through both major political parties. The organization grew in strength by coopting many of the CSO inspired Mexican American voters, and by addressing itself solely to the Mexican American community.

In 1962, for example, it reminded Mexican Americans that they did not have their proportionate share of elected or appointed government officials in California, and vowed to destroy "once and for all 100 years of almost complete exclusion /of Hispanos/ from participation in state and national government."[6]

MAPA has endorsed and actively worked for Mexican American candidates in California politics, and its effort has been significant in this respect. MAPA was a leading force in the East Los Angeles Incorporation movement which has generally yielded greater home rule powers to the large Chicano population of East Los Angeles. MAPA was instrumental in the election of two state assemblymen, three Superior Court judges, and three municipal court judges of Mexican American descent. The most notable success of MAPA to date, has been the election of Edward R. Roybal to Congress. MAPA's future prominence will probably depend on how well it can continue the process of politicizing the California Mexican American and reconcile it with the brokerage function they play on behalf of Chicanos between the two major parties. The power or full potential of the

Mexican American voter will not be felt until the group is more politicized. If MAPA fails to respond to that challenge, it may find itself supplanted by La Raza Unida Party, as has happened to its counterpart, PASO, in Texas.

The Political Association of Spanish-speaking Organizations (PASO)

In Texas, the counterpart of MAPA was the Political Association of Spanish-Speaking Organizations (PASO). PASO was formed from the remnants of Democratic Party "Viva Kennedy" clubs that had sprung up in Texas and elsewhere in the Southwest among Mexican Americans advocating the candidacy of John F. Kennedy for the Presidency. The first PASO chapter was formed in southern Texas in the early 1960s and soon spread to other towns in South Texas with large Mexican American populations such as San Antonio, El Paso, and Crystal City. Like MAPA, PASO was principally concerned with nominating and electing Mexican Americans to public office and supporting candidates from either party which were favorable to the interests of the Mexican American group. Unlike MAPA, however, PASO was more inclined to work within the Democratic Party.

PASO, because of the more hostile Texas social environment, was less ethnocentric than MAPA, striving as it did for coalitions with liberal and other ethnic groups.[7]

The most notable success of PASO occurred in Crystal City, Texas, in 1963 where the organization succeeded in defeating the Anglo mayor who had served for 38 years and replacing him and all of the City Council with Hispanos. After its initial success in Texas, PASO tried to expand to other parts of the Southwest, most notably Arizona, in an effort to create a Spanish-speaking political organization for all Hispanos in the Southwest.

It failed in this, and has, in the late 1960s declined, losing much of its support to La Raza Unida Party. Its victories in Crystal City were negated in 1965 when the Anglos returned to power.

The American Coordinating Council on Political Education (ACCPE)

In Arizona, the effort of PASO to establish a chapter failed, but led to the creation of the American Coordinating Council on Political Education (ACCPE) which eventually became Arizona's version of the Hispanic political organization. ACCPE grew to a membership of some 2,500 with chapters in ten of Arizona's fourteen counties. The ACCPE councils were able to secure the election of Hispanos to city council posts in several Arizona cities, but were most successful in Miami, Arizona, where they elected five of seven city councilmen in 1962.[8]

Chicano Political Parties

The high point in the development of Chicano political organizations has been the recent emergence of the separate ethnic minority political party. The most important of these has been La Raza Unida Party, (LRUP), and its most important difference from previous political organizations is its avowed political party designation. Before discussing LRUP it is appropriate to discuss previous ethnic party movements and to address related issues on the status of minor parties in American politics.

Minor Parties in American Politics

In order to appreciate the full importance of the separate ethnic political party to the ethnic group in the context of American society, it is necessary to consider the role - if any - that minor parties play in American politics, since the separate ethnic party is one form of a fairly common occurrence, the minor party, in American politics. V.O. Key, Jr. reflected on the role that third parties play when he said:

> A minor party can expect to win the pres-
> idency only if the party system is undergoing a
> radical transformation, with one of the major
> parties in process of dissolution. . .If they
> play a role it differs from that of the major
> parties.[9]

In other words, a minor party stands a scant chance of

success in terms of traditional standards for judging

success of major parties, i.e. victory at the polls, since

a minor party can compete for major offices such as the

Presidency only if it becomes a major party. Since this

has only occurred once (Republican Party) in American

history, the chances of a minor party, judged by this stand-

ard, are very slight indeed. On the other hand, as Key

infers, taken from a different perspective or alternate

standard for measuring success, it is possible that minor

parties perform an equally important though _different_ role

than the major parties. Hugh A. Bone summarized the theme

when he said that "the presence of minor parties is felt

in three ways - as exponents of dissent, champions of

change, and critics of the major parties."[10] Thus it is

possible to argue that minor parties by serving as purveyors

of protest, criticism and change, by raising and clarifying

issues, by suggesting innovative ways of responding to

existing problems, force the major parties to adopt change,

thus indirectly strengthening the two party process.

The point is, that a separate ethnic Chicano political

party can be seen as a viable political force in either of

two ways, either as a viable alternative to the major

parties in local and state elections where Chicano voters

present a sizable bloc vote, or in a gadfly role (in the

tradition of the minor party), in state or national elections.

This dual perspective of the potential importance will be

illustrated later when comparing the different roles which

the LRUP has played in the different political environments

of New Mexico and Texas.

Early Chicano Political Party Movements

It may come as a surprise to current day activists, to

discover that the modern La Raza Unida Party is not the

first, or second Chicano political party movement. The

first separate political party organized primarily by

Mexican Americans was El Partido del Pueblo Unido (The

United People's Party) organized on September 8, 1890, in

Las Vegas, New Mexico. The Partido was organized by a

coalition of disaffected Mexican American politicos from

both the Democratic and Republican parties in San Miguel

County, who were joined by a group of organizers for the

Caballeros de Labor (Knights of Labor) which had also been

active in the social activist activities of Las Gorras

Blancas (the white caps), in the county.

The Partido coalition reflected the most pressing

economic, social, ethnic and political issues of the period

that included (a) opposition to growing Republican Party

bossism, (b) the desire to resolve land grant title contro-

versies, (c) the pressure for expanded free public education,
and (d) the general anti-capitalist fervor of the period.

The Partido held its first party convention in the
Fall of 1890 with representatives from all of San Miguel
County's sixty precincts in attendance. The convention
nominated a full slate of county candidates and drew up a
party platform reflecting the main social, economic,
political, ethnic bases of the coalition. The party carried
the county in the elections of 1890. In 1892 the Partido
once again carried the county for its slate, as well as for
the National Populist Party which had been endorsed by the
Partido.

Although the Partido declined by the 1894 elections
and was disbanded, its temporary success proved to Hispanos
in New Mexico that a coalition built on economic, social,
and ethnic issues could alter the outcome of elections in
spite of the dominance of political machines. At a time
when Mexican Americans were considered a docile, easily
manipulated group, it is significant that Mexican Americans
in New Mexico's largest and most populous county successfully supported a minor party effort.[11]

A second political party that emerged among a few
Mexican Americans, was the Mexican Liberal Party (MLP)
which was Mexico-oriented. The MLP was made up of Mexican

expatriots who sought to overthrow the Mexican government.
The MLP headquartered in Los Angeles actually attacked and
captured the town of Tijuana causing an international
incident between the United States and Mexico. When the
raiders were forced to evacuate Tijuana and returned to
the U.S. they were promptly arrested.[12]

The People's Constitutional Party

The first modern example of a separate Mexican American
political party came at the impetus of the Alianza Federal
de Pueblos Libres in 1968. The idea for the formation of
a separate political party originated some time after the
famous "Tierra Amarilla Raid" undertaken by Reies Lopez
Tijerina and the national publicity that accompanied the
trial and subsequent activity of the fiery Chicano leader.
As early as the fall of 1967, when Tijerina visited and gave
speeches to Chicano groups in southern California, there was
talk of a Black/Chicano coalition in the Peace and Freedom
Party which would see Black Comedian Dick Gregory running
for President, with Tijerina as his Vice-Presidential running
mate. These plans, however, fell through even though
Gregory actually appeared in some states on ballots for
the Presidency.

The idea of a separate Chicano party in New Mexico was

spawned by Alianza leaders in June 1968 as the Alianza

participated in the Poor People's Campaign in Washington,

and as the campaign for the August primaries was beginning

in New Mexico.

When Tijerina returned to New Mexico, the discussion

had reached a serious stage and the Mesa Cosmica (Board of

Elders) finally decided to launch a separate third party to

be known as the Partido Constitucional del Pueblo (the

People's Constitutional Party).[13] In its choice of name,

the Alianza selected the euphemism "pueblo" or community

of people instead of Hispano as a way of underlining the

spirit of unity and brotherhood among poor people which

was so current in the summer of 1968 after the Poor People's

Campaign in Washington. Although there was little doubt

that the core support for the party would come from Hispano

Alianza sympathizers, there was an effort to make the party

a party for the poor people of all ethnic groups.

A founding convention was held on August 4, 1968, in

Albuquerque, New Mexico, where a body of rules and regula-

tions for presentation to the Secretary of State, and a

party platform was adopted. In addition, Tijerina was

selected as the Party's candidate for Governor, and indica-

tive of the Party's true desire to be a party of the poor,

an Indian, Jose Alfredo Maestas of San Juan Pueblo, was

selected to run for Lt. Governor.

Basic to the PCP platform was a provision calling for bilingual education for Mexican American children and a restoration of teaching of the Indo-Hispano culture. Working from Tijerina's premise that the two most cherished possessions of the Mexican American were his land and his culture (including the Spanish language), and that the former had been taken away illegally while the latter was slowly eroding away due to assimilationist tendencies, the Alianza felt that bilingual and bicultural education was basic to the preservation of Mexican American culture, and to prevention of its decay. Indicative of this mood, Tijerina said at the August convention:

> I never wanted anything to do with politics, but this is why I changed my mind. Not only the land has been stolen from the good and humble people, but also their culture and something else very valuable--their vote. I have seen how the bad politicians abuse it. . .I'd enforce that law for bilingual education, even if I had to call out the National Guard to do it.[14]

Other planks included in the original platform or included as time and necessity dictated were those calling for: an independent civilian police review board to investigate instances of police brutality and misconduct; investigation of corporations and banks that speculated in land; ending discrimination against minorities in local selective service draft boards (the Vietnam War was then at its height); increases in state welfare checks; pardon for convicts who had been convicted as a result of inadequate defense stemming from poverty; lowering of the voting age to 18; and protection of the rights of hippies and "all who want to live their own way of life."[15]

The PCP staged conventions in six northern New Mexico counties: Bernalillo, Rio Arriba, Santa Fe, Sandoval, Valencia, and San Miguel. Tijerina appeared in all of the county conventions and in his speeches reflected on the theme of rich vs. poor in the campaign. In San Miguel County, for example, Tijerina read names from a list of local farmers receiving annual government subsidies as high as $30,000 for not planting crops, or as Tijerina put it, "rich man's welfare." In Rio Arriba County, the PCP Convention nominated a whole slate of county officers to accompany the state candidates.

Almost from the outset, the PCP found itself in legal wrangling with the Secretary of State over their appearance on the ballot. The legal requirement was simple enough; at the time all that was needed were 100 signatures of qualified voters. On September 27, the PCP filed its petition with the Secretary of State and its slate of officers, headed by Tijerina for Governor, and for state, district, and county officers. On October 2, 1968, Secretary of State Ernestine Evans announced the disqualification of eight PCP candidates. Tijerina was disqualified because of his conviction on a felony in federal court for charges arising from an Alianza confrontation with the U.S. Forest Service. Candidates for Congress Wilfredo Sedillo and William Higgs were disqualified for failure to meet residency requirements. Dr. Roger Anderson, a geologist and candidate for State Board of Education, was disqualified on another technicality; Preston Monongye, candidate for District Attorney, First Judicial District, was disqualified because he was not a member of the bar. The other three disqualified candidates were given no explanation.

The arbitrary disqualification by the Secretary of State provided PCP and Tijerina with a ready-made issue, that being that poor candidates did not possess a chance of running for political office. Tijerina announced that the disqualification was a result of a fear by the "Democratic machine" of his candidacy and of the fact that he would get a "fantastic turnout."

On October 5, 1968, in accordance with Tijerina's avowal of October 2, the New Mexico Civil Liberties Union filed a petition on behalf of Tijerina and the PCP before the State Supreme Court, requesting an order that the

Secretary of State replace the names on the ballot or show cause why she should not. The Civil Liberties Union argued that the Secretary of State had acted arbitrarily and capriciously in removing the names without providing the public a full explanation and without affording the candidates an executive hearing. It also questioned the legality of the disqualifications, arguing that the candidates for Congress met all the U.S. Constitutional requirements and that any state requirement for these offices was unconstitutional. In Tijerina's case, the CLU argued that his conviction involved a federal offense which was being appealed and thus had nothing to do with New Mexico's statutes.

On October 28, the Court ordered that the Secretary of State replace all PCP names on the ballot with the exception of Tijerina, whose suspension from the ballot was upheld and the PCP thereupon moved Jose Alfredo Maestas up to run for Governor, and named Crucita Chavez to run for Lt. Governor. Especially significant in the Court's decision was that it found the state law requiring residency in the district in relation to Congressional races unconstitutional. The late decision created great confusion in the closing days of the election. Since the ballots had already been printed, the names of PCP candidates were to be placed on the ballot by gummed stickers. This did not include some 10,000 absentee ballots (4,000 of them to Vietnam) which the Secretary of

State had already mailed out. In a last minute effort to

disrupt the election, the PCP filed suit on November 2, two

days before the election, requesting an order for the

Secretary of State to put PCP candidate names on absentee

ballots. This effort failed and the election was held as

planned.

That the PCP challenge was not a serious threat to the

major parties became manifest in the election, as the highest

vote a PCP candidate received was 2,884 in the race for

State Treasurer. The votes received by the PCP candidate

in the races for State Auditor, State Corporation Com-

missioner, and State Commissioner of Public Lands were high

enough that it could possibly have affected the outcome of

the election. The candidate for Governor, Maestas, received

some 1,540 votes, less than the margin between the winner,

David Cargo, and the loser, Fabian Chavez, and probably

less than Tijerina would have received.

Notwithstanding its disastrous defeat at the polls,

the PCP certainly seems to have served in 1968 as an exponent

of dissent and criticism of the major parties. Tijerina

probably gained more by his removal from the ballot in

dramatizing the electoral inequities than he would have, had

he remained on the ballot. The mere fact of having a whole

slate of unknown, common, and mostly Hispano candidates
from presidential electors, to Congress, to state, district,
and county office was itself a novelty. Moreover, the legal
hassles with the Secretary of State added color to an otherwise drab campaign. Certainly, the legal position of the
PCP, as presented by the NMCLU, set important new precedents
in the Congressional races and engendered serious discussion
of issues relating to the accessibility of office to people
other than the wealthy. Most importantly, the introduction
by the PCP of planks calling for bilingual, bicultural
education certainly struck a responsive cord in the minds
of Hispano Democratic and Republican Party politicians, and
re-introduced issues that had long been ignored in New
Mexico politics.

In the 1970 elections, during Tijerina's imprisonment,
the PCP once again participated in the elections, this time
under the impetus and guidance of William Higgs, the anglo
lawyer, who had advised and guided the Alianza in Tijerina's
absence. The PCP presented a platform divided into seven
main headings entitled Government, Education, Welfare,
Youth, International Civil Liberties, and Drugs, that was
reflective of Higg's influence.

The Alianza repeated its commitment to the poor with
a statement under government, calling for "self-determination

of peoples and preservation of their language, culture, and way of life." Under education, the platform called for greater local control of school systems, with a school board for every district. In welfare, the platform called for a "minimum floor" as a living standard. In its youth plank, it called for full voting and legal rights for 18-year olds. In international affairs, it called for "an abandonment of foreign relations based on military and economic might and conceived in ideas of . . .political and economic imperialism." It also went on record as opposing the War in Vietnam. In relation to drugs, the platform urged "non-criminal controls on the use of marijuana or legalization."[17]

The Party ran a full slate of officers for U.S. Congress and state officers, and though their showing was somewhat better than in 1968, it still failed to influence the outcome of major races.

Shortly after the release of Tijerina from prison, the Alianza reported that the PCP would be disbanded, claiming that the party had fulfilled the purpose for which it had been created. That this was not an empty claim is evidenced by the fact that by 1972 the New Mexico Legislature "liberalized" candidate certification procedures designed to make it easier for poor people to run for office and also by subsequent passage of federal and state bilingual education bills. Though it is not appropriate to credit the PCP for these reforms it is possible to say that the PCP did occupy the traditional third party role in lobbying for those changes in 1968 and 1970, foreshadowing their advocacy by the major parties.

La Raza Unida Party in Texas

The single most important political organization that has emerged within the Mexican American community is La Raza Unida Party (LRUP, or, the United Chicano People's Party). The Party was founded in 1969 in Crystal City, Texas, by Jose Angel Gutierrez, and grew out of a mass Chicano student walkout in the spring of 1969 and an even greater walkout in December, 1969, organized by the Mexican American Youth Organization then headed by Gutierrez. The walkout involved 1,700 out of 2,300 students from all grades, and virtually closed the Crystal City schools, climaxing a long series of efforts by Chicanos in Crystal City to make the schools more responsive in its programs to the Hispano majority. The immediate cause of the walkouts was the refusal of the school board to respond to demands by the Mexican American Youth Organization (MAYO), involving bilingual education, participation in federal programs such

as lunch programs, better school facilities, and hiring of
Chicano counselors.[18]

The student walkout led to protest marches, reprisals
and counter-reprisals that served to weld the Chicanos
closer together. Employers who fired participating students
from their part-time jobs, for example, were faced with
boycotts by Chicanos. So unified was the Chicano community
that even after the school board capitulated, some two and
one-half months after the walkout began, two MAYO organizers
in each of four south Texas counties, Hidalgo, Dimmit, La
Salle, and Zavala, set about launching La Raza Unida Party
through voter registration drives that put the party on
the ballot in three Texas counties. On April 4, 1970, LRUP
candidates were elected to three school board seats in the
Crystal City school board. With the support of the lone
Hispano remaining on the board (previously the seven-man
board had consisted of five anglos and two hispanos), the
LRUP controlled the board.

Also, in April, LRUP gained two city council seats in
the Crystal City Council as well as winning the mayor's
race and one city council position in Cotulla and Carrizo
Springs, Texas, respectively.

In Crystal City, the LRUP controlled school board
promptly set about restructuring the school system to better

serve the Mexican American community. Jose Angel Gutierrez was selected chairman of the Board of Education, and under his leadership, the Board instituted a bilingual education program from the kindergarten to the third grade, a free lunch program for every child in Crystal City schools, prohibited use of culturally biased IQ testing, and adopted policies to adopt culturally relevant textbooks, encourage hiring of Chicanos to staff, custodial and administrative positions, and the implementation of bicultural education programs.[19]

From that beginning, the party grew rapidly as a result of voter registration drives conducted principally in the south Texas counties with high Hispano populations. In the November, 1970 elections LRUP nominated candidates for selected county offices in Zavala, Dimmit, La Salle and Hidalgo counties. Although ruled off the ballot on technicalities in Zavala, Dimmit and La Salle counties, LRUP quickly launched a write in campaign that resulted in election of one county official, Raul Rodriguez, in La Salle county, and close contests in two other races.[20] The successes further encouraged LRUP voter registration drives that continued following the election.

In a state party convention held on October 30, 1971, the party voted against Gutierrez' recommendation to field candidates for state office. Gutierrez had argued that the party should consolidate its strength on a sub-state regional basis before moving to the state level. On June 10, 1972, the party held its first state nominating convention in San Antonio, Texas, with Gutierrez as its keynote speaker. Attending were some 500 delegates from 25 Texas counties, including the most populous Harris, Dallas, Torrant, Bexar, Travis, Nueces, and Lubbock counties. In addition to naming its permanent party officials headed by state Chairman Mario Campeon (Gutierrez' close ally since the MAYO days), LRUP selected a slate of state officers to run in the November General Election. Heading the ticket would be a popular Chicano lawyer from Waco, Ramsay Muniz, who had been a star football player at Baylor University. The state party lists were to be accompanied by LRUP slates for county officials in some counties where the party had reached sufficient strength in its organizational drives.[21]

The party made a formidable showing in the November elections in Texas. Although Muniz with over 214,118 votes trailed both the Democratic and Republican Party candidates (each of which polled over a million votes) by large margins, his showing was strong enough to influence the outcome of the very close governor's race, and his 6.3 percent of the vote automatically qualified the party for the 1974 elections.

LRUP also made a strong showing in Zavala County (Crystal City) where it won the races for sheriff, county attorney, and one county commission position.

The 1972 statewide and selected county returns encouraged LRUP organizers who stepped up voter registration drives. As the 1974 elections approached, LRUP once again called on Ramsay Muniz to head the state LRUP slate in the race for Governor. Although Muniz' vote total of 93,295 was less than in 1972, he again received 6% of the total vote thus once again qualifying the party for the 1978 elections. La Raza Unida also consolidated its control of Zavala (Crystal City) County, as LRUP candidates swept offices for County Judge, District Clerk, County Clerk, County Treasurer, two County Commission seats, and three Justice of Peace positions, which together with the 1972 elections put LRUP in full control of Zavala County government. Gutierrez was himself elected as County Judge, and Muniz carried the county in his race for Governor. The only LRUP candidates who lost in the county lost to Hispano opponents, and all the LRUP candidates defeated Anglo opponents.[22] The successes in Zavala County have thus given it a strong base from which to expand to other south Texas counties.

Undoubtedly, the greatest strength of LRUP is concentrated in Texas, especially in the south Texas winter garden
region, both because it originated there among the endemic
Mexican American population, and because of the traditional
disfranchisement of Mexican Americans who form the basis for
the party's recruitment and registration drives. The LRUP
movement has, however, made significant progress in other states

La Raza Unida Party Outside of Texas

Although the progress of LRUP outside of Texas has
been variable, it has achieved a firm foothold in California
and Colorado where the political position of the Mexican
American has been very much like that of its counterpart
in Texas.

In Colorado, LRUP was launched as a result of the
second National Chicano Youth Liberation Conference sponsored
by the Denver Crusade for Justice in March, 1970 in Denver.
Although the LRUP has not secured as noteworthy success at
the polls as its Texas counterpart, the Colorado LRUP
leaders view the appearance of LRUP candidates on the ballot
as significant in itself, in view of stringent requirements
third parties must meet in order to appear on the ballot.
The party ran 30 candidates for state and local offices in
the November, 1970 elections, and though none was elected,

the party did receive more votes than any third party in the history of Colorado. The LRUP has expanded outside of Denver's barrios (where it is closely allied to the Crusade for Justice) to other cities in the "el valle" area of Southern Colorado, Pueblo, La Junta and Las Animas. The party has a state party organization which has coordinated the continuing voter registration drives and helped carry out LRUP campaigns. In the 1974 elections two LRUP candidates for the State Board of Regents made impressive showings. The candidate for a Denver seat drew over 7,000 votes and the at-large candidate drew over 24,000. In May, 1975, an LRUP candidate for the Denver City Council drew enough votes to force a runoff election though the candidate was defeated.

LRUP leaders in Colorado feel that LRUP has indirectly contributed to the victories of Mexican American candidates running as Democrats, since these appeared on the Democratic ballot partly as a result of LRUP pressure. For example, several Hispanos have been elected to the State Legislature in Colorado, something which had not occurred before. Probably the most important contribution of the Colorado LRUP to the national LRUP movement has been the leadership of Rodolfo "Corky" Gonzales, the organizer and leader of the Colorado LRUP (and Crusade for Justice) who has provided the party with its basic national structure and philosophical base. Gonzales is not only one of the two top leaders of the national LRUP structure, but one of its most popular and able strategists.[23]

In California, the LRUP first emerged in the Bay Area with chapters in Oakland, Hayward, Berkeley and Union City, and spread south to San Jose, Fresno and other cities in central California, and ultimately chapters were formed in East Los Angeles, San Diego, and Long Beach. The influence of LRUP was first felt in Oakland in 1971 when LRUP supported candidates made impressive showings in races for city council and board of education. Progress in voter registration drives has continued as reflected by the registration figures for a four month period in 1971 which showed that almost half of the total registrations in East Los Angeles were with LRUP.[24] In a recent study, Alberto Juarez pointed out that the presence of LRUP in California politics has been to challenge the traditional Hispano support for the Democratic Party. In one election for a state assembly seat the presence of an LRUP candidate was enough to withhold victory from the Hispano Democrat. Thus in Juarez' view, "the potential of La Raza Unida cannot help but haunt the Republican and Democratic leadership."[25]

In New Mexico, the impetus for LRUP has largely been external, although the leadership has come from within the state. Both of these factors help explain the uniqueness of the role of the party in New Mexico and the nature of the corps of supporters that it has attracted in the state.

Because the Hispano in New Mexico has been highly politicized, the function and base of support of LRUP in the state assumes a marked difference from its role in other states. The party in the first place, does not have a vast unregistered, unpoliticized corps of voters from which to draw electoral strength. The bulk of the Hispano population in New Mexico is not only registered, but has established, as is the general pattern among the American electorate, fairly rigid partisan preferences that influence the voting behavior of the group. Moreover, these partisan identifications are not easily altered.

The LRUP has, therefore, been forced to rely on the bulk of their support from young Chicanos who have not yet developed any form of rigid partisan loyalties, and at the same time, have held an awareness about the nature and activities of LRUP and the Chicano movement per se in other states. In New Mexico, LRUP membership has been notably absent of older and middleclass Hispanos whose loyalties generally lie with existing parties.

Because LRUP, like its predecessor PCP, has had serious difficulty in making serious inroads among that group of people that it has chosen to address itself, it must of necessity assume more of the gadfly role described earlier, forcing the traditional parties consisting of Hispano politicians to adopt specific policies aimed toward the Hispano group. This is not to say that the role of the group is not significant; it is to say that the role of the group differs from the roles attributed LRUP in other states.

The first efforts to form a La Raza Unida Party in New Mexico were undertaken in the summer of 1972, and were the result of simultaneous drives in Bernalillo County (Albuquerque), and San Miguel County (Las Vegas). The seeds for the party had been planted in the winter of 1972 when Jose Angel Gutierrez had visited at the request of Chicano students and spoken at several university campuses and encouraged young Chicanos to form chapters of the party. Gutierrez spoke of the problems faced and the success of the group in Texas.

In the summer of 1972, LRUP organizing conventions were held in Bernalillo and San Miguel Counties, where groups of young activist Chicanos laid the groundwork for permanent local party organizations. At the impetus of the two county organizations, a state party convention was held in the

Fall of 1972 when a permanent state party committee structure

was set up and officers elected.

The impetus for the creation of LRUP in New Mexico

and for its peculiar role in New Mexico were outlined by

Juan Jose Peña, the state party Chairman as follows:

> Partido La Raza Unida was founded this summer
> in New Mexico because the two major political
> parties were not serving the needs of 'our people.'
> . . .the Chicano, or Indo-Hispano, in the South-
> west has been under-represented by both of the
> major parties; this is especially true where the
> Chicanos' socio-economic position, language, and
> culture are concerned. The Partido intends to
> attempt to fill this vacuum which has existed for
> a long time and which has been detrimental to our
> people. . .The partido intends to work with their
> elected officials and the community to represent
> the people at all levels of social interaction. . .
> so that the poor people of the county can have their
> needs vocalized. The Partido also intends to bring
> many other issues, grievances, and injustices to
> light in order that the public may become more
> aware of them. The Partido will be acting as a
> public party, and invites all interested persons
> from San Miguel County to attend the convention
> and to aid the Partido in its attempt to help the
> people.[26]

Thus the party was created in New Mexico on the

assumption that the two major parties, in spite of the fact

that Hispanos had always been active in both parties, had

not served the Mexican American people, and that LRUP's

objective would be to "raise new issues relating to the

particular problems of Chicanos."

The San Miguel County (Las Vegas) chapter of the LRUP

headed by Pena has been the most active and compelling force for the party in the state, having dominated state party conventions and frequently participating in local elections in Las Vegas. For this reason, the following summary will focus on the San Miguel (Las Vegas) chapter of LRUP.

The San Miguel County LRUP organization has been an important political force in the county primarily because it has been built around a small core of loyal party workers who have devoted most of their energies to the LRUP or Chicano cause. The small core consists of young activist Chicanos, mostly college students, who are also active in the university Chicano student organization and other Chicano organizations in the community.

The first appearance of LRUP candidates was in the San Miguel County elections of 1972 when candidates were certified in races for County Clerk and Probate Judge. Together with these, LRUP sponsored a write-in campaign for three candidates for County Commission. The certified candidates drew slightly over 200 votes and the write in candidates sixty votes, indicating that LRUP had established its small base of loyal supporters, and more importantly that of the 231 LRUP registered voters in the county virtually all went to the polls.

In January, 1973, the Las Vegas LRUP initiated its efforts in the upcoming school board election, although it

had to forego its formal party label in the non-partisan
election. The first decision made was not to contest the
board positions in West Las Vegas since that board was then
controlled by liberal Chicanos who had already instituted
some programs advocated by LRUP. Instead, the party
selected Peña and another Chicano to run as an independent
slate in the East Las Vegas school board election since
the East Las Vegas Board had traditionally been controlled
by Anglos. The LRUP candidates ran on a platform that
emphasized bilingual and bicultural education, and recruitment of Hispano teachers and administrators for the school
system. The campaign was largely low key and personalized,
since the party lacked extensive funds to advertise; mimeographed statements of intent were distributed. This was in
contrast to the well organized and well financed campaign
of the Parents' Ticket, made up of a prominent Anglo
physician and a well-known Anglo rancher in the area.

Not surprisingly, both Anglos won handily. What was
surprising was the strong showing of the two LRUP candidates.
Peña, received 25% of the vote and a higher percentage than
two other Hispanos in the race, and his running mate
received 26% and a higher percentage than the other Hispano
in the race. Had the two LRUP candidates been running alone
against the two Anglos, the race would undoubtedly have been

much closer.

Although LRUP made an impressive debut in a local election, the fact that LRUP candidates had split the ethnic vote with the other Hispano candidates thus allowing the Anglos to win posed a problem for LRUP.

Encouraged by its showing in the school board elections, LRUP next turned its attention to the 1974 municipal elections in Las Vegas. Again the party in the spirit of bi-partisanship chose to forego its own designation and ran instead as the "Pueblo Unido" (united people) slate, but the candidates it posed for city offices left little mystery about its true affiliation. Peña once again headed the slate as candidate for Mayor, and five LRUP party members were candidates for four council seats and police magistrate. The Pueblo Unido slate stressed issues of greatest concern to the poor Chicano in the tradition of LRUP:

> The Pueblo Unido ticket will work to establish
> ordinances to aid the poor people of the community
> and will work to repair. . .pave and illuminate
> streets in the barrios; and to deal with other
> problems of the barrios; /and/ to direct revenue
> sharing funds for these ends.[27]

The outcome of the city elections once again dramatically bore the impact of the LRUP effort, and once again posed the problem of dysfunctional ethnic vote splitting. Of the two other slates competing in the city elections the

"Greater Las Vegas Ticket" was an all Chicano, but more moderate slate, while the "United Citizens" slate represented a coalition of conservative Chicanos and two Anglos. In the race for Mayor the appearance of Peña on the ballot (Pena received 8% of the vote) probably resulted in his drawing votes away from the liberal Chicano candidate, thus contributing to the victory by the conservative Chicano. In the races for City Council, the Pueblo Unido slate definitely influenced the outcome in favor of the two Anglos. The two Anglos running on the United Citizens slate were elected by 34 and 50 votes, over the liberal Chicanos of the Greater Las Vegas ticket, while their LRUP opponents were drawing 371 and 410 votes. Since it is most unlikely that LRUP voters would have favored the Anglo candidates, it is likely that the Anglos won because of LRUP participation.

The election clearly underscored the fact that Chicanos were splitting the ethnic vote, enabling more conservative and Anglo candidates to win. LRUP has viewed such a strategy as necessary in some areas as a way of pressuring Hispano candidates to adopt a more responsive tone in regard to LRUP sponsored issues, and as a way of embracing coalitions with LRUP candidates.

Another factor that has contributed to LRUP's role in

New Mexico as a gadfly minor party movement is the close

affiliation of LRUP with various activist Chicano groups.

In Las Vegas for example LRUP has drawn its basic core of

support from university students active in the Chicano

Associated Student Organization (CASO) which has figured

prominently in activist activity at Highlands University.

Most of the same people were also quite active in Chicanos

Unidos Para Justicia (CUPJ) another activist group that was

involved in the Las Vegas city schools protest of 1973 and

the Montezuma demonstration of 1974 and took part in setting

up an alternative school at Montezuma, New Mexico. The

theme is well described in a feature article appearing in

a Santa Fe newspaper on LRUP:

> Partido de La Raza Undia may not win elec-
> tions in the near future, but it unquestionably
> is the most dynamic force in the Las Vegas area
> today. The leadership and members of La Raza
> Unida are avowedly and proudly activist. They
> believe in protesting publicly against whatever
> upsets them, and demonstrating publicly to
> underline their protests. They frighten a lot
> of non-activist people. . .La Raza Unida and
> another organization, known as /Chicanos Unidos
> Para Justicia7 whose leadership is inter-
> changeable and almost identical with the party,
> have won some solid victories. . .Raza Unida
> and Chicanos Unidos demonstrators do not make
> their points by scholarly debates, learned
> discussion of the facts, or gentle appeals to
> reason and understanding. They shout in unison
> in picket lines; they stomp their boots in
> unison in marching through the streets. They
> wave in unison their red and black Chicano
> flags.[28]

Invariably, the ethnic basis of LRUP would of necessity imply a broad social reformist orientation that would involve the party in many problems relating to the Hispano. It is in this respect that LRUP finds itself more closely associated with the have-not segments of the Hispano community, and it is among this group and its loyalties that it poses the greatest challenge to the traditionally dominant political parties and its Hispano politicos. It is this challenge, posed first by PCP and more recently by LRUP, which has served to sensitize politicians in New Mexico, but more specifically Hispano politicians, to the needs and problems of the group on which they must rely for electoral support.

La Raza Unida as a National Minor Party

That the La Raza Unida Party has indeed taken hold in many parts of the country became manifest on September 1, 1972, in El Paso, Texas, when the first national political convention of the party was held. Over 3,000 delegates, including young activists, older middle-class Chicanos, and about half of them women, representing 17 states and the District of Columbia, convened in the Hotel El Paso del Norte to discuss national organization, resolutions to be adopted, and strategies for the November presidential

election. In addition to the southwestern states, the
convention included delegates from the Pacific Northwest
(Washington), the Midwest (Michigan, Illinois, Indiana),
the Plains Area (Kansas, Nebraska), and East Coast (Mary-
land, New York).[29]

The convention opened with speeches from three of the
current big four among Chicano leaders, Rodolfo "Corky"
Gonzales, leader of Denver's Crusade for Justice, Jose Angel
Gutierrez, LRUP founder and leading organizer, and Reies
Lopez Tijerina, Alianza leader. Absent was Cesar Chavez
of the United Farm Workers Organizing Committee.

All three leaders emphasized in their speeches that
ethnic cohesion or unity was the basic element requisite
for political power among Chicanos. Gonzales and Gutierrez
spoke against continued loyalty to either of the two major
parties, neither of which has served the interests of the
Hispanos. Gonzales called the two major parties a "two-
headed monster eating from one trough." Gutierrez maintained that "our vote has been taken for granted for too
long, especially by the Democratic Party."

The first action taken by the convention was the
adoption of a resolution declaring the political independence
of the party from either of the two major parties, and to
maintain that political independence in the race for

President. Neither George McGovern, the Democrat, nor
Richard Nixon, the Republican, was endorsed for the office.

The convention also adopted resolutions which were
consolidated and approved in a "national priorities platform." Heading the list of planks was a resolution calling
for bilingual, bicultural education for Mexican American
youth. Other planks reflected the multi-faceted nature of
the problems faced by the Chicano community. They included
an end to police brutality in the barrios; more Chicanos
to serve in judgeships; wage and employment parity for
Hispanos in the federal government; a more concentrated
effort against drug problems in Chicano communities; programs to increase recruitment of Chicanos to medical schools;
free legal aid; an end to the war in Vietnam; parity for
Chicanos in jury selection; support for the struggle of the
farm workers; a call for enforcement of the treaty of
Guadalupe Hidalgo; and several others.

The convention then moved toward establishing a permanent national organization for the party. The idea of a
permanent congress, or concilio, which had been advocated
long before by "Corky" Gonzales was presented to and adopted
by the Convention. The delegates voted to select a "Congreso
de Aztlan" (Congress for Aztlan) which would serve as the
permanent steering committee for the party. In the selection

of the Chairman for the Congress, a power struggle quickly
developed between the Colorado delegates supporting Gonzales
and the Texas delegates supporting Gutierrez, with the other
delegations taking sides according to preference. In the
end, Gutierrez was selected over Gonzales. After the
voting, the two leaders met and embraced beneath the banner
reading "unidos quedaremos" (united we stand), signifying
the spirit of ethnic unity of the convention.[30]

The spirit of cohesion with which the El Paso convention
ended was short-lived however, and the party soon became
hopelessly divided between the followers of Gonzales and
Gutierrez. The split has involved not only conflict in
styles of leadership, but also the philosophical basis.
Gutierrez is more the practical politician, intent on
using the party as an instrument to obtain immediate change
or concessions. Gonzales sees the party more as an
embodiment of an effort to secure a nationalistic Chicano
consciousness, which is consistent with his concept of
AZTLAN.

The philosophical split was exacerbated in 1974 when
Watergate-related revelations hinted that Gutierrez had
illegally received "payoffs" from the Republicans to steer
the 1972 LRUP convention away from a McGovern endorsement.
More recently Gutierrez has been criticized by Gonzales'

supporters for his own lucrative income (about $45,000) and status, which they claim is inconsistent with the LRUP objective of representing the poor Chicano.

The split between Gonzales and Gutierrez therefore is not one that can easily be reconciled. In the meantime it has split the national LRUP in half with the Texas contingent following Gutierrez, the Colorado delegation following Gonzales, and the remaining states either following one or the other, or themselves reflecting the split. While the division may affect the LRUP as a viable national party movement, it will probably not drastically affect the local efforts because of the decentralized nature of the party.

The Principles of La Raza Unida Party

It would be inappropriate to leave the topic of LRUP without considering some of the philosophical bases for and objectives of the Party. The preamble of the draft for the Congreso de Aztlan which is the permanent machinery for LRUP, states some of the rationale for a separate Chicano party:

> El Congreso de Aztlan, whose basic purpose is to provide direction for the platform, goals, and chair-person of La Raza Unida Party, proclaims the people of la raza to be a nation within a nation, endowed with the right and obligation to struggle for self-determination. For over a

century in the United States, la raza has been a
victim of political and economic exploitation and
oppression, one of the tools of that oppression
being the two-party system--the Democratic and
Republican parties. . .serving only the needs of
our exploiters and oppressors. . .La Raza Unida
activity will focus primarily on the local level,
on those issues which affect la raza and which are
ignored by the traditional parties. . .[31]

Included in the national constitution are a statement

of principles that are subdivided as follows:

I. Self-determination of La Raza: We, the
people of la raza have a right to control those
institutions which affect our lives. . .

II. Our relationship to other oppressed peoples:

La Raza Unida Party supports the struggles
of self-determination of all oppressed peoples consistent with our principles. . ./LRUP/ may participate
in coalitions on the basis of principles when it is in
the interest of all parties involved.

/LRUP/ does not endorse, work or form coalitions with the Democratic or Republican Party nor with
other parties who are not consistent with our principles; nor does it endorse their candidates.

III. Sexism: La Raza Unida Party is opposed to
the domination of one sex by another. . .both women
and men of la raza must provide leadership.

IV. Labor: La Raza Unida will struggle for full
employment and the end of exploitation of all working
people.

V. Health: Medical care is a basic right. La
Raza Unida Party will fight for free medical care for
all people.

VI. Housing: Decent housing is a basic human
right. . .over-taxation, racial exclusion, discriminatory denial of funds by credit institutions should be
opposed by La Raza Unida Party.

VII. Education: . . .Bi-lingual, bicultural education is a right of la raza.

VIII. Penal and Legal System: . . .We will work to abolish the present penal system which confines and brutalizes the victims of an exploitative society . . .the entire concept of prison as punishment should be abolished and replaced with a concept of true rehabilitation, education, and health.

IX. The Land: We support the right of the campesinos to organize to attain their basic human rights and while we oppose all those who exploit their labor, La Raza Unida Party believes that that land must belong collectively to those people who work it and fight for it. We will uphold and support the Treaty of Guadalupe Hidalgo. . .There can be no nation unless there is ownership of the land.

X. Imperialism: We call for the immediate end to United States imperialism and colonialism as epitomized by the United States presence in Indochina. . .[32]

The constitution itself established the National Convention as the supreme organ of the LRUP, the Congreso being responsible to the Convention, and being the policy-making body between the national conventions. Within the Congreso, a special executive committee known as the Consejo (council), made up of the national president, ten regional delegates (two from each region), and two at-large delegates was to be the permanent policy-making body between meetings of the Congreso. The remaining officers, vice-president, recording secretary, treasurer, corresponding secretary, and parliamentarian were to be selected from within the Consejo. The national conventions are to be held bi-annually on odd numbered years.[33]

Essentially, the objectives of La Raza Unida Party are best articulated in the statements of Gutierrez and Gonzales who have reiterated the same theme. Gutierrez argues that:

> Internally /at state and local levels/, we will be for our candidates at state levels; externally, /on national elections/, our position means that we are pro-Chicano. . .we can either be the deciding factor in a close election, or we can defeat the greater of two evils.[34]

Gonzales, in a different context, but on the same subject, has argued that:

> . . .when we organize in an area where we are a majority, we can control. Where we are a minority, we can be a pressure group. And we will be a threat.[35]

What both of these alternatives point to is to mobilize as much of the Hispano vote as possible under the banner of LRUP. In situations primarily at the local level where the Hispano population is a majority, LRUP can secure control of municipal governments, school boards, county and district offices, and state legislative representation from those areas. Moreover, when the group is a minority, the same bloc of voters will serve as a balance of power which will yield to the group a brokerage function wherein it can force the two major parties to adopt policy alternatives promoted by the group in return for their support. Finally, in settings where the party can neither win nor influence the outcome, the party can serve as a purveyor of protest, as critic and innovator of new policies. The party will, in other words, serve the dual role of full-fledged party in areas with Hispano majorities, and as a minor party pressure group, innovating policy changes, in areas where Hispanos do not control.

In theory, this strategy seems to offer a viable alternative for the Mexican American, if LRUP could swing the enormous job of politicizing the large ethnic blocs of voters in areas such as south Texas, southern California, and Arizona. It is certainly conceivable that Hispanos could control some municipal, school boards, and county governments in these states, and wield considerable influence in state and national elections. In New Mexico, of course, the thrust of LRUP takes on a different perspective.

The record of LRUP thus far seems to indicate at least preliminary success in both areas. In south Texas, the party has successfully challenged the dominance of the major parties in at least one county, and is growing in others. In New Mexico and elsewhere the party has contributed to dramatizing Mexican American problems such as those in education, and pressuring the major parties to embrace programs such as bilingual-bicultural education in their program appeal to Hispanos.

Summary

This chapter has described and analyzed Chicano
political party and quasi-party political organizations.
It begins by emphasizing the importance of political parties
and organizations in American politics. Descriptions of the
main quasi-party organizations (organizations that perform
most functions of a party but do not call themselves a
party) the Community Service Organization, the Mexican
American Political Association (MAPA) in California, the
Political Association of Spanish Speaking Organizations
(PASO) in Texas, and the American Coordinating Council on
Political Education (ACCPE) in Arizona, were presented.

The chapter then explored Chicano political parties.
It began by analyzing the role which minor parties play in
American politics thus setting the perspective for the
study of Chicano parties. It summarized previous Chicano
party movements, and described the Alianza's People's
Constitutional Party. A detailed description of the origin
and development of La Raza Unida Party, and its present
status in Texas, Colorado, California and New Mexico
followed. The principles of La Raza Unida and its potential
importance as a regional and national party movement was
discussed. LRUP is seen as one of the most important
political forces in the Chicano movement at the present time.

NOTES

[1]Clinton Rossiter, *Parties and Politics in America* (Ithaca, New York: Cornell University Press, 1960), 39.

[2]Guzman, "The Political Socialization of the Mexican American People," *op. cit.*, 246-49.

[3]*Ibid.*, 249-252.

[4]Tirado, *op. cit.*

[5]Lamb, *op. cit.*, 120.

[6]Guzman, *op. cit.*, 260-262.

[7]Moore, *op. cit.*, 148.

[8]Lamb, *op. cit.*, 120-121.

[9]V. O. Key, Jr., *Politics, Parties and Pressure Groups* (New York: Thomas Y. Crowell, 1958), 282.

[10]Hugh A. Bone, *American Politics and the Party System* (New York: McGraw-Hill, 1965), 141.

[11]See Robert Rosenbaum, "Las Gorras Blancas of San Miguel County, 1880-1890" in *Chicano: Evolution of a People*, Renato Rosaldo *et. al.*, eds. (Minneapolis: Winston Press, 1973), 134-135.

[12]Guzman, *op. cit.*, 232-233.

[13]Patricia Bell Blawis, *Tijerina and the Land Grants* (New York: International Publishers, 1971), 146.

[14]*Ibid.*

[15]*Ibid.*

[16]*Ibid.*, 147-150.

[17]*People's Constitutional Party Platform, 1970.*

[18]Antonio Camejo, "A Report from Aztlan: Texas Chicanos Forge Own Political Power," in *La Raza Unida Party in Texas* (New York: Pathfinder Press, 1970), 7-8.

[19]Ibid.

[20]Richard Santillan, La Raza Unida (Los Angeles: Tlaquilo Publications, 1973), 17.

[21]Joy Cook, "La Raza Unida Party," LA LUZ I (August, 1972), 24-26.

[22]Zavala County, Official Election Returns for Zavala County (Crystal City: Zavala County Clerk), 1975.

[23]Santillan, op. cit., 19-24.

[24]Ibid., 52-57.

[25]Alberto Juarez, "The Emergence of El Partido de La Raza Unida: California's New Chicano Party," in La Causa Politica: A Chicano Politics Reader, op. cit., 204-321.

[26]Las Vegas Daily Optic, August 3, 1972.

[27]La Raza Unida Party "The Pueblo Unido State: The Candidates, the Platform," February, 1974.

[28]Richard Everett "Area Raza Unida Party a Dynamic Force," Santa Fe New Mexican, August 12, 1973.

[29]John L. Espinoza, "Raza Unida Conference: Unidos Quedaremos", LA LUZ I (October, 1972), 10-12. Also Albuquerque Journal, September 5, 1972.

[30]Ibid.

[31]Draft of Constitution of La Raza Unida Party adopted as governing instrument for La Raza Unida Party in the El Paso Convention, September, 1972.

[32]LRUP Constitution.

[33]Ibid.

[34]Albuquerque Journal, September 5, 1972.

[35]La Raza: Why A Chicano Party? (New York: Pathfinder Press, 1970), 8-9.

FURTHER SUGGESTED READINGS

Joy Cook, "La Raza Unida Party," La Luz, X (August, 1972),
24-26.

John L. Espinoza. "Raza Unida Conference: Unidos
Quedaremos," La Luz I (October, 1972), 10-12.

Alberto Juarez, "The Emergence of El Partido de La Raza
Unida: California's New Chicano Party," in La Causa
Politica: A Chicano Politics Reader, F. Chris Garcia,
ed.,(Notre Dame: University of Notre Dame Press, 1974.

La Raza Unida Party in Texas. New York: Pathfinder Press,
Merit Pamphlet, 1970.

La Raza: Why A Chicano Party? New York: Pathfinder Press
Merit Pamphlet, 1970.

Richard Santillan. "El Partido La Raza Unida: Chicanos
in Politics," The Black Politician III (July, 1971),
45-52.

Richard Santillan, "Third Party Politics: Old Story, New
Faces," The Black Politician, III (October, 1971),
10-18.

CHAPTER VI

CHICANO LEADERS

A movement is pioneered by men of words,
materialized by fanatics, and consolidated by
men of action.*
                                    Eric Hoffer, 1951

No consideration of Chicano politics would be complete

without a look at the leaders of the Mexican American com-

munity. Like any social group the Chicanos have generated

quite an array of leaders who differ markedly in their

leadership style, in their ideology, in their objectives,

in their sense of issue priority, and in their personality.

Modern Chicano leaders have been politicians, social

reformers, radicals; they have been young or old, conserva-

tive or liberal, middle class and poor. The diversity of

Chicano leaders described above underscores the first

important pattern of Chicano leadership, and that is its

differentiation. The most logical explanation for this is

that the minority community naturally emulates the larger

society in its patterns of leadership.

The previous chapters on Chicano organizations and

political party and quasi-party organizations considered the

types if not the specific personalities of leaders that have

        *Eric Hoffer, The True Believer: Thoughts on the
Nature of Mass Movements (New York: Harper and Row, 1951),
147-148.

emerged in many organizations among the Mexican American community. Needless to say, these social, political, economic, religious, youthful, educational, professional and civic leaders, largely at the local level, are the vanguard of the Mexican American community and its main combatants. The present chapter is devoted to a more in-depth look at the most prominent and important leaders that have been associated with the modern Chicano movement and its most vital motive force, Reies Lopez Tijerina, Cesar Chavez and Rodolfo "Corky" Gonzales. It will also provide a brief sketch of the most prominent Chicano politicians.

Patterns and Problems of Leadership

Before discussing specific leaders, it is appropriate to address general problems of leadership in the Mexican American community. There are two facets of the problem of leadership, first is the problem the ethnic group has in developing legitimate leaders and second is the problem leaders face in unifying their constituency or consolidating their leadership. It is probable that some of the "problems" derive from unrealistic expectations of ethnic homogeniety, which does not exist because of the diverse nature of the group and its leaders.

One of the most often cited "problems" of Chicanos is

the lack of leaders of national stature. Observers have
often pointed to the fact that Chicanos lack a leader of
the stature of a Dr. Martin Luther King. Instead, observers
have said Chicano leaders are essentially regional leaders
whose main source of support or following comes from a
specific state. Perhaps the expectation that Chicanos
develop a national leader is an unrealistic one in light
of the fact that Chicanos unlike Blacks have had a more
diverse political experience. The issue of a lack of
national leaders is thus inextricably related to the
question of a single-compelling national issue to unify
the group, and to weld the ethnic community together. The
Black experience of a forced migration to this country,
into a condition of slavery, followed by the development
of a black American sub-culture, and the emancipation into
a condition of second class citizenship, was simply not
duplicated by Chicanos. Chicanos as a matter of fact had
a far different experience, some were colonists and were
conquered and colonialized, others were integrated into
the polity (New Mexico), the great majority are immigrants.
Thus the presence of the single compelling issue of civil
rights to the blacks, and the emergence of the single leader
espousing that issue, was more difficult to replicate among
the Mexican American community, because not all Chicanos

were directly affected by the problems of the land grants, the farm workers, or the urban Chicano.

A third "problem" that has been cited is the "political disunity" among the Mexican Americans. Stemming from both the failure to generate a single national leader and from frequent failures - as in Mexican American conferences - to present a united front, it is again perhaps a reflection of the diversity of the Chicano group. There are perfectly logical reasons, including regional fragmentation, (as manifested by the many ethnic labels still used), different historical experiences, different socio-economic position, differences in ideology, differences in style of leadership, which help explain the failure to achieve group consensus. Perhaps this problem is a problem born from an unrealistic "fetish for la raza unida", rather than from unique racial cultural characteristics as is often argued.

Perhaps a more realistic premise relative to the "problems" of leadership can be gained if one takes the perspective that group cohesion can be built around an ethnic association or identity, but is not necessarily the product of it. Moreover, a realistic assessment of the Mexican American group is that it is not a homogeneous group, but rather a complex differentiated group, made up of people with varying historical experiences and origins, varying sense of issue priorities, varying preferences in styles of political and social action, and varying ideologies. Given such diversity, perhaps it should be expected that the group will act cohesively in rather selective circumstances as when ethnic candidacies are clearly distinguishable, when ethnic issues clearly create cleavages, and in essence when ethnic over other identifications are most compelling. Greater ethnic solidarity can be systematically nurtured and built as a viable instrument for political action, but it is perhaps unrealistic to expect it to emerge from the womb.

Charismatic Chicano Leaders and Their Organizations

The Chicano movement of the 1960s and 1970s which has dramatically focused America's attention on the formerly "forgotten" minority, the Chicano, has largely been inspired and led by three Chicano leaders, Reies Tijerina, Cesar Chavez and Corky Gonzales. Since Chavez' and Tijerina's movements were largely simultaneous, it is most difficult to identify one or the other as the first of modern Chicano leaders. It is safer to say that their's were parallel movements, which though involving different constituencies, and different styles of political action, together focused national attention on and catalyzed the

Chicano movement. The ensuing discussion of Tijerina, Chavez, and Gonzales will focus on the man, his background, his political philosophy, the organization he built, his style of political action, and his contribution to the Chicano movement.

Reies Lopez Tijerina and the Alianza

Background

Although much conflicting information has emerged from the many studies of Reies Tijerina's background, it has been established that he was born in the obscure Texas town of Falls City, on September 21, 1926. The circumstances surrounding his birth and early life were largely typical of the south Texas Mexican American. His father, although an heir to the defunct Laredo land grant, had been a share-cropper before entering the ranks of migrant workers in the central migrant labor stream, a livelihood which Tijerina himself adopted when he became old enough. The most compelling influence in Tijerina's early life was his mother whose religious piety deeply influenced Tijerina into selecting the ministry as his vocation. At the age of eighteen Tijerina attended a Bible school operated by the Assembly of God church in Isleta, Texas, and though remaining for only a year he embarked for the next fifteen years in a rather erratic migrant ministry traveling throughout the Southwest and even engaging in the interim in the establishment of a utopian theocratic community known as "Valley of Peace" in the mid 1950s in Arizona.[1]

His first appearance in New Mexico was sometime in 1958 following the demise of the Arizona utopian venture after conflicts developed with law enforcement authorities. If much of Tijerina's early life was spent searching for a cause - as it seems - he found such a cause in New Mexico, where he became imbued and obsessed with the problems of the land grants. Tijerina became acquainted with hundreds of poor Mexican Americans in the towns of Chama, Tierra Amarilla, Espanola, El Rito, and in the smaller villages such as Coyote, Canjilon, Gallina, and Cebolla in north central New Mexico. Tijerina could see, as these people recounted the tales of the loss of their land that here was a cause which was just and which required attention. Tijerina became more and more interested, meeting with more heirs, reviewing more of their deeds and titles, and studying the Spanish archives and the Laws of the Indies providing for the administration and distribution of lands. Tijerina also rediscovered the Treaty of Guadalupe Hidalgo and the explicit guarantees made by the United States to Mexicans in New Mexico following the Mexican War. Tijerina saw how much of the land in New Mexico had been granted through a series of proprietory and community land grants. He became especially interested in the "pueblo" or community grants the most numerous, which provided large blocs of land given to a group of families who subdivided some land among the members and heirs and retained other land (ejido) for common use (as in grazing, lumber, firewood and so on). This ejido Tijerina, found, had largely been declared surplus land and taken over by various federal government agencies such as the U.S. Forest Service, the Bureau of Land Management and so on, when specific individual title could not be proven. Tijerina saw how inspite of guarantees by the U.S. Government in the Treaty of Guadalupe Hidalgo of the integrity of land grant titles, Hispanos had lost about half of the approximately fifteen million acres in granted land. The loss was systematically carried out through a series of legal and illegal devices, including property tax foreclosures, payment of land in lieu of money for legal fees incurred in clearing titles, and often out-right fraud on the part of government officials and land speculators. Tijerina was especially interested in the ejido land, which was most intact since it had been con-verted to U S. Government property, and as such still contestable.

Formation of the Alianza

In 1962 Tijerina founded the Alianza Federal de Mercedes (Federal Alliance of Land Grants) which essentially was an organization made up of the remaining heirs of the land grants (some of them now defunct). The Alianza was to serve as an instrument to accomplish a return of the lands. The first four years after the founding were uneventful, as Tijerina sought to enlist new members and land grants, and as his research into the land problem continued.

On July 4, 1966 the Alianza staged its first public protest in a march from Albuquerque's Old Town Plaza to the state capitol in Santa Fe where a list of demands relative to land grant problems was presented to then Governor Jack Campbell. No action on the demands was forthcoming.

The Echo Amphitheatre Incidents

In October, 1966, the 4th Alianza Convention reflected the growing activism of the membershp and pessimism that the problems could be resolved peacefully. At this convention the Alianza voted to reinstitute or recreate the defunct "Pueblo de San Joaquin del Rio Chama," and in an election involving heirs to that grant, elected an alcalde (mayor) and Concilio (council). The Alianza publicly announced its action and pronounced intentions of re-

occuping the original grant. The objectives of the Alianza
have since become known. First it was felt that the
publicity generated by the audacious act of recreating a
sovereign community within the boundaries of the state of
New Mexico in forest service land would dramatize the issue
of the land grants. Secondly, the Alianza sought to con-
front the United States Government in the form of the U.S.
Forest Service, hoping to get Aliancista heirs to the
original grant arrested for trespassing. Since proof of
trespass requires proof of clear title to the land, the
Alianza hoped to place the Forest Service in an embarassing
position since the onus for proving ownership would fall
on the U.S. Government.

On October 15, 1966 the Alianza staged a publicly
announced occupation of the Echo Amphitheatre, a public
recreation park located in the Carson National Forest, and
according to the Alianza, in land originally part of the San
Joaquin Grant. No action was taken by the Forest Service
against the Aliancistas but the head of the New Mexico office
of the Forest Service announced that such activity would not
be tolerated in the future. Dutifully, Tijerina announced
and carried out a second occupation on October 22 when a
confrontation between Aliancistas and Forest Rangers took
place. The Aliancistas greatly outnumbering the Rangers,

arrested one Ranger, charged him with trespassing, held a
mock trial and released him but impounded his Forest Service
vehicle. The Forest Rangers retaliated in force and arrested
Tijerina and five others on federal charges of converting
government property (the pickup truck) and interferring
with a federal officer carrying out his job.

Although much publicity resulted from the Echo Amphitheatre incidents, the Alianza failed in its effort to
raise the trespass issue. Tijerina and the others were soon
released on bail, but Tijerina was to be convicted later.

The failure of the confrontations to focus the government's attention only exacerbated the frustration and anger
of Aliancistas, and for unexplained reasons forest fires,
barn burnings and general harassment of Anglo landowners
was stepped up in northern New Mexico, though no specific
connection to the Alianza was made.

The Tierra Amarilla Raid

The Spring of 1967 presented an ominous atmosphere in
New Mexico, as rumors of a second impending confrontation
between the Alianza and the Forest Service were rampant.
The Alianza announced a meeting to be held on June 3,
1967, a Saturday, in the small village of Coyote, and it
was expected that the confrontation would then take place.

Upon hearing the rumors, First Judicial District, District Attorney Alfonso Sanchez determined to take preventive action to prevent any such confrontation. He decided to use any and all means necessary to prevent the Coyote meeting from taking place. In addition to making a public pronouncement on radio and circulating notes in the area warning Aliancistas not to attend the Coyote meeting, the District Attorney filed state charges and obtained warrants for the arrest of Tijerina and other principals involved in the 1966 Echo Amphitheatre incidents. By Friday morning the arrests of Aliancistas, including Tijerina's brother had begun. Although Tijerina himself escaped the warrants, the combined public threats and arrests by D. A. Sanchez prevented the Coyote meeting from taking place as planned. Sunday's edition of the Santa Fe New Mexican could thus proclaim in headlines "Coyote Meeting A Bust." According to Tijerina, these actions by Sanchez infuriated the Alianza members who met in a private ranch that weekend and mapped out plans for a citizen's arrest of District Attorney Sanchez, on the charge of violating their constitutional right of assembly. Tijerina maintains that they had been advised by a competent attorney of their right to perform citizens arrests, and had even been provided with prototype warrants to use in such an exigency.

Thus the Tierra Amarilla courthouse raid, the "grito de
Dolores" of the Chicano movement carried out on June 5,
1967, was actually an effort by the Alianza to make a
citizen's arrest of Sanchez, who had been expected to be
at the Tierra Amarilla courthouse supervising the arraignment of the Alianza members who had been arrested the
prior weekend. The "raid" itself was conducted by twenty
Aliancistas who came in five cars and a pickup truck.
The raiding party held the courthouse for two and one-half
hours, during which they shot and wounded a deputy sheriff
and state policeman, and held various county officials and
employees, prisoners. The raiders escaped with two host-
ages who were soon released, touching off the largest manhunt in the state's history. If the event itself was not
dramatic itself, then its dramatization by the mass media
multiplied its effect. Newspapers and network television
reporters ingeniously translating Reies Tijerina's name for
effect, portrayed him as "King Tiger" leading a guerilla
insurrection in northern New Mexico. The lack of information
on Tijerina and the Alianza, and the extent of its activities
and following, only complicated matters, leading state
officials to understandably overreact, thus further dramatizing the event. Crude maps and papers confiscated by
state policemen who arrested Cristobal Tijerina (Reies'

brother) ominously depicted "battle plans", and organizational
charts which along with weapons and ammunition also captured, yielded rumors of a wide scale insurrection in the
hills of New Mexico. Governor David Cargo called out units
of the New Mexico National Guard which together with state
policemen, mounted patrol and various other law enforcement
agencies and volunteers consisted of a combined force of
some 500 persons. In addition to other military equipment
the National Guard employed two Patton tanks in the manhunt.
Within a week most of the participants in the raid including
Tijerina himself were arrested.

The Tierra Amarilla raid, needless to say, catapulted
Tijerina into national prominence, and the Alianza into the
role described by Frances Swadish as a "catalyst" for social
change. Tierra Amarilla became the rallying cry for Chicano
activists throughout the nation.

Other Arenas for Tijerina

The national attention only inflated Tijerina's
egotistic nature, making him even more reckless and nihilistic.
At the first arraignment on charges stemming from the Tierra
Amarilla incident, Tijerina boldly announced he would defend
himself. Although antagonists gloried at the prospect of
Tijerina tightening his own noose, his handling of the

defense not only resulted in his acquittal, but enabled him to use the trial itself to further his own growing fame and his growing popularity among Chicano activists. Tijerina showed remarkable ability to extract key information from key witnesses underscoring the awkwardness of public and law enforcement officials in the handling of the whole affair. Tijerina skillfully turned the trial into a forum for airing land grant issues, by injecting testimony by land grant experts. The climax to the trial came when the Judge, in his instructions to the Jury, underscored the sacred right of private citizens to legally employ the citizens arrest in situations where they felt the law had been violated, and their right to employ force to bring about such an arrest.

This preparation for his own trial did not deter Tijerina from further activity. Tijerina had been designated by Dr. Martin Luther King (before his death) to head the southwestern (primarily Mexican American) contingent of the Poor People's Campaign", thus in June 1968, Tijerina appeared in Washington, D.C. as the titular head of the Chicano poor peoples' delegation. Once again, Tijerina used the campaign as a further arena to further his own cause, emerging according to journalist observers as the most creative leader of the otherwise dismal undertaking.

Tijerina organized peace councils between the Black, Indian and Chicano delegations to foster cross-ethnic understanding; he charged discrimination on the part of Black leaders when he felt the Chicanos were being slighted; he confronted the State Department over the Treaty of Guadalupe Hidalgo, and organized a mass demonstration march on the Mexican Embassy to demand Mexico's intervention on behalf of Mexican Americans in the U.S.

On his return to New Mexico, Tijerina became involved in the launching of the People's Constitutional Party (see Chapter 5) and in the 1968 campaign, and again this served as a further forum for airing land grant problems.

Following his acquittal in December, 1968, on the Tierra Amarilla charges, Tijerina and the Alianza stepped up their tactics of confrontation. Unwittingly, Judge Larrazolo's edification of the legal validity of the "citizen's arrest" gave Tijerina his next tactic. Within a few weeks, Tijerina attempted citizens arrests of Chief Justice Warren Burger (for decisions as Judge discriminatory to minorities), Norris Bradbury, Director of Los Alamos Scientific Laboratory (for building weapons for mass human destruction) and Governor David Cargo (for violating civil rights of Alianza members).

In June, 1969, the escalating militance of the Alianza

led to the burning of U.S. Forest Service signs in the Carson National Forest.

Tijerina was arrested for "aiding and abetting the destruction of government property," and assault on a Forest Ranger. Tijerina's bond on previous federal charges (the Echo Amphitheatre incident) were revoked and Tijerina remained in prison for the next two years. During this time, he was tried for the Echo Amphitheatre and sign burning incidents and served a minimum time on both convictions. He was also tried again on new state charged for the Tierra Amarilla raid and after exhausting appeals served six months in state prison in 1975.

Since his release from prison, Tijerina has displayed a less activist and more benevolent temper. The strict conditions of his parole which explicitly eschewed Alianza leadership and activity, and the pending appeal on new convictions probably restrained Tijerina. Tijerina soon re-gained symbolic, if not titular control of the Alizanza and steered it on a more pacifist direction, sponsoring several Brotherhood conferences in 1972 and 1973. In the Spring of 1976 Tijerina led an Alianza caravan to Mexico and personally appealed to Mexican President Luis Echevarria asking for his support in presenting Alianza claims of U.S. violtation of the Treaty of Guadalupe Hidalgo before the United Nations. The moderate posture that Tijerina has display

since his release from prison has alienated many of the
young activist Chicanos and obviously diminished his influence as a Chicano leader, but his contributions to the
Chicano movement cannot be challenged.

The Impact of Tijerina and the Alianza

The successes or impact of Tijerina and the Alianza can
be viewed from two perspectives; that is, their impact on
the immediate problem of the land grants and their impact
on the Chicano movement as a whole. Although the Alianza
has not accomplished the main objective of mass reversions
of public land to original grantees, they have succeeded
in drawing national attention or publicity to the land
grant problems. They have also accomplished the introduction of the Community Land Grant Bill by California
Congressman Augustus Hawkins, in two sessions of Congress,
thus laying perhaps the groundwork for some future remedy.
The National Presbyterian Church has independently acted
to restore some church land in the Ghost Ranch area of
northern New Mexico, to original heirs. Also, Alianza
pressure has made the U.S. Forest Service, Bureau of Land
Management and other federal agencies more responsive and
aware of the problems of Mexican American small farmers and
ranchers who they deal with.

The importance of the Alianza, however, goes beyond its own immediate objectives in that it has been a major catalyst of the Chicano social movement.[2] It has helped dramatize the human problems experienced by the Mexican American people in the United States. The Alianza has publicized the socio-economic deprivation of the group as manifested by inadequate health facilities, high disease and mortality rates, high incidence of dependence on public assistance, substandard housing, and high evidence of crime among Chicano youth. The Alianza has also been very critical of cultural, linguistic, and educational discrimination against the group. By being one of the first groups to raise these issues and problems, it has set the mood for reform that has been taken up as part of the movement.

Tijerina: The Man, The Philosophy, The Motives

What factors have motivated Tijerina? What is his personal philosophy or justification for his chosen cause? Tijerina's own account of his past and the forces that brought him to New Mexico go far in explaining his personality, motivations and goals. He maintains that he was a Protestant minister searching for ways to help the poor. He admits his ministry was unorthodox, even fanatical in some ways. He felt as if much of his early life was a

a searching for himself, his identity, his role, his way.
When they burned his home in Arizona and he was driven from
"Valle de la paz" he came to New Mexico and found his cause.
He says he could hear from the "pueblo" (the people) "the
anguish, the cries, the tears, over the loss of their land."
As he talked with more and more people, he could see the
"agony that had as its root the loss of their land". He
perceived from the accounts of the people, from his studies
of their land documents, from his study of the laws of the
Indies, and the Treaty of Guadalupe Hidalgo, that a great
moral injustice had been perpetrated against the Mexican
American people. He perceived that underlying the poverty,
the alienation, the discrimination against the Mexican
American was the loss of his land, wherein lay the Hispanos'
culture, language and heritage.

His focus upon the land was based on his conception
that the original land grants were not simply "parcels" of
land, but that the grants, as specified in the laws of the
Indies constituted a spiritual and symbolic presence of a
"pueblo". A pueblo or free community embodied not only a
people's culture, language, tradition, history, and value
system, but connoted utopian ideals of fraternity, peace,
security, welfare and morality of the people. Thus the
grant was not just a materialistic phenomenon. The land

however, was basic to the existence of the pueblo, for without land the community would disintegrate, the people would
stray as lost sheep, losing their sense of identity, language,
culture and value system. That is why the recovery of the
land was so important and basic a struggle in the wider
effort to ensure the suvival of Chicano culture. What moved
him he says were the same motives that moves a mother to
feed or change a baby that is crying for attention. The
Alianza says Tijerina was one   "instrument" or "vehicle"
among several, along with various strategies and tactics
that were employed along the way.[3]

In the last analysis the Tijerina phenomenon represents
a combination of forces - personal egoism, genuine concern
for the plight of his fellow men and ethnics, a messianic
quality, extraordinary charismatic leadership qualities
and abilities, that combined to inspire a social movement -
in a crucial period for Chicanos in American history.
Tijerina was truly the right person, in the right place,
at the right time.

Cesar Chavez and the Farm Workers

A coequal with Reies Tijerina as an inspiration to the
modern Chicano movement is Cesar Estrada Chavez, whose
organizing and leadership of California's migrant farm workers

(mostly Mexican Americans) has made him probably the best known Mexican American as well as one of the most admired men in the United States. Chavez has been identified as the symbol for the aspirations of the most oppressed segment of one of the most oppressed minority groups in the country. If one were to seek out a most appropriate man to lead the farm labor movement, it is unlikely that one could find a more fitting personality than Cesar Chavez. Chavez' whole life has envolved in the shadow of the problems and plight of the migrant farm worker.

Chavez: Background and Affiliation with the CSO

Chavez was born in Yuma, Arizona in 1927 into a family of five children, who lived on a small farm. The loss of their farm during the depression forced the Chavez family to join the ranks of the migrant workers in California, and the "grapes of wrath" existence which characterized much of Chavez' young life. Even after Chavez became married and settled in San Jose, California, his livelihood was that of a farm worker. Although his father had been a staunch advocate of unionization of the farmworkers, there is little else in Chavez' background that would foretell his involvement. The first signs of an interest, according to Peter Mathieson,[4] in the migrant worker unionization, emerged in conversation with Father Donald McDonnel whom Chavez met in "Sal si puedes" (get out if you can) barrio in San Jose. Chavez, according to Mathieson, became a constant companion to Father McDonnel in his visits to migrant camps, where he would talk about labor history, social justice, social movements and the role of the church in these issues. It was Father McDonnel who recommended Chavez to Fred Ross, then an organizer of Mexican American groups for the Community Service Organizations. Chavez, though initially skeptical of "Anglo do gooders" soon became a great admirer of Ross and enlisted at Ross' recommendation as an organizer for the CSO. It was from Ross that Chavez learned many of the organizing skills that would assist him in his own struggles later. Chavez soon became the most effective organizer for CSO, expanding it's influence in Bakersfield, Oakland and the Bay Area. In 1958 Chavez became national director of the CSO, and it was at that time that Chavez began to focus his and the CSO's attention on the plight of the farm workers. Chavez hoped to use the CSO as a base for organizing the farm workers. In 1958 Chavez entered the dispute that had developed between the growers and migrant workers in Oxnard, California. Chavez organized the farm workers in protest of the policies and practices of the growers in combination with state labor regulatory

agencies. At the time, under provisions of the Bracero
Program, growers were required to exhaust all domestic
labor before hiring Mexican braceros for farm work. The
California Farm Placement Service (CFPS) and the U.S. Employment Security Commission, the agencies responsible for
enforcing the provisions were violating the basic provisions by allowing growers to hire braceros, who usually
settled for lower wages. Chavez unified the domestic
workers and insured that they were duly registered for work.
When they were bypassed by growers in the hiring of braceros,
Chavez led public demonstration in which the domestic
laborers burned the CFPS registration cards. The ensuing
publicity resulted in an investigation of the CFPS which
uncovered illicit bribes and resulted in resignation of
some CFPS officials.

Chavez and the Farm Workers Union

The success at Oxnard convinced Chavez that the
growers were not as invincible as had been supposed, and
that a systematic organizational effort with publicity
and resultant public support could bring the growers to
their knees. Secondly Chavez became convinced that it was
possible to organize the farm worker. At the 1962 CSO
convention, Chavez proposed that the CSO direct all of its

energies toward organizing the farm workers. When his proposal was rejected by the convention Chavez resigned as national director. Following his resignation Chavez was offered well paying jobs in the Peace Corps and by the AFL-CIO's American Farm Workers Organizing Committee (AFWOC), but Chavez, foreshadowing his independent posture, refused, and decided to organize a separate independent farm workers' union. He moved to Delano, California and from there launched his organizing efforts.

The National Farm Workers Association (NFWA) was organized in September, 1962 with about 300 members as a "strictly independent grass roots organization committed to obtain human dignity and to guarantee by contract, improved living and working conditions through collective bargaining with their employers." By 1964 Chavez' union had grown to 1,000 members, and some success had been felt in securing higher wages for workers in the rose fields of McFarland, California. The union had also become involved in litigation involving violations of minimum wage laws and in hiring discrimination.

In September, 1965 the first step in the eventual merger of Chavez' union with the AFL-CIO affiliated Agricultural Workers Organizing Committee (AWOC) was taken. The NFWA joined a strike against the DiGiorgio, Schenley

and Giumarra grape producers launched by the AWOC. In
1967 the two unions combined, forming the United Farm Workers
Organizing Committee (UFWOC) and eventually Chavez embraced
AFL-CIO affiliation partially out of his need for financial
support and partially as a result of growing competition
from the Teamsters Union.

Strategies and Tactics of Chavez

The successes of Chavez in organizing the farm workers
and securing concessions from the growers are attributable
to the unique strategies and tactics that have been employed
as well as his ability to combine elements of a labor
struggle with those of a broader social movement. Thus
the struggle of the migrant farm worker is not just
a typical example of a labor/management conflict, but takes
the form of a social movement involving an effort by an
oppressed ethnic minority, the Mexican American, against the
monolith of the American Agribusiness corporation. Thus
part of the struggle is to secure wide public sympathy
and support for the struggle of the farm workers. For this
reason some legally questionable tactics such as the boycott
have been successfully employed by Chavez.

The first strategy was of course the huelga (strike)
but the most familiar labor tactic was itself subject

to variation by the farmers unions. The initial phases of the grape strike were selective strikes against the major table grape producers since their product requires greater care in the growth and harvesting because of the importance of appearance to its market value. The wineries (where the appearance of the grape is not as important) were brought into the strike later when the second strategy of boycott could be successfully used to pressure them.

The strike and the picketing would not have yielded success to the farm workers since this was an industry where a plentiful supply of alternate scab labor was available. Further, the impoverished condition of the workers, most of whom were transients, the great number of growers involved, the stigma against unionizing agricultural workers were additional obstacles which Chavez faced. Since the farm workers were struggling for the basic contract acknowledging their "right to organize and bargain collectively," they possessed absolutely no rights in terms of job security as they carried on the strike.

To supplement the strike Chavez launched a second and more effective tactic, the nation wide boycott of the name and products of the larger growers such as the Schenley and DiGiorgio farms. These larger agribusiness concerns were quite vulnerable to a boycott where a trade or brand name

and a whole line of products (not only grapes) were involved. Schenley Industries for example, saw its whole
line of food and condiment products in jeopardy because of
its comparatively small interest in grapes. DiGiorgio
farms whose products were sold under familiar S & W,
Treesweet and White Rose brands was also less than enthus-
iastic about placing their well established brand names
on the line for their grape holdings. The boycott was
entirely a grass roots undertaking carried out by volunteers
who used their own resources in organizing and publicizing
their boycott.

To focus nationwide attention on the grape strike
and boycott, Chavez in March, 1966, staged his "peregrinacion,"
or protest march from Delano to the California state capitol.
The theme of the march "penitence, pilgrimage and revolution"
combined racial/cultural/religious elements with the
economic motive reflective of the social movement emphasis
of the farm workers' struggle. Chavez patterned the march
after Lenten processions of Catholic Mexicans, and a banner
with a picture of La Virgin de Guadualupe (the patron saint
of poor Mexican campesinos) headed the column. As Chavez
planned, the procession ended on Easter Sunday. The march
also revealed, before the nationwide television audiences,
the farm workers flag (a bold red flag with a black Aztec

eagle in a white circle) which would thereafter be taken
up by other Chicano groups as symbolic of the Chicano
movement.

The first grape producer to capitulate was Schenley
products which signed a union contract with NFWA in June,
1966 providing for an hourly wage of $1.75. The elation
over the contract with Schenley was short-lived, as Chavez'
union became engaged in a bitter struggle with DiGiorgio
farms, that foreshadowed future troubles for Chavez.
DiGiorgio, anticipating the inevitable, had signed a "sweet-
heart" contract with the Teamsters union to represent
DiGiorgio workers. The contract, smacked of collusion
between the growers and union officials and was designed to
undermine Chavez' organizing efforts. Although Chavez'
retaliation ultimately forced the calling of new elections
to allow DiGiogio workers to choose their own union (which
Chavez' union won) the pattern for future efforts to undermine UFWOC was established. After the capitulation of two
of the larger producers other grape producers followed
suit, and by 1968 most of the grape producers including
wineries such as Gallo, Almaden, Christian Brothers and Paul
Massoin had signed union agreements. Between 1968 and 1970
UFWOC continued strike and boycott efforts against other
unions while consolidating their union organization.

Giumarra, the largest grape producer, Bianco fruit corporation and the Despoto Company also signed agreements. The
climax came on July 28, 1970 when 26 growers signed contracts
with UFWOC calling for $1.80 hourly wage, fringe benefits
and union recognition.

By 1972, when most of the grape industry was under
contract, Chavez announced that UFWOC would shift its focus
to producers of other crops, specifically the lettuce
producers. The major difference in the strategy was that
UFWOC now directed the boycott against the super-market
chains such as Safeway, that purchase and sell lettuce. The
successes in the lettuce industry have been limited,
primarily because UFWOC had to redirect its attention to
the grape industry where a new threat emerged. As contracts
with grape producers began to expire in the 1970's, UFWOC
has faced severe competition from the Teamsters Union which
has made important headway in organizing in the migrant
worker ranks. Bitter, often violent confrontations have
occurred between the unions as elections are held among
workers on respective farms to determine which union will
represent them. The Teamsters, aided by the grower's
desire to destroy Chavez' union were successful by 1974
in securing the bulk of the contracts with growers, and
reducing UFWOC to a handful of contracts.

In 1974 the California legislature passed a law providing
for mandatory supervised secret elections to allow the
approximately 250,000 farm workers to select the unions that
would represent them. The elections held since that time
have been favorable to UFWOC, 56 percent of the workers
having chosen it and 38 percent having chosen the Teamsters.

The victory of Chavez' union in the state supervised
elections indicates that the majority of the farm workers
still favor Chavez over other leaders. The fact however,
that the movement has evolved into a clash among unions,
and thus lost its social movement fervor has of course
diminished the overall impact of UFWOC on the American
conscience, and cost it some of its public support.
As Chavez' union takes on more of the familiar character of
a labor organization, the immediate challenge is to further
consolidate its contracts and organization and to move into
other agricultural products such as the lettuce and date
industry. It must also cope with the challenge of mechanization in the agricultural industry.

Chavez: The Man and His Impact

The impact of Chavez and UFWOC can be measured in
terms of long range impact on the Chicano community as well
as immediate successes in the case of the farm workers.

The association, by Americans, of the plight of the farm
workers with the plight of Mexican Americans as a whole
has had a spillover effect on the Mexican American community. Like Alianza activity the struggles by farm workers
contributed to a widespread refocusing of attention on
America's second largest ethnic minority. Moreover,
inspired by Chavez, other groups emerged in California
addressing other problems of the minority group.

Also important has been Chavez' willingness to associ-
ate himself with voter-registration drives among Mexican
Americans in California and his endorsement of candidates
such as John and Robert Kennedy for President and most
recently Edward Brown, Jr. for Governor. The politicians
have favored the cause of farm workers and Mexican Americans.

As for the immediate successes, it is unlikely that
unionization of farm workers would have proceeded so rapidly
if at all, without Chavez' leadership. The long history of
failure at efforts to organize the farm workers is testimony
to that. It is unlikely that a leader matching the organizational skills with the ideal personality, commitment
and background so necessary for the success of the labor/
social movement would have emerged.

The personal qualities that Chavez brought to the
struggle probably meant the difference between success and

failure. Chavez as a Mexican American and as a former migrant worker himself could speak with authority on the plight of the farm worker. Second his personal qualities - humility, self-sacrifice, non-violence, religious fervor - reflected his own intense commitment to the cause. To the workers who suffered abject poverty, only an individual who could prove that he suffered more (as Chavez often manifested on his prolonged fasts) could generate the respect and support necessary to sustain a prolonged union struggle. Chavez' personal sacrifice and commitment was also crucial in generating the public support which made the boycott successful.

What has been gained by the struggle? Critics have argued that Chavez' gains will only stimulate mechanization of the agricultural industry. While the higher wages paid farm workers will make previously expensive mechanization a more economical enterprise, it is unlikely that such progress will occur quickly. The immediate changes that have occurred are quite impressive. The contracts gained by both UFWOC and the Teamsters have given farm workers privileges and rights they never possessed, including the basic right to organize and bargain collectively for higher wages, better working conditions and living conditions. The struggle has thus contributed to improving the lot of thousands of farm workers, many of them highly politicized, who will probably be able to settle down because of their new found economic success, and this will probably have some political consequences in future California politics.

The prospect that Chavez will graduate from the struggle of the farm workers and assume a wider role of leadership in the Mexican American community is unlikely, since Chavez himself has continuously rejected such a prospect, and since he has shown no ambitions beyond furthering his own union.

Rodolfo "Corky" Gonzales and the Crusade for Justice

The third important charismatic leader of the Chicano movement is Rodolfo "Corky" Gonzales. Gonzales is the principal leader and inspiration of the Chicano movement in Denver where he organized, and is leader of the Crusada para Justicia (Crusade for Justice). In addition to being the only leader whose principal interests lie in urban civic action Gonzales is the uncrowned "poet laureate" of the Chicano movement and one of its leading political philosophers.

Background

Corky Gonzales was born in the barrios of Denver, Colorado, and typically for the Colorado Mexican American into a condition of poverty and discrimination.[5] Like

thousands of barrio residents, Gonzales' family used Denver

as the winter headquarters and worked as migrant laborers

in the sugar beet and other field crops in Colorado. Al-

though experiencing the typical problems of migrant worker

children in attending school, Gonzales did complete high

school, the only one of the big three Chicano leaders who

did so. Gonzales' first claim to fame was as a scrappy

featherweight boxer, having been good enough to achieve

national ranking before abruptly quitting the ring and

opening an insurance agency in Denver.

The insurance agency afforded Gonzales time to pursue

his growing interest in urban civic action. He became

active in youth programs including the opening of a free

boxing gym for barrio kids. At the same time he became

active in Democratic Party politics, becoming at age 29

the youngest ward captain. In 1960 Gonzales was designated

as Colorado state coordinator of the Viva Kennedy clubs.

During this time he also became head of "Los Voluntarios"

(the volunteers) a Chicano barrio political action group

involved in representing barrio residents in conflicts

with municipal government. "Los Voluntarios" was quite active

for example, during Gonzales leadership, in uncovering and

protecting against unnecessary police brutality in the

barrios of Denver. It published a Chicano newspaper "VIVA" which was a forum communicating ongoing barrio concerns. The dual role of Gonzales, as a loyal and active party worker and his popularity with barrio residents in civic action, made Gonzales an important leader for Denver's Democratic Party. His part in the successful Kennedy campaign led to other important positions for Gonzales including Chairman of the Board for Denver's War on Poverty, membership in the Steering Committee for Anti Poverty programs in the southwest, and other similar boards and committees. Gonzales' involvement with these programs and with the Democratic Party grew into disenchantment as he coped with bureaucratic ineptitude, red tape, waste and inefficiency. He grew tired of attending conferences which repeated the familiar rhetoric of promises and projects, yet little was being done to change the barrios.

In 1965 Gonzales resigned all his positions in the party and in the poverty programs and formed the Crusade for Justice, declaring that it was a "movement born out of frustration and determination to secure equality with dignity." Gonzales insisted that the Crusade be separate and independent of private or governmental agencies.

The Crusade has become Gonzales' base for expressing Chicano demands for better housing, equal educational

opportunities, jobs, and land reform, as well as his medium
for articulating his own philosophical pronouncements on
the Chicano movement. The Crusade publishes a newspaper,
"El Gallo" which communicates activities of the Crusade
as well as expressing la raza philosophy.

The Crusade has served as the self-appointed representative for Denver's Chicanos. It has served as representative for Chicanos in any kind of conflict with
municipal authorities, it has served as critic and purveyor
of protest relative to the ills of the downtrodden. Much
of the Crusade's efforts are directed toward Chicano youth,
who have been the most vehement supporters. One of the
Crusades youth projects is its Freedom School for children
aged 6 through 16 where courses offered include Chicano
history, culture, and Spanish.

Gonzales: Philosophy

Gonzales, more than any other contemporary Chicano
leader has contributed to the spirit, ideology and philosophy of the Chicano movement. This is manifest by frequent
utterances by activist leaders about "Chicano nationalism,"
and "Aztlan" which were popularized by Gonzales. Gonzales'
epic poem "I Am Joaquin" is one of the outstanding literary
pieces reflecting an effort to capture the unity and

diversity of Chicano identity, as well as an effort to argue

for cultural revitalization. The poem captures the his-

torical diversity (Spanish and Indian influences) that went

into the formation of la raza, as well as the main themes,

repression and confrontation, that have characterized the

Chicano experience in American life.[6]

To Gonzales "nationalism" is the key to the liberation

of Hispanos. At a symposium on "Chicano liberation" at

Hayward College in California, Gonzales outlined his conception

of nationalism and elaborated on how "nationalism" was to

serve as a tool for Chicanos:

> . . .Now what are the tools? We said
> nationalism, which means that we have to be able
> to identify with our past and understand our
> past, in order that we can dedicate ourselves to
> the future, dedicate ourselves to change. . .we
> are for meaningful coalitions with organized
> groups. . .we have to consider ourselves a nation.
> We can create a Congress or a Concilio. We can
> understand that we are a nation of Aztlan.[7]

Thus, nationalism implies an internal symbolic unity

among Chicanos which can serve as a common denominator for

mass mobilization of the Chicano community, "a commitment

to the concept of la raza plan of Aztlan. . .which implies

a commitment to social, economic, cultural independence. . .

a struggle that must involve control of our barrios,

campos, pueblos, lands, culture, economy and political life

. . .that commits all levels of Chicano society, the barrio, the camp, the ranchero, the writer, the leader, the worker, the professional. . .to la causa."[8]

The Crusade for Justice has served as Gonzales' main instrument for pursuing the goal of nationalism. In March, 1969, the Crusade sponsored the first National Chicano Youth Liberation Conference, a five day session attended by up to 1,500 Chicano youth who participated in workshops on philosophy, self-defense, poetry, art and cultural identity. At the end of the Conference the Conferees adopted "El Plan Espiritual de Aztlan" which bore the indelible literary and philosophical imprint of Gonzales. El Plan states:

> . . .Brotherhood unites us, and love for
> our brothers makes us a people whose time has
> come and who struggle against the foreigner
> 'gabacho' who exploits our riches and destroys
> our culture. With our heart in our hands and
> our hands in the soil, we declare the independ-
> ence of our mestizo nation. We are a bronze
> people with a bronze culture. Before the world,
> before all of North America, before all our brothers
> in the bronze continent, we are a nation; we are a
> free people. We are Aztlan.[9]

The Plan encompassed both the spirit of Chicano nationalism based on common language, culture, history and tradition, and a rejection of the dominant Anglo American culture.

The implementation of a specific strategy to bring about Chicano nationalism was begun by the Crusade in its sponsorship of the second national Chicano Youth Liberation

Conference in March, 1970. The second conference launched Colorado's version of La Raza Unida Party, which had been envisioned by Gonzales since the 1969 Hayward College symposium.

It was the Colorado LRUP under the leadership of Gonzales which formulated the organizational structure providing for a Congreso and Concilio which was adopted by La Raza Unida Party in its first national convention in El Paso in 1972. It was natural and appropriate that Gonzales would be one of the leaders at the La Raza Unida Conference and one of the two candidates for leadership of the Party. Although Gonzales was defeated for the position by Jose Angel Gutierrez, Gonzales graciously endorsed the selection of Gutierrez. Since the conference Gonzales has withdrawn his support for Gutierrez due to differences over philosophy, ideology, and strategy for the party. Many members of the Party have aligned with Gonzales in the intra-party split.

Chicano Politicians

The American political arena has been a most conducive setting for the emergence of minority politicians, and the Chicano community has been no exception, having produced a number of Chicano politicos who have distinguished themselves in national and state politics. Again New Mexico has led other southwestern states in both setting the pattern for Chicano politicians and in producing the most famous of these. As Ernest Fincher has observed, the Mexican American politicians in New Mexico have benefited from the patron-peon socio-political tradition that was firmly embedded in the Spanish and Mexican culture in New Mexico.[10] The medieval feudal tradition introduced by the Spanish along with a strong hierarchical tradition among the indigenous Indian populations established a strong tradition in New Spain whereby political "patrones" (bosses or overlords) essentially dictated public policy. The patrones generally came to their position by virtue of their social and economic status which rendered them not only the esteem of peones (vassals) but their un-qualified following. Patrones were the leaders in the Hispanic pueblo. The Patron not only provided the base for the economic life of the community, but was the religious and social leader. The Patron represented the pueblo, and resolved problems. In this sense he was the highest patriarch in a patriarchial culture. Often the pattern of New Mexico history through the colonial and early statehood period witnessed Hispano patrones wielding power by their ability to manipulate large blocs of Hispano votes. The tradition of following a dynamic, charismatic, Hispano patron has not completely faded among Mexican Americans even though the passage of time and governmental reforms have reduced the all pervasive social and economic power once held by patrones.

The modern Hispano "jefe politico" (political boss) benefits from this tradition, and by blending   an ability to appeal to ethnic symbolism he is often able to employ familiar techniques (organizational skills, patronage, favors), of American political bosses in establishing a strong base of political power.

Ezequiel C. de Baca

Ezequiel C. de Baca, a Democrat from Las Vegas, was probably one of the first of the modern Mexican American political jefes. C. de Baca had been a leading party figure for many years before seeking and winning his first political office as Lt. Governor in 1911. C. de Baca served four years as New Mexico's first Lt. Governor, and although very ill in 1916, he was nominated and elected New Mexico's second Governor. C. de Baca died a few weeks after his inauguration.

Octaviano Larrazolo

Octaviano Larrazolo, a Mexican-born immigrant to New Mexico, was a contemporary of C. de Baca. Larrazolo a

lawyer, was initially a Democrat and made several tries for
Congress during the Territorial period. He later switched
to the Republican Party. Larrazolo was one of the first
Hispano's to exploit racial cleavages between Anglo and
Hispano. Although an acknowledged Republican Party leader,
in 1916 he actively campaigned for Democrat and fellow
Hispano, C. de Baca. In 1918, Larrazolo deftly played up
Anglo-Hispano cleavages within the Democratic Party to
capture the nomination of his own Republican Party and
proceeded to defeat his Democratic opponent in the
race for Governor, on the strength of Hispano Democratic
support. Larrazolo was elected United States Senator in
1928, but died shortly after assuming office.[11]

Dennis Chavez

Dionisio "Dennis" Chavez is probably the best manifestation of the most recent Hispano jefe politico. Chavez,
unlike previous Hispano patrones was born into a poor family
and had no early formal education. Chavez entered Democratic Party politics as a local party worker, even before
he could vote. His first big opportunity came in 1916 when
he served as Spanish interpretor for then Senator A.A. Jones.
His service won him a job as a clerk in the U.S. Senate which
enabled Chavez to earn a law degree at Georgetown University.

Thus Chavez set the pattern to be followed by dozens of
Hispanos who received patronage jobs, were educated in
Washington, and returned to New Mexico to become prominent
political leaders.

Chavez was elected to the U.S. House of Representatives
where he served until 1934 when he challenged Bronson Cutting
for the U.S. Senate. Although Chavez lost to Cutting by
a narrow 1,000 vote margin, he was appointed Senator in
April 1935 when Cutting was killed in an airplane accident.
From 1935 until his death in 1962, Chavez remained in the
U.S. Senate and personally dominated New Mexico politics.
Basing his power in the Hispanic counties, Chavez was able
to inject his influence over all state political offices,
legislative and administrative politics in the state.
Chavez' dominion over state politics was parallelled also
by his position of power in Washington, built by over two
decades of seniority. Chavez at the time of his death was
Chairman of the Senate Public Works committee (over which
he exercised authority typical of the most powerful committee
chairman) and a high ranking member of the Senate Finance
Committee, making him one of the most powerful men in
Congress. Chavez' stature in New Mexico politics is manifested by the fact that he was accorded the first of two
statues reserved for New Mexico Congressmen in the rotunda

of the nation's Capitol Building. That singular honor underscores the fact that Chavez has achieved the highest stature
of any Mexican American in American politics.[12]

Joseph M. Montoya

Joseph M. Montoya, elected U.S. Senator in 1964 to fill
the unexpired term of Senator Chavez, not only fell heir to
Chavez' Senate seat, but also his position as leading "jefe
politico" for New Mexico's Mexican Americans. Montoya, a
Democrat, has very closely emulated Chavez' career in the
United States Senate, and is without question the highest
ranking and most powerful Hispano politician in the country.

Montoya, whose biography reads like a Horacio Alger
political success story was born in Peña Blanca, New Mexico
in 1915, attended Regis College in Denver and Georgetown
University Law School in Washington. His political career
began in 1936 at the age of 21 while still in college when
he was elected as the youngest member ever, to the New Mexico
House of Representatives. He was re-elected in 1938 and
became Majority Floor Leader. In 1940, Montoya stepped up
to the State Senate and there also, was the youngest ever
elected. Montoya served as Majority Whip and chaired the
Judiciary Committee in his four years in the Senate. In 1946
Montoya was elected Lt. Governor and served two terms. In
1950 he returned to the New Mexico Senate and served until 1952

when he again was elected Lt. Governor and served another
two terms. In 1957 Montoya was elected to Congress in a
special election to fill the unexpired term of Congressman
Antonio Fernandez who had died in office. Montoya served
in the U.S. House until 1964 when he was elected to the
United States Senate to fill the unexpired term of Dennis
Chavez. Montoya has been re-elected twice and is in his
twelfth year in the Senate. Montoya is a member of the
powerful Senate Appropriations Committee, the third ranking
member in the Public Works Committee, the Joint Atomic
Energy Committee and the Democratic Steering Committee.
A liberal, Montoya has been a staunch advocate of liberal
legislation in civil rights, social security, medicare,
education, labor, health and environmental protection.
Montoya was one of the primary sponsors of the Wholesome
Meat Act of 1967, the Wholesome Poultry Act of 1968, and
other consumer protection legislation. He was a sponsor
of the Bilingual Education Act of 1968 and its amendments
in 1974.[13] His major claim to national attention came as
a member of the Senate Select Committee investigating the
Watergate affair.

Other Hispano Politicos in New Mexico

In addition to the heavyweights, Chavez and Montoya,

there have been a number of important politicos in New
Mexico politics, among them Antonio Fernandez, New Mexico
Congressman for several terms in the 1950s, and Tibo Chavez,
who served in the New Mexico House of Representatives,
in the Senate and as Senate Majority Floor Leader, longer
than any other person. Chavez is most recently a New Mexico
District Judge. Congressman Manuel Lujan is a rare Hispano
who has succeeded as a Republican. Lujan who had been
quite active in Republican Party activity was elected to
Congress in 1968 and has been re-elected three times. Lujan,
a conservative Republican, has combined support in the
northern Hispanic counties because of his ethnicity with
strong backing in the Albuquerque suburbs because of his
conservatism to defeat comparatively strong opponents.[14]

The rising star in Hispano politics has to be the
youthful, energetic, charismatic Jerry Apodaca who was
elected New Mexico's Governor in 1974. Apodaca, a former
star halfback at the University of New Mexico, was a teacher
before opening his own insurance firm in Las Cruces. Apodaca
served several terms in the New Mexico State Senate before
making his successful try for the Governorship. Apodaca in
his short time as Governor has acquired a reputation as a
tough, energetic executive.

Consideration of New Mexico's Hispano political jefe's would

be incomplete without mention of some of the Hispanos who
have distinguished themselves as Party Chairmen. Emilio
Naranjo, Democratic Party Chairman of Rio Arriba County is
the last of the great mould of Chairmen who had a firm grasp
on their county. Naranjo's stewardship and control of Rio
Arriba County rivals the most successful of the great American political bosses, Big Bill Thompson of Chicago, Tom
Pendergast of Kansas City, Tweed of Tammany Hall, Edward
Crump of Memphis and Frank Hague of New Jersey, though in a
smaller setting. Naranjo has amazed political analysts by
his ability to bring in the Rio Arriba vote for his endorsee
regardless of how obscure the candidate and regardless of
how the rest of the state goes. In 1974, for example, Naranjo's
endorsement of Fabian Chavez gave him the victory over the
nominee Jerry Apodaca in the Primary election, but in the
general election his endorsement of Apodaca gave Apodaca
the largest vote, 79.9%, than any county in the state,
contributing significantly to Apodaca's victory.

Edward Roybal

Although the pattern of political patrones of New Mexico
has not been duplicated in California, the state has produced its own brand of Hispano politicos, and Edward Roybal
has been the most successful. Roybal, a Democrat from Los

Angeles, was by profession a social worker, public health educator and administrator with the Los Angeles and California Tuberculosis Association in the 1940s. Roybal was one of the prime organizers and leaders of the Community Service Organization (CSO) and later the Mexican American Political Association (MAPA) in California. He was elected to the Los Angeles City Council in 1949 and served until 1962 when he had reached the position of President Pro-tempore of the Council. Roybal was elected to the 88th Congress from Los Angeles in 1962 and has been re-elected six times and is presently in his thirteenth year of service in the U.S. House. Roybal is a member of the powerful House Appropriations Committee and of various appropriation sub-committees including the Labor, Health, Education and Welfare sub-committee which is quite important to the Hispanic and Black constituency Roybal represents.[15]

Roybal, a liberal, has been an active supporter of civil rights, social security, and education programs. He was instrumental in the passage of the Bilingual Education Act of 1968, the creation of the Cabinet Committee on Opportunities for the Spanish Speaking, and has been an advocate for bilingual court systems.

Henry Gonzales

The state of Texas, long before providing the setting
for the emergence of La Raza Unida Party, also contributed
successful practitioners of conventional political party
activity. Henry Gonzales is probably the most astute and
best known Hispano politician in the state. Gonzales was
born in San Antonio, Texas in 1916, educated in San Antonio
schools and graduate of the University of Texas and St.
Mary's school of law. Gonzales' first run for public
office was in 1950 when he ran for the Texas state legislature and was defeated by a narrow margin. In 1953 he
was elected to the San Antonio City Council and served
for three years, during which time he pushed for the de-
segregation of San Antonio recreational facilities and
served as Mayor pro tempore.

In 1956 Gonzales was elected to the Texas state Senate
and was re-elected in 1960 for a second term. In the state
legislature, Gonzales developed a reputation as a fiery
civil rights advocate conducting filibusters against
segregation bills. Gonzales was a vehement opponent to
sales tax legislation. In 1961, Gonzales was elected in a
special election to fill the unexpired term of Congressman
Paul Fidlay. Gonzales has been re-elected seven times by
his predominantly San Antonio constituency, and his victories, reflecting his tremendous popularity, have been so

overwhelming (Gonzales received 90% of the vote in 1966

and 82.2% in 1968), that he did not have opposition in 1970

and 1974, and only token minor party opposition in 1972.

Gonzales, although branded as conservative by activist

Chicanos in Texas, has been a moderate Democratic Congress-

man, especially liberal on Civil Rights issues. Gonzales

generally has been a friend of labor, protector of the

interests of the poor and advocate of social security and

social legislation. He is a high ranking member of the

House Banking and Currency Committee and Chairman of its

sub-committee on International Finance. Gonzales is a

"zone whip" in majority whip structural organization

representing the House Democratic leadership among

the Texas Democrats. He is also a member of the House Small

Business Committee. Gonzales was one of the prime movers

for San Antonio's sponsorship for Hemisfair.[16]

E. (Kika) de la Garza

During the same period that Gonzales was consolidating

his base in the south-central Texas city of San Antonio,

E. Kika de la Garza was developing his power base in the

southern point cities of Mission, McAllen and Edinburg,

Texas. de la Garza, a lawyer by profession and a Democrat,

served in the Texas State House of Representatives prior

to making his first successful run for the U.S. House in
1964. He has been re-elected five times and is in his
twelfth year of membership in the House.[17]

Raul Castro of Arizona

The most important Hispano politician in Arizona is
Raul H. Castro, a Mexican immigrant born in the state of
Sonora, Mexico in 1916. Castro, came to the United States
with his parents and settled in Tucson, Arizona. Castro
attended Arizona State College at Flagstaff and law school
at the University of Arizona at Tucson. Castro was in the
U.S. Foreign Service diplomatic corps in Mexico from 1940
to 1946 when he returned as an Instructor of Spanish at the
University of Arizona while attending law school. In 1949
Castro entered law practice in Tucson in the firm of Castro
and Wolfe. In 1952 Castro became Deputy District Attorney
for Pima County, Arizona, and was later elected as District
Attorney serving from 1954 to 1958. In 1958 Castro was
elected Judge of Superior Court serving in 1963 and 1964
as Presiding Judge for Juvenile Court. In 1964 Castro was
appointed Ambassador to El Salvador serving until 1968, when
he became Ambassador to Bolivia. In 1969 Castro returned to
Arizona and private law practice.[18] In 1974 Castro was
elected Governor in Arizona. Although he received strong

support from Arizona's Hispanic voters in South Tucson and in the core areas of Phoenix, Castro's victory reflected the fact that he appealed to conservatives and moderate Democratic Party elements as well.

Summary

This chapter has focused on leaders of the Mexican American community. It began by emphasizing the diverse patterns of Chicano leadership as to style, ideology, personality, objectives. It addressed the problems of leadership of the Mexican American community or at least presumed problems such as lack of a single national leader, lack of a single unifying issue, and the fetish for Chicano unity.

It then focused attention on the big three leaders who have been associated with the modern Chicano movement, Reies Tijerina, Cesar Chavez and Rodolfo "Corky" Gonzales. The emphasis in these analyses was on the background of the leader, the man's philosophy, the organization he built, the style of political and social action he employed, the nature of his particular struggle, and his particular and unique contribution to the Chicano movement.

The chapter concluded with a consideration of more conventional leaders, the Mexican American politicians.

After a brief discussion of the importance of the Patron tradition in New Mexico politics, short profiles of some early Hispano jefe's politicos (political bosses) in New Mexico politics was presented. Among these were profiles of Ezequiel C.de Baca, Octaviano Larrazolo, Dennis Chavez and Joseph M. Montoya. Additional profiles of other New Mexico Hispano leaders, Antonio Fernandez, Manuel Lujan, Tibo Chavez and Jerry Apodaca were also offered.

Last but not least, the chapter offered profiles on Congressmen Henry Gonzales and Kika de la Garza of Texas, Congressman Edward Roybal of California and Governor Raul Castro of Arizona, all of these the most prominent Hispano politicos in their own state.

NOTES

[1]This description of Tijerina and the Alianza has relied extensively on the accounts provided by the main works on the subject, especially Richard Gardner, GRITO: Reies Tijerina and the New Mexico Land Grant War of 1967 (New York: Harper Colophon Books, 1971), also Peter Nabokov, Tijerina and the Courthouse Raid (Berkeley: Ramparts Press, 1970); Patricia Blawis, Tijerina and the Land Grants, op cit.

[2]See Frances Swadesh, "The Alianza Movement: Catalyst for Social Change in New Mexico," Proceedings, 1908 Annual Spring Meeting, American Ethnological Society, Seattle, Washington, 1968, 162-177.

[3]This analysis is based largely on an extensive observation of and discussions with Mr. Tijerina. Personal interviews on March 25, 1972 and April 20, 1972 formed some of my analysis of his personal philosophy.

[4]Peter Mathieson, Sal Si Puedes: Cesar Chavez and the New American Revolution. New York: Dell Publishing Co., 1969. Much of this description of Chavez' early life and activities relies on Mathieson. Also very useful was Ruth Lamb's, Mexican Americans: Sons of the Southwest (Claremont, California: Ocelot Press, 1970), 131-137, and Stan Stieners, La Raza: The Mexican Americans (New York: Harper Colophon Books, 1969), 272-338.

. [5]The narrative on "Corky" Gonzales has been pieced together from short written descriptions on the man, conversations, and from Stan Steiner's epilogue "The Poet in the Boxing Ring" in his work La Raza: The Mexican Americans, op. cit.

[6]See Rodolfo "Corky" Gonzales, "I Am Joaquin."

[7]La Raza: Why A Chicano Party? (New York: A Pathfinder Press pamphlet, 1970), 9-12.

[8]Ibid.

[9]"El Plan Espiritual de Aztlan", Documents of the Chicano Struggle (New York: A Pathfinder Merit pamphlet, 1971), 4-6.

[10]See Fincher, "The Spanish Americans of New Mexico as a Political Factor," op. cit., 135.

[11]Ibid., 138-140.

[12]Ibid., 140-145.

[13]United States Congress, 1974 Congressional Directory, (Washington: U.S. Government Printing Office, 1974), 120.

[14]Ibid., 120.

[15]Ibid., 22-23.

[16]Ibid., 182.

[17]Ibid., 181.

FURTHER SUGGESTED READING

Rodolfo Acuna. "Goodbye America", Chapter 9 and "The Road
to Delano" Chapter 7 in Occupied America: The Chicano's
Struggle Toward Liberation (New York: Canfield Press,
1972).

Patricia Bell Blawis. Tijerina and the Land Grants: Mexican
Americans in Struggle for Their Heritage. (New York:
International Publishers, 1971).

"El Plan Espiritual de Aztlan" Documents of the Chicano
Struggle (New York: Pathfinder Press pamphlet, 1971).

Ernesto Galarza. Spiders in the House and Workers in the
Field. (Notre Dame University Press, 1970).

Richard Gardner, GRITO: Reies Tijerina and the New Mexico
Land Grant War of 1967. (New York: Harper Torch
Books, 1970.)

Rodolfo "Corky" Gonzales, I Am Joaquin, An Epic Poem, 1967.

Horowitz, George D. La Causa: The California Grape Strike.
(New York: MacMillan, 1970.)

Peter Matthieson. Sal Si Puedes: Cesar Chavez and the
New American Revolution. (New York: Dell Publishing
Co., 1973.)

Peter Nabokov. Tijerina and the Courthouse Raid. (Berkeley:
Ramparts Press, 1970.)

Stan Steiner. "The Poet in the Boxing Ring", in La Raza:
The Mexican Americans. (New York: Harper and Row,
1969).

CHAPTER VII

CHICANO VOTING BEHAVIOR

The study of voting. . .is concerned with
a fundamental process of political decision. . .
It would be difficult to overstate the significance of popular elections for democratic theory
and practice. If politics has to do with 'who
gets what, when, and how,' the free competitive
election has proven an essential means of insuring
that the current solution of this problem enjoys
the broad consent of the government.*
Angus Campbell, 1964

Assumptions and Patterns of Chicano Voting Behavior

Probably the most neglected topic in the research on

Chicano politics is Chicano voting behavior. Even the most

recent book of readings on Chicano politics[1] contains only

a handful of studies on this important topic. Voting

behavior is the most important manifestation of political

participation of a group simply because it is the most

common political activity engaged in by most of the popula-

tion.

Generally speaking, the most documented characteristic

of Chicano political behavior is the notorious lack of

participation of Chicanos in voting. Quite apart from this

general assumption, a number of important questions present

*Angus Campbell, et. al. The American Voter (New York:
John Wiley and Sons, 1964), 4.

themselves relative to Chicano voting behavior. For
example, is Chicano non-participation a universal characteristic attributable to all the group in all parts of the
country? Also, are there possible explanations as those
suggested in Chapters I and II which might clarify or
suggest possible reasons for the lack of participation?
Finally, considering these explanations what is the like-
lihood that the situation will change?

The present chapter will address these questions, by
reviewing the available literature on Chicano voting behavior and by presenting contrasting case studies analyzing
the voting behavior of Chicanos in New Mexico.

Two different sets of explanations have been offered
for the tendency of Chicanos towards non-participation in
politics, those are the racial/cultural explanations and
the legal or structural explanations. Those who "explain"
Chicano non-participation on racial/cultural grounds suggest
that Mexican culture (the Chicano's parent culture) is a
subject political culture wherein the common citizen is
prone to expect and rely on elites to govern. Others
suggest that Mexican American culture is too individualistic,
that Chicanos are withdrawn, not prone to interaction,
anti-social, all attributes that discourage active participation in politics.

On the other hand, those who point to legal and
structural explanations argue that the dominant society
(Anglos to Chicanos) have controlled political structures
and have imposed legal or procedural barriers that have
served to exclude Chicanos. Examples would be the California English language requirement, the Texas poll tax
and annual registration requirement. These observers also
suggest that intimidation by the dominant group has also
discouraged Chicano participation. In this they point to
the fact that in Texas, Klu Klux Klan activity was directed
at Chicanos as much as at Blacks. Gerrymandering of
electoral districts - say other observers - has resulted
in discriminatory patterns that has minimized the importance and impact of large blocs of Mexican American voters
thus contributing to their political exclusion. Others
maintain that Chicano non-participation is a manifestation
of the culture of poverty, that is that Chicanos are a poor
population, and poorly educated, all characteristics that
preclude active participation since such groups feel
isolated from government, they distrust it, and they do not
feel capable of influencing it.

As indicated before in the consideration of Chicano
political culture, it is difficult to quarrel with the fact
that all (the cultural characteristics and the legal

barriers) contributed to the political culture of the group
and thus it's tendency to remain outside of politics.

On the other hand, the fact that New Mexico's Chicano
population has participated extensively and effectively in
politics presents an important exception to the general
pattern.

This chapter will illustrate how the regional differences in the socio-political experience of the Chicano in
the southwest has resulted in the disparate patterns
of political participation evident among Mexican Americans
in New Mexico and other parts of the Southwest. In focusing
on the high levels of participation among New Mexico's
Mexican Americans, it will challenge certain assumptions
that have generally been held about Chicano political
behavior as a whole.

It will also suggest that given a favorable and conducive environment, and political socialization process,
the Chicanos (in spite of antecedent political cultural
orientations), could have, and can still develop the skills
and traits for effective political participation in American
life.

What is needed to bring this about is an elimination
of the restrictive legal barriers, combined with a systematic
and concerted effort by the parties to integrate, politically,

the Chicano population.

The Political Culture of New Mexico's Mexican Americans

In what way is the political culture of Chicanos in New Mexico different from that of his counterpart in California or Texas or elsewhere? Why would its participation orientations differ so markedly from Chicanos elsewhere?

Most of the explanations for the difference of New Mexico's Mexican Americans can be attributed to historical circumstances. First of all, New Mexico contained the largest (some 50,000) Mexican population of all of Mexico's northern provinces at the time of the American occupation. Naturally, because of this, it would have proven quite difficult for the Americans to govern without the collaboration of some acknowledged leaders of the Mexican population. This led the Americans, beginning with the occupation Army of Gen. Kearny to call on individuals such as Donaciano Vigil who became the first territorial secretary under the civil government, and later became Governor after the assassination of Governor Charles Bent in the Taos rebellion of 1847. This participation in the political affairs from the outset, served to socialize important Mexican officials in the affairs of the new American government. A second factor relates to the nature of Mexican leaders in New

Mexico. New Mexicans had been quite isolated from Mexico, and governed themselves as a self-contained province. As such, these circumstances had allowed the development of distinct political institutions and an elite group of leaders. These leaders were quite sophisticated not only in the political affairs of the Mexican government, but on the nature of the American political regime. Many leaders had been quite critical of the benign neglect of the province by the Mexican government, especially with regard to affording protection from the depradation of warring Indian tribes. Thus the coming of the Americans was viewed by Mexican leaders in a variety of ways. Some saw genuine promise of democracy in the coming of the Americans; others visualized a more effective administration to cope with the Indian problem; others visualized the possibility of establishing perhaps a separate nation; others anticipated the prospect of improving their own economic and political position. In all cases, however, the leaders foresaw and grasped the opportunity to share in the administration and governing of the territory, thus establishing a pattern of participation that both trickled down to the Mexican population, and became part of the political structure in the territorial period and later statehood in New Mexico. Mexican American leaders such as Vigil, Antonio Jose Martinez,

Gregorio Vigil, Manuel A. Otero and others became active in establishing a territorial government and in launching efforts for statehood, realizing that such a development would contribute to the prompt political integration of the new territory into the American system while allowing it to progress independently. Contributing to this state of affairs was the fact that New Mexico was not engulfed and overwhelmed by Anglo American immigration, and even after the coming of the railroad and with it Anglo immigration, Mexican Americans continued to constitute a majority of the territorial and later state population. Today they constitute the single largest ethnic group and at 40.1 percent close to half of the state's population.

What all this has meant, is that the Mexican Americans have been a most important political group in New Mexico politics since territorial days, participating most effectively in every dimension of political affairs. Mexican Americans, for example, have held all Congressional positions and presently hold one of two positions in the U.S. Senate and one of two positions in the U.S. House. Hispanos have held all state elective offices including the Governorship, except for the office of State Treasurer, and presently occupy six of the ten state elective positions. Hispanos have served in every level of the state judiciary from the Supreme Court down and presently occupy two of five positions

in the State Supreme Court and State Court of Appeals and
seven district judgeships. They have continuously been
highly represented in the state legislature and in legislative positions and presently hold the highest leadership
positions (Speaker of the House and Majority Floor Leader)
in the state legislature. Hispanos also serve in hundreds
of county, municipal, school board and special district
offices. Hispanos have consistently occupied high appointive
offices in state and local government, and occupy leadership positions in the party structure of both major political
parties.[2]

The circumstances in New Mexico have, of course, not been
duplicated in other states. In Texas, the Lone Star independence movement wiped out all vestige of Mexican influence
in government. In Arizona, the pattern of Anglo domination
was established in the colonization of that state. In
California and Colorado, the Mexican population and leaders
were overwhelmed when the onset of Anglo immigration engulfed those states following the gold strikes of 1849
and 1859. In all cases, as was described before, the
pattern resulted in the political subordination of the
Mexican American population.

Review of Voting Behavior Research

A brief overview of the existing literature on the
voting behavior of the Mexican Americans illustrates not
only the paucity of such literature, but reflects the
recurring theme of Chicano voter apathy and non-participation. One of the first efforts to evaluate systematically
the voting behavior of Chicanos outside of New Mexico was
conducted by the Mexican American Study Project at UCLA in
1965. The M.A.S.P. conducted field interviews to ascertain
information about voting behavior and political attitudes
among the Mexican Americans in Los Angeles, California and
San Antonio, Texas.

The results of the survey indicated that in Los Angeles
County although Mexican Americans constituted about 12.5%
of the total population only about 5.5% were registered
to vote. In the 1964 elections, only 55.8% of the eligible
Mexican American voters were registered to vote, and of
these only 49.8% actually participated in the election.
The project also noted a significant decline of 20.2%
in voter registration percentages among Mexican Americans
between 1958 and 1965, indicating that the decline of voter
registration activities of organizations such as the C.S.O.
was having an adverse effect.

In San Antonio, Texas, the project found that although

Mexican Americans constituted approximately 40.0% of the population, they constituted only 20.1% of San Antonio's registered voters. In the 1964 elections only 49.3% of the eligible Mexican American voters were registered, and then only 41.6% actually voted in the elction.[3]

The findings of the study conducted in two major centers of Mexican American population in two different states seemed to reinforce the notion that "Mexican Americans, as a group, have long appeared to be less disposed to exercise the franchise of 'good citizenship' than have other minorities" and thus: "In terms of the American political system Mexican Americans have had a limited impact and their political efficiency seems low."[4]

A second study of Mexican American voting behavior, this time in Harris County (Houston), Texas, was conducted by Clifton McCleskey and Dan Nimmo and not only reinforced the Mexican American Study Project findings, but showed that Mexican Americans in Harris County were even less disposed to register and vote than Blacks. This study will be discussed later.

In 1967, Donald Freeman[5] contributed one of the first studies on the voting behavior of Mexican Americans in Arizona. Freeman observed that Mexican Americans make up over 60% of the population of South Tucson and dominate city government there. He finds an overwhelming attachment of Mexican Americans to the Democratic Party, but is perplexed that in spite of their dominance of South Tucson and the relative lack of clear obstacles, that Chicanos simply do not participate in politics. In 1964, for example, 51.6% of Mexican Americans were not eligible to vote and of these, 13.9% did not vote, thus contributing negatively to a Goldwater victory in Arizona, since their participation would have been favorable to Lyndon Johnson, the Democrat. The clear assumption in the Freeman selection is that since Hispanos dominate South Tucson's population, and since they control city government, there are seemingly no clear legal obstacles to their participation, yet it is not forthcoming. Again the presumption that Chicanos should take to democratic participation "like a duck takes to water" ignores the fact that strong and efficatious participation and attachment to a regime is built over a long period of socialization, and even then depends on the antecedent political orientations of the group. Also, the Freeman analysis suffers from a lack of comparative context. How frequently American scholars have decried the low levels of political participation in American democracy in spite of its "democratic" basis and the essence of voting to that basis. Freeman, for example, might have compared Hispano participation to other Arizona ethnic groups such as Blacks or Indians.

Among the more sophisticated recent studies of Chicano

voting behavior was that of Rudolph de la Garza.[6] Garza

addresses the "causes" of low levels of Chicano participation,

and argues that the lack of participation is more a result

of "systemic variables" operating to inhibit participation,

than intrinsic cultural traits of the group itself. Garza

reiterates the themes of attachment of Chicanos to the

Democratic Party, of the lower levels of Mexican American

participation, but he also finds that Chicano political

participation has been structured by the dominant society.

In El Paso, for example, the Anglo majority constrains the

Mexican American minority from independently selecting its

own leaders thus Chicano leaders are essentially legitimized

by their acceptance by the Anglo community.

One of the most recent behavioral analyses on the

Mexican Americans in Texas is that of Clifton McCleskey

and Bruce Merrill.[7] These writers found that although

Hispanos constitute 18.4% of Texas' population, and con-

stitute a majority of the population in 21 of the state's

254 counties, "the Mexican Americans have not qualified

and voted in the same proportion as the rest of the

citizenry."[8]

Analyzing several indices of Mexican American political

behavior and attitudes, McCleskey and Merrill find that voter

registration rates among Mexican Americans in the fifteen
Hispano counties are about the same as other Texas counties,
but active participation in voting is anywhere from 5 to
15 percent less. Outside of these fifteen counties both
Mexican American voter registration and voting were below
that of the population as a whole. The authors also
reiterated the theme that 86% of Mexican Americans identify
with the Democratic Party, but found that Hispanos do not
perceive themselves as often as "strong" Democrats, as do
Blacks. McCleskey and Nimmo found a less pronounced liberal,
ideological, self-perception among Chicanos than Blacks.
In measures of political efficacy and alienation, the
authors found very high indices of low levels of efficacy
combined with political alienation which to them portends
a "volatile, potentially disruptive situation."

By and large, the studies on Mexican American voting
behavior reflect then, the low levels of political participation of the group in American politics. This conclusion
- aside from its application to New Mexico - is not
challenged here. Some of the more recent studies such as
those of de la Garza, and McCleskey and Merrill, have
appropriately addressed their studies to analyze reasons
for these patterns. This, should be the main concern of
scholars. Other of the voting studies have, unfortunately

gone beyond stating limited findings, to draw questionable

inferences beyond the realm of their limited data. These can,

and must be challenged. One recent example (1973) is that

of Mark Levy and Michael Kramer[9] who state categorically:

> On balance, Chicano voters seem to lack
> the political activity that makes the southern
> black voter. Years of political neglect have
> made the Chicano voter apathetic. Even when
> a Chicano politician stands on the verge of a
> political triumph, Chicano voter response is
> often lackadaisical. Futher, Chicano voters
> are generally disinterested in attempts to
> create third-party movements that would speak
> directly to their needs or force the powers that
> be into dealing with Chicano problems. No
> third-party Chicano candidate has done well with
> his own people, and Chicano voters appear little
> interested in ideology.[10]

That such analyses are being made in such recent years,

in spite of clear evidence in New Mexico, in Crystal City,

Texas, to the contrary, indicates that the little literature

on Chicano voting behavior suffers from misinterpretation.

The remaining portion of this chapter is devoted to a

detailed analysis of the 1974 Democratic Primary election

and the 1974 General Election in New Mexico. This analysis

will address the familiar issues of Chicano voter apathy

but illustrate quite different voting patterns. The

selection of the 1974 elections was made because it was a

particularly important and successful year for New Mexico's

Mexican American voters, but it reflected a long consistent

pattern of political participation that has been documented by this and other writers before.[11]

Voting Behavior of New Mexico's Mexican Americans: The 1974 Elections

The present discussion is an attempt to provide some balance to the philosophical arguments that have been made regarding the political participation of the Mexican American people. The objective here is to challenge the basic generality of the assumptions of Mexican American apathy and docility by describing the case of the Mexican American in New Mexico. By illustrating the invalidity or inapplicability of the generalization to the case of the Chicano in New Mexico, it is argued that more reliable and valid explanations than those previously offered can be discovered for the traditional low-levels of participation of the group in other states.

The 1974 Democratic Primary elections conducted in the state of New Mexico present an excellent opportunity for evaluating the validity of the above generalization. It was an election in which the substantial political potential and power of the Chicano group was translated into dramatic political victories in state politics.

In a state where the Democratic Party has predominated since 1936, and which at present holds about 66 percent of the voter registration as compared to the Republican Party's 30 percent, Hispanos were nominated for six of eight elective state offices. These included the offices of Governor, Secretary of State, State Auditor, Attorney General, Land Commissioner, and State Corporation Commissioner. Hispanos were also nominated to one of two positions for Congress, and one of two positions to the State Court of Appeals without opposition.

There are, it seems, two basic questions that could either validate or lay to rest the traditional assumption of Mexican American apathy and docility as regards political affairs. The first question would appropriately focus on levels of political participation and could be phrased as follows:

To what extent do Mexican Americans exercise the voting franchise? A corollary would be: In a given setting how do Chicanos compare with other groups or the general population in their exercise of the franchise?

A second question addressing the issue of Chicano docility would read: To what extent do Chicanos exhibit a tendency toward ethnic bloc voting in the presence of ethnic issues or candidates?

The 1974 Democratic Primary in New Mexico: An Hispano Sweep

The 1974 Democratic Primary in New Mexico is an election
that especially lends itself to an analysis and evaluation
of both questions since it can be described as the banner
year for Hispanos at least as far as primaries are concerned.
Although Hispanos had previously contested for and held every
major state elective office except State Treasurer, few
elections had yielded such overwhelming Hispano success
as the 1974 Primary. The first part of the study of the
1974 election considers only the Primary and not the General
Election because of the effort to control for the variable
of ethnicity in a given election in New Mexico. This
objective is made more difficult when the additional variable
of partisanship is operational as it would be in a General
Election. In other words, the importance of ethnicity can
be more readily identified in a situation where an Hispano
Democrat selects between an Anglo or Hispano Democrat, than
in a situation where an Hispano Democrat selects between an
Hispano Democrat and an Anglo Republican as was likely to be
the case in the 1974 General Election. While it would be
desirable to illustrate the greater importance of ethnicity
over partisanship among most Hispano voters which is the
case in most electoral situations, in this writer's view, this

particular facet of Hispano voting behavior will be taken up later.

Highlighting the Hispano sweep in the 1974 Democratic Primary was the surprisingly strong victory of Jerry Apodoca, the former star-halfback at the University of New Mexico and two-term State Senator from Doña Ana County, who capitalized on a strong statewide organization and his youthful energetic public relations campaign. Apodoca captured the Democratic Party Gubernatorial nomination with 30.6 percent of the vote and a plurality of over ten thousand votes over his nearest competitor, Tibo Chavez, also an Hispano and former Senate Majority Floor Leader of the New Mexico State Senate, who received 23.6 percent of the vote. Trailing in the race for Governor were four Anglos: Odis Echols, Majority Whip of the New Mexico State Senate (17.3 percent); Bobby Mayfield, former state representative (15.3 percent); Drew Cloud, former State Democratic Party Chairman (8.6 percent); and Boston Witt, former State Attorney General, who trailed the slate with 4.6 percent.

The race for Secretary of State presented the unique race between former Secretary of State Ernestine D. Evans, an Hispana with an Anglo married surname, and Betty McDaniel Lujan an Anglo woman with a Spanish surname. This

race presented interesting results in some Hispano precincts
where the voters did not identify the true ethnic differences as will be shown later. Evans won the race with 56.3
percent of the vote. In the race for State Auditor, Max
Sanchez who trailed his Anglo opponent, Earl Davidson, for
most of the election-night tabulations, emerged a close
victor on the strength of his support in the late-reporting
Hispano counties. Sanchez received 51.3 percent of the
vote to Davidson's 48.7 percent. In the race for Attorney
General, the Hispano, Toney Anaya, although like Sanchez
trailing through the early returns, emerged victorious on
the basis of his strong support in the Hispano counties.
Anaya received 50.9 percent of the vote to Fred Howden's
49.1 percent. In the race for Land Commissioner, Phil
Lucero, the only Hispano in the race, benefited from this,
since opposition by two Anglos, Johnny Taylor and Anthony
Fiorina, largely split the non-ethnic vote. Lucero received
45.9 percent to Taylor's 37.3 percent and Fiorina's 16.8
percent of the vote. The race for Corporation Commission
also presented a unique slate. Charles Rudolph, an Hispano
with an "Anglo" surname generally identified as Hispano in
the northern Hispano counties, but not recognized as such
in other parts of the state benefited in all areas as a
result, and very convincingly defeated the incumbent John

Abraham and the other Hispano in the race, Joe Barela.

Rudolph received 48.1 percent, to Abraham's 29.5 percent

and Barela's 22.4 percent of the vote. In the race for

State Treasurer, Alex Pacheco, though losing in his bid for

nomination, made the first competitive effort ever by an

Hispano for that office on the basis of his strong support

in the Hispanic counties.[12]

The Hispano victories in the Democratic Primary were

attributable in large part to two factors, the high levels

of voting by Hispanic voters, especially in the counties

with majority Hispano populations, and the very strong

preference for Hispano candidates exhibited by Hispanic

voters. This can be illustrated by a careful analysis of

the primary election returns.

Larry Calloway, an able political reporter and analyst,

conducted one such early investigation and wrote that "the

results of the New Mexico primary elections, certified last

week, show Democrats in the predominantly Spanish-speaking

counties were the most active voters." Calloway concluded

that the pattern which was very favorable to Hispano

candidates was significant if it carried into the General

Election.[13]

If it can be shown that Hispano participation was in-

deed higher in the primary, and that the higher participation was translated in 1974 into victory for the Hispano

candidates because of the preference of Hispano voters for

Hispano candidates, such convincing evidence will cast

serious doubt on the validity of the aforementioned assump-

tions about Mexican American apathy and docility.

The following commentary will attempt just that, first,

by comparing levels of turnout and candidate preference of

Hispano counties with other regions and statewide, and

secondly by exploring in detail the returns for one of

those Hispanic counties.

Comparisons in Registration and Turnout: Hispanic and Little Texas Counties

Although New Mexico is a state with quite a complex

and diverse population including rural/urban cleavage

patterns, a sizable Indian population, and a varied array

of economic interests, it is possible as Jack Holmes and

other analysts have done, to isolate fairly homogeneous

"political groups." Holmes, for example, describes such

groups as the "Hispanics," "Little Texas," and "Los

Alamos" as among the more important.[14] The "Little Texas"

counties are those counties in the southeastern corner of

New Mexico, which are very similar in population and

economic and cultural orientation to the Lone Star State.

They are appropriate for the present analysis because they

are counties with low Hispano populations, which is in
sharp contrast to the Hispanic counties whose designation
derives from their large Hispanic populations. Thus
electoral comparisons between these two fairly homogeneous
political groups are appropriate as well as instructive of
the political environment of the state of New Mexico.

Table 1 which compares registration and turnout not
only verifies Calloway's conclusion but illustrates the
significant differences between the turnout in Hispano
counties with those of the state as a whole and with the
Little Texas counties. The turnout in Hispano counties
was 8.5 percent higher than the statewide turnout and 10.2
percent higher than the Little Texas county turnout.
Viewed another way, the Hispanic counties though constituting
18.7 percent of the registered Democrats in the state, cast
21.9 percent of the votes for Governor in 1974 while the
Little Texas counties, though constituting 19.5 percent of
the registered Democrats, cast 18.8 percent of the votes.
This represents a significant difference between the
registration and voting of the Hispano and Little Texas
counties (x^2 = 851.07 df = 1 p $\leq$ .01). The difference was
due to a combined Hispano county increase in voting of
17.1 percent and a Little Texas decrease of 3.6 percent
which resulted in the proportional increase of Hispanos

TABLE 1

Comparison of Registered, and Actual Voters in "Little Texas" and Hispanic Counties for 1974 Democratic Primary

	Statewide	Hispanic Counties[a]	Little Texas[b]	Difference Between Hispanic & Little Texas
Registered Voters	294,017	55,096	57,358	+2,262
Percent of State Totals	100%	18.7%	19.5%	+1.8%
Voted for Governor in 1974 Primary	148,608	32,559	28,006	-4,553
Percent of State Totals	50.5%	21.9%	18.8%	-3.1%
Percent Voting	50.5%	59.0%	48.8%	10.2%

Source: State of New Mexico, Official Election Returns, 1974 Primary Returns (Santa Fe: Secretary of State, 1974), pp. 2-3.

a Hispanic counties are those counties with Hispanic populations greater than 60% of total county population. These counties are in north central New Mexico. The counties are Guadalupe, Mora, Rio Arriba, Sandoval, San Miguel, Santa Fe, Socorro, and Taos.

b Little Texas counties are counties with generally low Hispano populations, which because of their southeastern location and bordering on Texas reflect many of the social, economic and cultural patterns of the Lone Star State. The counties are Chavez, Curry, De Baca, Eddy, Lea and Roosevelt.

Similar designation of counties were used by T. Phillip Wolf "The 1968 Elections in New Mexico," Western Political Quarterly, XXII, No. 3 (September, 1969), Table 2, p. 512.

voting of 3.29 percent (18.7 to 21.9%) and a proportional
decline of Little Texas voting of .7 percent (19.5 to
18.8%).

The higher turnout in Hispanic counties is more
significant when one looks at the showing of Hispano and
Anglo candidates in the respective counties. Table 2
provides a breakdown of the percentage votes won by all the
candidates in the Hispanic and Little Texas counties. The
table shows that, indeed, the higher turnout of voters in
Hispanic counties was generally favorable to Hispano
candidates. Apodaca received 43.6 percent of the vote in
Hispanic counties but shared the Hispanic county majorities
with Tibo Chavez who got 31.3 percent. Together these
candidates received 74.9 percent of the vote. Apodaca and
Chavez each carried four of the eight Hispanic counties.
The vote for Secretary of State shows that Betty McDaniel
Lujan fared better probably because of her surname - in the
Hispanic counties than she did statewide although she lost
these counties by 1 percent. In the race for State Auditor,
Max Sanchez' precarious 2.6 percent margin was aided by the
75.4 percent of the vote he received in the Hispano counties.
Sanchez carried all eight Hispano counties. In the race
for State Treasurer, Alex Pacheco, although losing and
receiving only 32.6 percent of the vote statewide, received

TABLE 2   330

Comparison of Percentage Votes Cast for Hispano and Anglo
Candidates in "Hispanic" and "Little Texas" Counties

	Statewide Percentage	Hispanic Counties[a]	Little Texas Counties[a]
Governor			
Boston Witt	4.6	6.3	4.2
Drew Cloud	8.6	4.7	9.9
Odis Echols	17.3	9.3	26.8
Bobby Mayfield	15.3	4.8	29.1
Jerry Apodaca	30.6	43.6	14.2
Tibo J. Chavez	23.6	31.3	15.8
Apodaca/Chavez	54.2	74.9	30.0
Secretary of State			
Betty McDaniel Lujan	43.7	49.1	33.1
Ernestine Evans	56.3	50.9	66.9
State Auditor			
Max R. Sanchez	51.3	75.4	25.9
Earl Davidson	48.7	24.6	74.1
State Treasurer			
Carl Folkner	29.2	20.0	41.3
Edward Murphey	38.2	23.1	44.5
Alex Pacheco	32.6	56.9	14.2
Attorney General			
Toney Anaya	50.9	66.5	33.9
Frederick Howden	49.1	33.5	66.1
Commissioner of Public Lands			
Phil Lucero	45.9	69.5	25.6
Johnny Taylor	37.3	15.6	54.8
Anthony Fiorina	16.8	14.9	19.6
Corporation Commission			
Charles Rudolph	48.1	49.3	59.6
Joe Barela	22.4	26.3	18.2
John Abraham	29.5	24.4	22.2
Rudolph/Barela	70.5	75.6	77.8

Source: State of New Mexico: Official Election Returns
1974.

a See Table 1 for description of each category.

56.9 percent of the Hispanic county vote, carrying all
Hispano counties except Sandoval. In the race for Attorney
General, Anaya's very slight victory of less than 1 percent
was aided by his strong showing in Hispanic counties where
he received 66.5 percent of the vote. Anaya carried every
Hispanic county. In the race for Commissioner of Public
Lands, Phil Lucero received 69.5 percent of the Hispanic
county vote which contributed to his impressive victory
statewide. The race for Corporation Commission was
especially interesting because Charles Rudolph, the Hispano
from San Miguel County, benefited in every respect from his
surname. Rudolph, capitalizing on the recognition of his
name as Hispano in the north, carried all the Hispanic
counties except Taos with a total of 49.3 percent of the
vote. He also carried the Little Texas counties where the
Rudolph name is not identified as Hispano with 59.6 percent
of the vote. These two factors combined to give Rudolph
an impressive victory in his first try for elective public
office, capturing 48.1 percent of the vote statewide in a
three man race.

The second significant point manifested in Table 2
is that in addition to a very strong ethnic vote in the
northern counties, there is an equally strong anti-ethnic
vote in some parts of the state as in Little Texas. This

is reflected in the almost complete reversal of the percentage votes received by Hispanos in Hispanic counties
and in Little Texas counties. Thus, because of the prominence of the ethnic factor (both in ethnic and anti-ethnic
voting) in New Mexico politics, the specific electoral
circumstances will determine what impact the ethnic factor
will play. Candidates (both ethnics and non-ethnics) must
therefore allow for the ethnic factor in planning their
electoral strategy. The 1974 Democratic Primary election
is one example of an electoral situation that was most
favorable to Hispano candidates and less favorable to
Anglos.

San Miguel County: A Typical Hispanic County?

An in-depth look at one of the Hispano counties which
contributed significantly to the victory of all Hispanos in
the statewide races will also provide evidence in response
to the two questions raised before.

San Miguel County located in north central New Mexico
and the center of Hispano concentration (81.7% Hispano) is
in some ways typical and in some ways atypical of the
northern New Mexico Hispano majority counties. Once the
most populous and important county in the state (up to the
1920s), it has maintained a strong reputation for being a

highly political county. In the heyday of patronage politics,

Hispano party bosses from both major parties regularly lined

the rolls of state jobs available in the county with party

loyalists and supporters. It was an old adage that

employees at the State Mental Hospital in Las Vegas, the

county seat, would change party affiliation in accordance

with which party controlled the state government. Although

the State Personnel Act and Merit System has reduced the

number of patronage jobs available for distribution by the

party chairman, the Democratic Party at least has partially

maintained its prerogatives by shifting its influence to

the West Las Vegas school board and municipal government in

Las Vegas. The Democratic Party in the county has, since

the mid-1950s, been characterized by extensive factionalism

often characterized by splits in which the regular and gadfly

organization hold separate county conventions, select separate

county officers, send separate delegations to state party

conventions, and endorse separate competing slates for

county and state offices.

In its extreme factionalism, San Miguel county is

unique among northern New Mexico counties, but in its

highly political environment it is not, since other counties

such as Rio Arriba County are equally, if not more, political.

Like most of the state outside of Bernalillo County,

San Miguel is a Democratic Party stronghold where 66 percent of the registered voters are Democrats. Democratic
candidates for state office, barring unique electoral
circumstances, usually fare well in the county, and a
Republican holding county elective office in San Miguel
is a rarity.

Comparison with the McCleskey-Nimmo Harris County Study

As the observations and findings that follow contra-
dict prior assumptions about Mexican American participation,
it is appropriate that they be formulated in some comparative context with previous studies. The research pro-
cedure employed in this part of the study thus parallels
the earlier study by Clifton McCleskey and Dan Nimmo.[15] In
analyzing the voting behavior of the population of Harris
County (Houston), Texas, in the 1964 elections, the authors
studied three populations: the potential (all citizens of
voting age), the qualified (those registered to vote) and
the actual (in 1964 elections) voters. Although their
study focused on several electoral variables such as age
and sex, their most significant findings were relative to
racial and ethnic differences. They found, for example, a
significant difference between Anglos and Spanish-surnamed
voters in the respective proportions the two groups dis-

played in the "potential" and "qualified" voter categories.
The Anglo population showed a proportional increase of
6.0 percent (75.5% to 81.5%) from the potential to the
qualified voter category which represented an actual 7.9
percent increase of Anglo registrants. The Hispanos on
the other hand showed a proportional decrease of 2.5 percent (05.6% to 3.1%) which represented an actual decrease
of 44.6 percent among Hispanos. This led the authors to
state that "the Spanish-surname population is significantly
distinguished by its poor record in qualifying to vote,"
and to conclude that "Latin American turnout /was/ much
lower than that of Negroes despite similarities in the
socio-economic status of the two minorities."[16]

These conclusions will be the focus of the commentary
which follows. The effort will be to uncover the levels
of voting participation of Hispanos in San Miguel County,
compared with the Anglo population, and additionally
attempts to yield inferences as to the ethnic preferences
of ethnic voters in San Miguel County.

The operational definitions of the three populations
parallels those of the McCleskey/Nimmo study even though
the sample derivations may differ. The <u>potential</u> <u>electorate</u>
universe as defined by constitutional decree are all
citizens aged eighteen years or older. Figures for this

age group are taken from the census reports for San Miguel

County and appropriate ethnic subgroups. The main limita-

tion in these figures is that they fail to exclude potential

non-qualified voters such as ex-felons, mental deficients

and others who may legally be excluded from voting.

The universe of qualified voters are persons who met

all voting requirements and were legally qualified to vote

in the 1974 elections by virtue of their registration.

These figures are taken from up-to-date voter registration

lists maintained on a precinct level by the County Clerk

in San Miguel County. Sixteen precincts well distributed

throughout the county and containing 56.3 percent of the

total Democratic Party registration of the county were

included in the sample. Five of the precincts are from

various parts of East Las Vegas where the Anglo population

is concentrated. Five more precincts from various parts of

West Las Vegas were also taken. Two precincts from Pecos

and one from the village of Villanueva, the most populous

villages in rural San Miguel, were also included. Four

additional rural precincts were selected on the basis of

their location in the various regions of the county. The

precincts included in the sample make it truly representa-

tive of the population of the county in terms of ethnicity,

region, age and so on and perhaps reflective of other

northern New Mexico counties such as Rio Arriba, Guadalupe,

Sandoval, Socorro, Mora and Taos. The method used to

specify Anglo versus Hispanic voters was by identification

of Spanish surnames, or other surnames generally identified

with the Hispano population in San Miguel County such as

Rudolph, McGrath, Leger and others, from the recent voter

registration lists.

The universe of actual voters was taken from the

Regular Precinct Poll Book for the June 4, 1974 primary,

wherein voters affix their signature just before voting.

Identification of Anglo/Hispano distinctions was made by

reading through actual lists of voters. Admittedly this

was the most difficult part of the identification process

because of the illegibility of an occasional name. However,

the large size of the sample would preclude gross misidenti-

fication. Election returns listed in Table 3 were obtained

from official election returns for San Miguel County in the

June 4 primary.

The 1974 Democratic Primary in San Miguel County

The 1974 Primary campaign in San Miguel County had as

a background the usual factionalism within the Democratic

Party. The regular Party organization headed by Donald A.

Martinez early endorsed the candidacy of Jerry Apodaca while the opposing Apolonio Duran faction endorsed Tibo Chavez.

Both organizations recognizing that an Hispano gubernatorial

nominee would have better prospects in the general election

if accompanied by an Anglo running mate for Lieutenant

Governor, endorsed Anglos for that position even though

two former Hispano legislators, Fred Chavez, Jr. and Raymond

Garcia were in that race. The Martinez faction however,

in keeping with Martinez' own recent Chicano activism,

endorsed the Hispano surnamed candidates for the remaining

state races while the Duran faction endorsed Anglos with

the exception of its choice of Phil Lucero for Commissioner

of Public Lands.

The first set of significant results yielded by the

1974 Primary in relation to the comparison of levels of

participation of Hispanos and Anglos in the Primary election,

are depicted in Columns A-D of Table 3.

A comparison of the potential electorate versus the

qualified electorate for the sample precincts reveals a

significant difference in the participation between the

Anglo and Hispano populations (x^2 = 34.59, df = 1, $p \leq$ .01).

The significance may be attributed to a 13 percent Anglo

decrease and 4.2 percent Hispano increase in registration.

The Anglo population showed a proportional decrease of 3.2

percent (24.4 to 21.2%) from the potential to the qualified

TABLE 3

Comparison of Frequencies, Percentages and x^2 for the Potential, Qualified and Actual Electorate in the San Miguel County Primary Election, 1974.

Ethnic Group	A Potential Electorate[a]	B Qualified Electorate[b] (N=6139)	C % Change (A-B/A)	D Qualified Democratic Electorate[b] (N=3992)	E Actual Democratic Electorate[c] (N=2452)	F % Change (D-E/D)
Hispano	75.6%	4839 (78.8%)	+4.2%	81.4%	2143 (87.4%)	+7%
Anglo	24.4%	1300 (21.2%)	-13%	18.6%	307 (12.6%)	-22%

x^2 = Potential (A) vs Qualified Electorate (B) = 34.59, df-1, p -.01.

x^2 = Qualified Democrats (D) vs Actual Democratic Electorate (E) = 58.44, df = 1, p=-.01.

a. Based on 1970 Census for San Miguel County. Population aged 18 or over. See U.S. Bureau of the Census, U.S. Census of Population: 1970. Characteristics of Population, Vol. 33 New Mexico.

b. Taken from lists of registered voters from sample precincts maintained by San Miguel County Clerk.

c. Taken from Regular Precinct Poll Book, San Miguel County Clerk, 1974 Primary Election.

voter category which represented a 13 percent decrease of

Anglo registration. The Hispanos on the other hand showed

a proportional increase of 3.2 percent (75.6 to 78.8%) from

the potential to the qualified voter category which repre-

sented a 4.2 increase in Hispano registration. These trends

represent a complete reversal of the voting patterns found

in the McCleskey/Nimmo study.

An interesting trend reflected in the Hispano per-

centage of potential voters is the fact that the Hispano

population though constituting 81.7 percent of the total

county population declines considerably (to 75.6 percent)

of potential voters, indicating the important fact that the

Hispano population is a "young" population. Also, the per-

centages in Column D indicate that the ethnic division of

the population very closely approximates each party's Anglo/

Hispano ratios, indicating that Anglos or Hispanos do not

generally prefer one or another party, but select party

affiliation in close proportions.

A second set of significant results are contained in

Columns E and F which compare the qualified Democratic

electorate and the actual voters in the 1974 Democratic

Party Primary. These columns indicate a significant

difference between the Anglo and Hispano populations

(x^2 = 58.44, df - 1 $\underline{p}$ $\leq$ .01). The difference was a result

of a 22 percent Anglo decrease and a 7 percent Hispano
increase from the registration to the voting phase of the
electoral process. The Anglo population showed a proportional decrease of 6 percent (18.6 to 12.6%) from the
qualified Democratic voter category to the actual Democratic voter category which represented a 22 percent decrease in Anglo voting. The Hispano population, on the
other hand, showed a proportional increase of 6 percent
(81.4 to 87.4%) from the qualified Democratic voter
category to the actual Democratic voter category which
represented a 7 percent increase in Hispano voting. Again,
this trend is different from that of the McCleskey/Nimmo
study which found no significant changes according to
ethnicity between the registration (qualifying) or election
(voting) phase of the electoral process.

The percentages described in Table 3 are further
broken down into actual numbers and percentages according
to precinct in Table 4. This table indicates that the
pattern of higher Hispano turnout and lower Anglo turnout
is consistent throughout the county. Only in the small
precinct of Trujillo with 5 Anglos and 40 Hispanos registered is the pattern interrupted. In Villanueva, also the
2 registered Anglos both voted in the primary. Aside
from these two precincts where the minute numbers largely

TABLE 4

342

Comparison of Democratic Party Registration and Voting in the 1974 Democratic Primary between Anglos and Hispanos. Selected Precincts in San Miguel County.

Precinct # and Geographic Location	Total Democratic Registration	Total Anglo Registration	Total Hispano Registration	Total Democrats Voting 1974 Primary	Total Anglo Voting in Demo Primary	Total Hispano Voting in Demo Primary
#3 McFarland Hall East Las Vegas (north)	114	78 (68%)	36 (32%)	64 (56%)	43 (67%)	21 (33%)
#4 Carnegie Library East Las Vegas Central	273	132 (48%)	141 (52%)	135 (49%)	48 (36%)	87 (64%)
#5 Paul D. Henry School East Las Vegas (central)	294	36 (12%)	258 (88%)	179 (61%)	18 (10%)	161 (90%)
#6 Home of J. Gallegos, Pecos Street East Las Vegas (south)	213	24 (11%)	189 (89%)	137 (64%)	7 (5%)	130 (95%)
#11 Rociada Rural - north San Miguel Co.	51	2 (4%)	49 (96%)	30 (59%)	0 (0%)	30 (100%)
#15 Legion Park School East Las Vegas (north)	389	243 (62%)	146 (38%)	224 (58%)	121 (54%)	103 (46%)
#17 Bernal Rural South San Miguel Co.	107	8 (7%)	99 (93%)	77 (72%)	2 (3%)	75 (98%)
#18 Trujillo Rural East San Miguel Co.	45	5 (11%)	40 (89%)	41 (91%)	5 (12%)	36 (88%)
#21 Armijo School West Las Vegas (north)	152	17 (11%)	135 (89%)	91 (60%)	5 (6%)	86 (94%)
#22 North Public School West Las Vegas (north)	529	25 (5%)	504 (95%)	342 (65%)	9 (3%)	333 (97%)
#23 Health Center West Las Vegas (central)	300	25 (8%)	275 (92%)	177 (59%)	11 (61%)	166 (94%)
#25 South Public School West Las Vegas (south)	383	19 (5%)	364 (95%)	248 (65%)	5 (2%)	243 (98%)
#26 Union St. School West Las Vegas (south)	433	17 (4%)	416 (96%)	277 (64%)	5 (2%)	272 (98%)
#32 Villanueva Village (rural)	253	2 (1%)	251 (99%)	169 (67%)	2 (1%)	167 (99%)
#37 Pecos Village (west)	241	41 (17%)	200 (83%)	140 (58%)	20 (14%)	120 (86%)
#38 Pecos Village (east)	215	18 (8%)	197 (92%)	121 (56%)	7 (6%)	114 (94%)
TOTAL	3992	742 (18.6%)	3275 (81.4%)	2452 (61.4%)	308 (12.6%)	2144 (87.4%)

Sources: San Miguel County Clerk, Lists of Registered Voters, and Regular Precinct Poll Books, 1974 Primary and State of New Mexico, Official Election Returns 1974 Primary.

explain the differences, Hispano voter registration and
participation was higher (anywhere between 1 to 12 percent)
than Anglo voter registration and participation.

This means that even in the East Las Vegas precincts
where Anglo registration was highest, the proportional
turnout of Hispanos was generally higher than that of Anglos.
In Legion Park School, where Anglos make up 62 percent of
the registered voters, they made up 54 percent of the votes
cast. In Carnegie Library where Anglos make up 48 percent
of registered voters they cast 36 percent of the votes.
In McFarland Hall with 68 percent Anglo registration the
Anglo turnout was almost equivalent with 67 percent.

The table also reflects the high levels of turnout
61.4 percent in the combined sample precincts, which has
to be considered by national norms inordinately high for
a Primary election in a non-presidential election year
where the highest contested state office was for Governor.
Also, the precincts with highest Hispano voter registration
were the precincts with the highest average voter turnout.

The third set of results contained in the 1974 Democratic Primary election in San Miguel County yield some
further inferences as to whether higher ethnic participation

necessarily translates into preferences and victories for ethnic candidates. Table 5 compares the percentage votes cast for the Anglo and Hispano candidates in the sample precincts in San Miguel County. The reliability of the sample precincts is underscored by the fact that all Hispano candidates received percentage votes in the sample precincts equal to or nearly equal (within 1.6%) to their county totals.

The figures in Table 5 indicate a clear and consistent preference of Hispano voters for the Hispano candidates since in most cases the Hispano percentages in the precinct table are very close to the totals received by the Hispano or Hispanos in a given race. For example, in the race for Governor, Apodaca and Chavez together got 85 percent of the vote in the sample precincts while the poll books showed that 87.5 percent of the voters were Hispano in the sample precincts. Max Sanchez with 77 percent, Toney Anaya with 75 percent, Phil Lucero with 78 and Charles Rudolph and Joe Barela with 85 percent received percentage votes in their respective races which varied in degree of closeness but which were quite close to the 87.5 percent of Hispanos voting in the sample precincts. Although the totals vary in the respective precincts and races, there is still a very close similarity between the percentage of Hispanos voting

TABLE 5

Comparison of Percentage Votes Cast for Hispano Candidates and Percentage of Hispanos Voting, Selected Precincts in San Miguel County

Precinct Number	Pct. of Hispanos Voting	Governor							Secretary of State		State Auditor			State Tres.		Att. Gen.		Land Commissioner				Corporation Commissioner		
		Witt	Cloud	Echols	Mayfield	Apodaca	Chavez	Apodaca/Chavez	Betty McDaniel Lujan	Ernestine Evans	Sanchez	Davidson	Folkner	Murphey	Pacheco	Anaya	Howden	Lucero	Taylor	Fiorina	Rudolph	Barela	Abraham	Rudolph & Barela
3	33	10	3	20	8	33	25	59	33	67	43	57	46	23	32	52	48	50	36	14	78	6	17	84
4	64	7	12	9	4	42	27	69	54	46	35	65	18	40	42	60	40	60	23	17	58	19	23	77
5	90	2	5	7	1	52	34	86	58	42	81	19	21	18	61	74	26	77	8	15	80	9	11	89
6	95	3	3	3	3	59	29	88	69	39	74	26	25	15	60	81	19	75	11	14	78	11	13	89
11	100	4	10	4	0	36	47	83	37	63	74	26	31	38	31	69	31	84	3	3	69	4	27	73
15	46	6	6	2	10	39	24	63	48	52	49	51	36	30	34	52	48	54	27	19	56	15	29	71
17	98	4	0	1	1	71	23	94	54	46	85	15	18	6	76	91	9	90	2	8	81	9	10	90
18	88	0	3	14	3	35	45	80	67	33	71	29	46	14	39	72	28	65	14	20	67	21	12	88
21	94	2	4	4	1	71	18	89	72	28	87	13	20	22	58	86	14	88	5	7	74	16	10	90
22	97	3	2	2	1	73	20	93	67	33	87	13	16	14	70	82	18	85	6	9	82	11	7	93
23	94	2	0	16	2	71	20	91	60	40	88	12	13	21	66	87	13	81	9	10	76	14	10	90
25	98	3	2	3	2	69	21	90	75	25	88	12	22	14	64	85	15	82	10	8	82	11	7	93
26	98	5	3	6	1	59	27	86	65	35	85	15	22	18	60	79	21	80	8	12	72	17	11	89
32	99	1	1	1	0	57	40	97	59	41	76	24	30	5	65	77	23	94	3	3	68	17	14	86
37	86	3	5	4	1	58	29	87	48	52	75	25	27	16	57	72	28	83	13	4	40	27	33	67
38	94	8	2	3	1	49	38	87	64	36	76	24	22	19	59	76	24	87	5	8	38	25	36	64
TOTALS	87.5	3	3	6	2	58	27	85	61	39	77	23	24	19	57	75	25	78	11	11	70	15	15	85

Source: State of New Mexico, Official Election Returns 1974 Primary.

with the percentage received by the Hispanos in the respective precincts. The two races which deviated more from this
pattern were for Secretary of State and State Treasurer.
In the former race Betty McDaniel Lujan received 61 percent
of the vote even though she lost the race statewide, but
her margin in the sample precincts was considerably less
than that of the Hispanos in other offices. The main factor
operating here was the recognition by many voters of Ernestine
Evans as an Hispana and/or as the former Secretary of State.
In the race for State Treasurer Alex Pacheco got 57 percent
of the vote even though he lost statewide, but his percentage
was also lower than Hispanos in other races.

The importance of the ethnic voting preferences of
Hispanos is more easily appreciated if one considers that
probably the same preferences are apparent in other Hispanic
counties where Hispanos obtained large majorities, and when
one looks at the very close contests for State Auditor and
Attorney General where the margin of victory was slightly
over 3,000 and 2,000 votes respectively.

I have tried in this analysis of the 1974 Primary to
outline and document what appears to be very convincing
evidence that certain assumptions and generalizations
currently in vogue about Mexican American political behavior are not supported by the evidence in New Mexico, and

that because this is the case that such generalizations are indeed inappropriate in their universal application to the whole population of Mexican Americans in the United States. By thus freeing the analysis of Mexican American political behavior from the straitjacket of pre-supposed generalizations and from "racial" or "cultural" explanations for that political behavior, it is hoped that serious scholars can concern themselves with searching for explanations in the differential patterns of political participation of the group across various regions. It is expected that these new researches will uncover the presence of social, legal, economic or other barriers in addition to perhaps cultural which explain lower levels of participation of Hispanos in Texas and California.

The theorizing payoff of a single primary election in a single locale is of course very limited, hence no argument is made as to theory building. However, several conclusions do emerge which sufficiently challenge existing theories.

The first and most important conclusion, is that the assumption so widely current about Mexican American apathy toward politics does not hold for New Mexico, and thus that generalization is soundly refuted. Mexican Americans in New Mexico not only participate extensively, but their participation at least in the 1974 Primary election was

higher than that of the Anglo population in the state,
yielding to the group a greater political importance than
its numbers would indicate, and contributing significantly
to victories by Hispanos in six of eight statewide races.

A second conclusion can be drawn from the comparison
with the McCleskey/Nimmo study of Harris County, Texas.
The data presented in this study indicates a complete
reversal of the voting patterns described by McCleskey and
Nimmo. In this study the authors found a significant
increase in Anglo participation and decrease in Hispano
population from the potential to the qualified voter category. The present study shows on the other hand a significant Hispano increase and Anglo decline in the same categories. Also, although McCleskey and Nimmo found no
significant change in the respective groups between the
qualifying and actual voting stage, the data presented in
this study found again a significant Hispano increase and
Anglo decrease in these categories. These findings not only
add further evidence to the first conclusion, but points
out the need for studying the social, economic, legal and
other such variables which may serve as barriers to certain
groups in the exercise of the elective franchise in different
regions of the country.

A third conclusion that can be made from the data is

that there is strong evidence of ethnic bloc-voting patterns.
The very strong victories of Hispanos in the Hispanic
counties, and the very strong showing of Hispano candidates
in the sample precincts of San Miguel County indicate the
very strong preference for Hispano candidates by Hispano
voters. This pattern casts serious doubt on the assumptions
of Mexican American political docility and arguments that
the group cannot and does not unify.

A fourth and final conclusion that can be inferred
from the study is that New Mexico is a state where the
ethnic factor in politics is most pervasive. Not only is
there strong evidence of ethnic bloc-voting patterns, but
there is a very strong anti-ethnic vote as manifested by
the data on "Little Texas" counties. All of this means
that in New Mexico the ethnic factor is something that
every candidate for political office must allow for in his
overall campaign strategy. The particular electoral circumstances will determine to what extent the ethnic factor is
operational.

Outcome of the 1974 General Election

On November 5, 1974, New Mexico's voters - with
Hispanos making an indelible mark - wrote the final words
to this epitaph to the myth of Mexican American political

apathy and docility.

On that day Jerry Apodaca became the first Hispano Governor in New Mexico in modern times and the third in New Mexico's history. In addition the five other Hispanos contesting state offices were also elected, making for the most overwhelming Hispano electoral victory in any election in any state in American history. Elected along with Apodaca were Ernestine Evans, Secretary of State; Max R. Sanchez, State Auditor: Toney Anaya, State Attorney General; Phil Lucero, Commissioner of Public Lands, and Charles Rudolph, Corporation Commissioner. There are presently more Hispanos holding state level office than ever in New Mexico history. This includes one of two positions of U.S. Senator (Joseph M. Montoya) one of two positions in the U.S. Congress (Manuel Lujan), the Governorship, the aforementioned state executive offices, two of five positions in the State Supreme Court and two of five positions in the State Court of Appeals. In addition Hispanos in the state legislature number 34 members (including the Speaker of the House and Senate Majority leader) hold seven District judgeships and hundreds of county offices.

A cursory analysis of the General Election will clearly illustrate that the victory of the Hispanos was attributable to the fact that they were Democrats in a state that rarely

elects a Republican for state offices below the Governorship,
and that the ethnic voting patterns of the Hispano population
contributed to the Hispano victories.

In the most important race for Governor, Apodaca won a
narrower victory than had been predicted by the pre-election
polls, as he received 49.95 percent of the vote to 48.80 for
Joe Skeen his Republican Anglo opponent, or a margin of
3,742 votes. Capitalizing on strong party organization,
and a mass-media campaign depicting Apodaca as "the man
nobody owns", as well as a young energetic leader (some TV
spot announcements depicted Apodaca jogging or throwing a
football, a throwback to his days as a star halfback at the
University of New Mexico) Apodaca was able to reduce the
Republican Party margin in the state's most populace
county, Bernalillo (Albuquerque) to 7,543 votes. Skeen
carried Bernalillo County with 53.5% of the vote to
Apodaca's 46.5%. Although Apodaca's vote total of 56%
and a 2,500 vote margin in his home county of Dona Ana
(Las Cruces) was far less than the 70% expected, the
Hispano candidate recuperated by cutting into Skeen's
margin in the normally anti-ethnic "Little Texas" counties.
In these counties Skeen received 59% of the vote and
Apodaca 40.4%. Apodaca even carried Eddy County one of the
more populous of the "Little Texas" counties.

It was the overwhelming support which Apodaca received
in the Hispano counties, however, which gave him the victory.
The predominantly ethnic voters in these counties gave
Apodaca 67.3% of the vote to Skeen's 31.8% and Gene Gonzales
of the American Independent Party, .99%. Apodaca amassed
78.0% of the votes in Rio Arriba, 73.3% in Taos and 69.3%
in San Miguel counties. Apodaca's largest vote margin came
in populous Santa Fe County where he defeated Skeen by
6,448 votes.[17]

Apodaca's overall margin in the Hispano counties of
21,690 votes was in itself enough to "offset" Skeen's
10,000 vote margin in "Little Texas", and 7,543 margin in
Bernalillo County, which when combined and compared approximates Apodaca's margin of victory. The election was clearly
a manifestation of large numbers of Hispanos going to the
polls in record numbers and supporting their ethnic representative overwhelmingly.

Aside from the most important implication of the
Apodaca victory which clearly repudiates the assumptions
about Mexican American political apathy, the election
clearly shattered the myth that an Hispano could not win
in the race for Governor in New Mexico.

The ethnic factor was also visible in the remaining
races. Ernestine Evans received 58.2% of the vote over her

Hispana opponent, Mary Ann Gomez. Mrs. Evans' victory was primarily due to her Democratic party affiliation and her former tenure as Secretary of State. Mrs. Evans did not fare as well as other Hispanos in Hispano counties as evidenced by the results in San Miguel County where she defeated Ms. Gomez by only 433 votes, while other Hispanos were winning victories of 3,000 votes and over.

In the race for State Auditor and Attorney General, Max Sanchez with 51.5% of the vote and Toney Anaya with 51.0% of the vote, respectively, won relatively narrow victories. In their case the anti-ethnic vote which was visibly manifest against them was off-set by the pro-ethnic support they received in the Hispano counties. In the race for State Land Commissioner Phil Lucero benefited from his partisanship, his prior service as Deputy Land Commissioner, and the strong support of the Hispano counties in winning 55.6% of the vote and a margin of over 34,000 votes. In the race for Corporation Commission, Charles Rudolph was favored by his partisanship, his youthful good looks, and the aforementioned universal appeal of his surname as he won an impressive victory over his Anglo opponent with 58.5% of the vote. In all cases except for the race for Secretary of State, where the ethnic factor was neutralized, the Hispano candidates benefited from the overwhelming support

of the Hispano counties which as in the past also reflected
a higher voter turnout (74.9%) than the state average of
67.25 percent.[18]

It is hoped that this analysis of the 1974 Primary and
General election will lay to rest the general assumption of
Mexican American political apathy and that the apathy is
reflective of cultural characteristics inconsistent with
or contrary to values of American democratic participation.
It is in essence a call for scholars to widen the range of
their observations so that they may attempt to analyze
and explain systematically and logically the differential
patterns of political participation that appear among,
between and within different groups in American society.
Political participation of Americans in general is hardly
commendable, so it should not be surprising that participation is lower among some minority groups.

Perhaps by addressing the basic problem of citizen
apathy in American politics, possible remedies such as the
elimination of all legal barriers to voting and the establishment of incentives to voting will begin to improve the
participation of all segments of the society.

Summary

This chapter has discussed the theoretical and practical

issues involving the voting behavior of the Mexican Americans.
It explored the problem of nonparticipation of Chicanos in
voting and summarized and analyzed the various explanations
that have been offered for it. The existing literature on
Chicano voting behavior was reviewed, and the recurring
theme was the non-participation of Chicanos, the close
affinity to the Democratic Party, and the failure of
Chicanos in spite of potentially important population
numbers to use the franchise as an effective instrument
for social and economic change.

Several logical explanations for Chicano non-participation were suggested, among them the fact that Chicanos came
from an antecedent political culture where political
participation was not very compelling, and became exposed
to legal barriers in the American system that only reinforced
existing predispositions.

The case of New Mexico's Mexican Americans and their
high levels of political participation and inclination to
support their own candidates was offered as evidence that
given a favorable political socializing experience Mexican
Americans can become a viable political force.

Most importantly, the chapter has attacked traditional
generalizations that have attributed to Chicanos certain
ingrained racial and cultural characteristics of political

passivity, and lethargy. It has rejected arguments that such characteristics will forever preclude the group from being politically integrated into the American system.

NOTES

[1]F. Chris Garcia, La Causa Politica: A Chicano Politics Reader (Notre Dame: University of Notre Dame Press, 1974).

[2]For more discussion of this see Vigil "Ethnic Organizations Among the Mexican Americans of New Mexico," Chapter 5.

[3]Guzman, op. cit., Chapter 9.

[4]Ibid., 392 and 403.

[5]"Party Vote and the Mexican Americans in South Tucson," paper delivered at the annual meeting of the Southwestern Political Science Association, March, 1967.

[6]Garcia, "Voting Patterns in 'Bi-cultural El Paso'", 250-266.

[7]Garcia, "Mexican American Political Behavior in Texas," 128-142.

[8]Ibid., 130.

[9]Garcia, "Patterns of Chicano Voting Behavior," 241-249.

[10]Ibid., 247.

[11]Vigil, Chapter 5. Also Ernest Fincher, "The Spanish Americans as a Political Factor in New Mexico: 1912-1950," unpublished Ph.D. dissertation, New York University, 1950, Chapter 14.

[12]State of New Mexico, Official Election Returns, 1974 Primary Election (Santa Fe: Secretary of State, 1974), 3.

[13]"Hispanic Americans Led Voting", Albuquerque Journal, July 21, 1974.

[14]Jack Holmes, Politics in New Mexico (Albuquerque: University of New Mexico Press, 1964).

[15]Clifton McCleskey and Dan Nimmo, "Differences Between Potential, Registered and Actual Voters: The Houston Metropolitan Area in 1964," Social Science Quarterly, 49 (June, 1968), 103-114.

[16] Ibid., 107-113.

[17] State of New Mexico, *Official Election Returns,
1974 General Election* (Santa Fe: Secretary of State).

[18] Ibid.

FURTHER SUGGESTED READINGS

Rudolph O. de la Garza "Voting Patterns in Bi-cultural El
    Paso: A Contextual Analyses of Mexican Americans
    Voting Behavior," in La Cause Politica: A Chicano
    Politics Reader, F. Chris Garcia, ed Notre Dame:
    University of Notre Dame Press, 1974.

Donald M. Freeman, "Party, Vote, and the Mexican American
    in South Tucson," in La Causa Politica: A Chicano
    Politics Reader.

Mark Levy and Michael Kramer, "Patterns of Chicano Voting
    Behavior" in La Causa Politica: A Chicano Politics
    Reader.

Clifton McCleskey and Bruce Merrill, "Mexican American
    Political Behavior in Texas" in La Causa Politica: A
    Chicano Politics Reader.

Clifton McCleskey and Dan Nimmo, "Differences between
    Potential, Registered and Actual Voters: The Houston
    Metropolitan Area in 1964," Social Science Quarterly,
    49 (June, 1968), 103-114.

Maurilio Vigil, "Ethnic Organizations Among the Mexican
    Americans of New Mexico: A Political Perspective,"
    unpublished PH.D dissertation, University of New
    Mexico, 1974, Chapter 5.

CHAPTER VIII

CHICANO PROSPECTS: THE END HAS NOT BEEN WRITTEN YET

> Nationalism as the key to organization
> transcends all religious, political, class and
> economic factions or boundaries. Nationalism is
> the common denominator that all members of La
> Raza can agree upon.
>
> El Plan Espiritual de Aztlan, 1970

This work has attempted to narrate, describe, and
analyze the various aspects of Mexican American political
activity. It has sought to provide one of the first comprehensive, systematic, integrated treatments of the subject
of Chicano politics. To accomplish this goal, the most
important topics relating to the theory and practice of
Chicano politics were selected, and then studied and
analyzed according to the most current literature available
and in accordance with current theoretical and analytical
models of the various disciplines. In addition much new
research data and information was generated and new perspectives on existing data offered in order to fill needed
gaps in the literature.

The various topics were grouped around a single conceptual approach or framework in order to provide as
systematic, coherent and ordered treatment as possible.
This may well be the most criticized aspect of the effort.

However, the conceptual framework and the selection of topics were purposely designed to serve as a heuristic model that will (a) encourage further testing of this model (b) encourage further theoretical speculation (c) stimulate further research in the field, and (d) help orient and structure future research on Chicano politics. This last goal will contribute toward establishing some order and cohesion in the field, something which has been lacking in the past. As the first comprehensive treatment it will undoubtedly be criticized also for its sins of "omission" as well as "commission," and if it encourages or stimulates further elaboration this is also welcome.

What can, in summary, be said about the state of Chicano politics in the United States? What are the prospects for the group? What impact has the Chicano movement had on American society and on the group itself? What new insight has been offered here about Chicano politics?

The study began by establishing the relationship between "Chicano" politics and American politics. It was suggested that it was most logical to consider the subject of Chicano politics in a broad theoretical perspective of American politics that encompasses conflict theory, groups in politics and widely dispersed and inequitably distributed sources of political power. American politics was perceived

as a conflict process, with different kinds of groups,
individuals, interests pursuing largely private objectives,
and that policy making was largely a product of these
interests competing and compromising. As the resources,
skills and services are unevenly distributed, the groups
possessed of the greatest of these are most successful,
and those lacking them are most deprived. The American
social milieu was perceived as consisting of a stratified
system in which some groups dominate largely because of
their control of the resources, skills and incentives that
produce political power. Other groups - ethnic, racial,
cultural - have been politically subordinated because of
their inability to marshall and utilize the resources,
skills and incentives.

What has been suggested here is that given the highly
pluralistic nature of American society and the open conflict system which characterizes and regulates the policy
process, that group politics is an inherent and natural
process in American politics. Thus group politics is not
only a logical but to an ethnic group like the Chicano a
most viable objective to pursue in search for political
and social change. It was suggested that though lacking
in some respects in the requisite resources, skills and
incentives, the Chicano group can compensate by strengths

in other aspects.

It was suggested that probably the greatest political resource Mexican Americans hold is their numbers, especially in light of the fact that these numbers are concentrated in a specific region (the Southwest) where they constitute the largest ethnic minority, and they have remained a relatively distinct group in spite of the American assimilationist tendency.

It was suggested that rather than such an effort being considered separatist or un-American, that it was a natural manifestation of the group process of American politics.

The historical profile outlining the making of the Mexican American people and their political development showed that Mexican Americans have not participated effectively in American politics primarily because of an antecedent political culture that eschewed active citizen involvement in politics and also a very hostile American political environment.

In spite of this condition, it was shown that Hispanos have proven quite capable, given a more appropriate socialization process of participating effectively as the study of New Mexico's Mexican Americans has shown.

It was further suggested that the political integration

of the Hispanic community could be accomplished by a systematic campaign that would stress the elements of ethnic solidarity involving the use of ethnic symbols and stressing ethnic values such as racial origins, historical experience and common culture. To the Hispano, notions such as mestizaje, la raza, Mexican American culture, bilingualism could be some of the unifying elements.

It was suggested that the antecedent culture of the Mexican American has been a primary factor resisting assimilation in the past, but that the traditional resistance was beginning to break down as a result of social, demographic and regional changes in the population.

The Chicano movement has temporarily halted that process, as Mexican Americans were once again reminded of their antecedent culture and its value, of their identity, and of their sense of ethnic community.

Although the Chicano movement began as a series of rather isolated events involving the land grants in New Mexico and the farm workers in California, it quickly spread and became a broader social movement. Thus the movement was perceived as more than a temporary aberration or a passing phase. The initial instances of activity by Tijerina and Chavez stimulated other leaders and organizations, and what has resulted is a multi-pronged reform effort in many fronts.

The Chicano organizations have served and continue to serve as the main instruments in "institutionalizing" and "regularizing" what was initially a protest movement. The Chicano organization, by emphasizing ethnic symbols, by stressing the need for ethnic community, by dramatizing the problems of the group, by generating a dialogue on common problems, by opening the lines of communication, by suggesting possible alternatives of action have not only contributed toward reviving ethnic solidarity, but laid out in their activity the path for social reform and change. Thus there are today, a great number and variety of Chicano organizations involved in different dimensions of the Chicano struggle.

In addition to the political organizations such as La Raza Unida Party, there are a great number of business, professional, youth and student, social service, community service, religious, literary and scholarly Chicano organizations involved in the movement. Moreover, the Chicano movement through the organizations has enlisted more and more Chicanos into its ranks, so that today more Chicanos of all ages, classes, economic station and professions (doctors, lawyers, teachers and other fields) are active in the struggle.

There are many visible manifestations of the impact
which the Chicano movement has had and is having. The
literature on Chicanos - in history, sociology, politics -
has multiplied reflecting a greater interest in the group.
Governmental agencies such as the Cabinet Committee on the
Spanish Speaking, the Civil Rights Commission, and State
Human Rights Commission have become active advocates of
Chicano rights and privileges, while disseminating more
information on or about the group and its situation in
this country. Legislation at both the national and state
level, such as the Voting Rights Acts, the bilingual
education acts, reflect not only the concern, but the
first steps taken by government to deal with the special
problems of the Hispanics in America. The manifestations
are also visible in the status of Chicanos. More and more
Chicanos are being appointed to higher offices in federal
and state governments. More and more Hispanos are
entering the professions and business community not only
as a result of affirmative action programs, but also the
opening of opportunities combined with incentives to enter
the professional schools.

While, in retrospect, it is true that the level of
political participation of Hispanos (as suggested by the
study of Chicano leaders and voting behavior) has not been

as much as could be expected or hoped for, it has undergone important changes since the 1960s, and is becoming more visible.

The important point in all the study is that the "forgotten people" or "forgotten Americans" as Chicanos have often been labeled are no longer forgotten, but are in the minds and conscience of most Americans.

What outcome will all of this have on American society? The activism of Chicanos combined with the activism of other groups like the Blacks and the Native Americans is likely to temper the traditionally WASP dominated value system. Notions of assimilation into an overriding WASP oriented core - cultural system will likely yield toward greater acceptance of cultural differences, toward perhaps acceptance of the notion that the diversity of the American people necessitates a diverse cultural and value system.

Governor Jerry Apodaca stated in his inaugural address that he hoped his service as Governor of New Mexico would once and for all shatter the ethnic walls that have kept Hispanos from the state's highest office. Perhaps it is too idealistic a hope, perhaps it is just as, or more idealistic than the hope of the little Chicanito in the barrios, who when asked what he wished to be replied, "President, of course."

Perhaps we Chicanos can never achieve that "level".

Perhaps we are doomed to our fate as some have suggested.

But as has been suggested here we can no longer sit back

and blame the "system." The "system" offers more opportunity

and flexibility to accommodate new political influence than

any other, provided the citizen embraces it, understands

it, and tries to make it work for him.